# Liberalism and Conservatism 1846–1905

David Paterson

**Series Editors**
Martin Collier
Erica Lewis

HEINEMANN ADVANCED HISTORY

Heinemann Educational Publishers
Halley Court, Jordan Hill, Oxford, OX2 8EJ
a division of Reed Educational & Professional Publishing Ltd
Heinemann is a registered trademark of Reed Educational & Professional
Publishing Ltd

OXFORD MELBOURNE AUCKLAND
JOHANNESBURG BLANTYRE GABORONE
IBADAN PORTSMOUTH NH (USA) CHICAGO

First published 2001

ISBN 0 435 32737 2
03 02 01
10 9 8 7 6 5 4 3 2 1

Designed and typeset by Wyvern 21 Ltd, Bristol
Printed and bound in Great Britain by The Bath Press Ltd, Bath

Index compiled by Ian D. Crane

Picture research by Elisabeth Savery

**Photographic acknowledgements**
The author and publisher would like to thank the following for
permission to reproduce photographs:
Fortean Picture Library/Janet & Colin Bond: 20
Hulton Archive: 23, 41
Hulton Getty/Sean Sexton: 73
Hulton Getty: 6 (right), 7, 18
Mary Evans Picture Library: 6 (left), 17, 28, 64, 79, 129, 138, 206, 241
Punch: 60, 95
The Bridgeman Art Library/Manchester City Art Galleries: 51

Cover photograph © Mary Evans Picture Library

**Author's dedication**
To Marie, with love and thanks

# CONTENTS

How to use this book

## AS SECTION: NARRATIVE AND EXPLANATION

## A2 SECTION: ANALYSIS AND INTERPRETATION

# HOW TO USE THIS BOOK

This book is divided into two distinct parts. The first part is designed to meet the requirements of AS-level history. The origin, meaning and significance of the Conservative and Liberal parties in nineteenth-century British political history are examined and particular attention is paid to the development of the ideas and careers of William Gladstone and Benjamin Disraeli. This part provides an explained narrative of the major political developments of the later nineteenth century. Summary questions at the end of each chapter are designed to get the student to re-enforce and check learning and understanding. The boxes at the side of the principal text can be used as useful explanatory points while reading the main body of the work, or they can be referred to separately.

The A2 part of the book examines similar themes but in the greater depth and analytical complexity required at a more advanced level. It looks at issues such as Ireland, foreign policy and free trade in more detail than the AS part, with a thematic approach and appropriate historiographical introductions.

For those students studying A2 a preliminary read of the relevant chapters of the AS part of the book is strongly recommended to help with necessary context and background. Likewise, those studying AS should find it useful to stretch their minds by seeing how the material is developed at a more sophisticated level in the A2 sections.

There are assessment sections at the end of both parts. Original questions have been devised, though these are in the style of the relevant examination board's AS and A2 papers. Practical guidance on how to answer these is given.

# AS SECTION: INTRODUCTION

The year 1846 was a significant one in British history. Tragically, it saw a major famine in British-controlled Ireland: linked with this crisis were the parliamentary debates in the House of Commons. Would the starving Irish be able to benefit from removing customs duties on imported corn? What effect would such a removal have on the aristocratic landed interest? These events led to the downfall of the Conservative government of Sir Robert Peel and a time of relative party political confusion. Yet it eventually became apparent that the political scene was now dominated by Conservatives and Liberals and competition between them would be a major political theme for the next 60 years and beyond. The year 1846 also saw the confirmation of the emergence of Liberal William Gladstone as a loyal defender of Peel, and the more sudden rise to fame of Conservative Benjamin Disraeli, who took a leading part in attacking Peel: these two had now become prominent parliamentary and political figures.

Since the extension of the right to vote in 1832, political debates in the Houses of Parliament had taken on a new importance and there were to be further reforms to the way the House of Commons was elected in both 1867 and 1884. It was a time when the class below the landed aristocracy but above the working class – the middle class – became increasingly important and active in political terms.

By 1905, however, there were signs of this era coming to an end. The Labour Party was emerging to represent working people, the power of the House of Lords was being questioned and the **Queen** who had given a unity –

## KEY PERSON

**Queen Victoria**
**1819–1901** Niece of the previous monarch, William IV, Victoria became Queen in 1837. Politically Whig in her early days, much admiring her first Prime Minister Lord Melbourne. Married Albert of Saxe-Coburg-Gotha in 1839. Never really recovered from Albert's death from typhoid in December 1861 and became rather reclusive. Later, she much preferred Disraeli to Gladstone. But such were the limits of her powers that she could not prevent Gladstone from holding office when he was electorally successful.

and her name – to the last two-thirds of the nineteenth century was no more.

However, in the intervening period the Conservative and Liberal parties dominated the politics of much of the Victorian era. In the late 1870s the writer W.S. Gilbert penned the words to a song in an operetta called *Iolanthe*, set to music by the most famous mid-Victorian British composer, Arthur Sullivan. It ran:

I often think it comical
How nature always does contrive
That every boy and every girl
That's born into this world alive
Is either a little Liberal
Or else a little Conservative.

Contemporaries were very well aware of the importance and domination of Liberals and Conservatives.

- What did Conservatism and Liberalism stand for in the nineteenth century?
- How did these names come to be used for the two main political parties?
- Who were the leading politicians most identified with their ideas?
- What were the overall philosophies of these parties if they had them?
- What did they believe and achieve in foreign policy?
- How did they view the dramatic economic expansion and urban development of the nineteenth century?
- Where did they stand on such issues such as the extension of the vote?
- Where did they stand on the amount that governments should interfere in the social questions of the day, such as public health, working conditions and the problems of poverty?
- How successful were they in their attempts to hold power and govern the country at this time?
- What kind of people in the country were attracted to support these groupings?

These are some of the questions that this book will attempt to answer.

# CHAPTER 1

## WHAT WERE CONSERVATISM AND LIBERALISM?

### INTRODUCTION

The words **Conservative** and **Liberal** are used in a number of ways today. When the words are used with capital letters in their political sense, their precise definition may change a little and vary according to time and circumstance. Nevertheless, in this political context, their meaning is likely to bear some resemblance to the more general explanation outlined in the margin.

Today in the early twenty-first century we are familiar with the words Conservative and Liberal with a large 'C' and a large 'L' to describe two of our major political parties. The Conservatives remain one of the major players in the political game; the Liberals, however (who have changed their name to Liberal Democrats), have long been displaced as the second of two major parties by the Labour Party. This was a twentieth-century development. In the second half of the nineteenth century the Conservative and Liberal parties were the two dominant parties in the British parliamentary system. Yet at the start of the century in 1800 the words were only being used with a small 'c' and a small 'l' and the two main parties were known as the Tories and the Whigs.

### What were Whig and Tory?

The terms **Whig** and **Tory** had been in use ever since the second half of the seventeenth century and stood largely unchallenged until the 1830s as describing the two major political groupings of the day. Parties and groupings emerged gradually after 1660 when it was clear that the role of the king after the **restoration of the monarchy** was not going to be all-dominant and there were different views on how he ought to be advised and how far his powers should be restricted.

## KEY TERMS

**Conservative** The word conservative can be used with a small 'c' to describe a particular attitude to a problem, question or situation. This attitude:

- is cautious, careful and apprehensive of too much change all at once;
- has regard for past traditions and ideas;
- believes that rapid upheaval may produce instability and uncertainty;
- feels that, at national level, this kind of alteration could result in the loss of valuable ideas or institutions.

**Liberal** Likewise, the word liberal with a small 'l' suggests:

- an open-minded and flexible approach to a problem;
- plenty of scope for free interpretation of the question in hand;
- that tradition, though respected, should not be adhered to over-rigidly;
- that change may be seen as desirable to prevent frustration and anger from building up.

**Whig and Tory** Like many names that stick they were not intended at first to be complimentary: a Tory was an Irish robber and a Whig his Scottish equivalent.

Parties began as informal groupings rather than being founded as an organisation in a formal manner with rules and regulations and a balance sheet. These parties were very different from today.

- Only a small number of Members of Parliament would have identified with Whig or Tory.
- Many MPs would regard themselves as independent country gentlemen who were above party and would vote as they chose.
- Those who did think about it frequently regarded themselves as Whig or Tory rather than members of the Whig or Tory parties. There was no mass membership of the parties in the country as a whole and little formal organisation.
- The proportion of adult males who were entitled to vote for MPs was quite small under the old **electoral system before 1832**. Moreover, many candidates who stood for Parliament were elected unopposed because of the property or land they owned and/or influence they possessed in a particular area. They did not have to win voters over to the policies they supported by the politics of persuasion.

When a dispute emerged as to whether Parliament should be reformed in 1831–2, the differences between Whig and Tory were clearly demonstrated. Tories opposed what they saw as an unwarranted, sudden and drastic interference with the stable and well-established **British constitution** and Whigs supported what they felt was a moderate, prudent and necessary change to include the respectable middle class among those privileged to vote for their choice of elected Member of Parliament. In passing the **Great Reform Bill of 1832** the Whigs seemed to have won an important struggle and taken advantage of the growing demand for reform, especially from the industrial middle classes.

## THE CHANGE TO 'CONSERVATIVE'

It was around the 1830s when the use of the terms 'Conservative' and 'Liberal' began to challenge the terms 'Whig' and 'Tory'. This challenge came at slightly different

Successfully proposed an extension of the vote in English boroughs to a group of men known as £10 householders. In effect this gave the franchise (right to vote) to the middle classes in the towns – shopkeepers, merchants, traders and small businessmen who had generally been excluded from voting before. It also abolished some of the very smallest borough seats and partially redistributed these to the new industrial towns in the north.

## KEY PEOPLE

**Duke of Wellington 1759–1852** Defeated Bonaparte at Waterloo 1815; subsequent political career as a Tory politician less happy. Prime Minister 1828–30; refusal of even the smallest degree of reform when faced with evidence of corrupt nature of electoral system brought his downfall. 1835–52 a senior yet background figure in the Conservative Party. In Peel's cabinet 1841–6 without holding office.

**Sir Robert Peel 1788–1850** From a wealthy Lancashire manufacturing family. His father was in Parliament before 1832. After brilliant academic success at Oxford, Peel was Irish Secretary 1813–20 and a reforming Home Secretary in the 1820s, but opposed parliamentary reform. Prime Minister 1834–5 and 1841–6. In the political wilderness for the last few years of his life.

times, in different ways and with different results. The historian of the Conservative Party, Robert Blake, records that the first use of the word Conservative to describe the Tory party was in an article in January 1830. This was at the start of the Reform Bill crisis and related to the idea of 'conserving', or preserving, the old electoral system. However, it came into common use soon afterwards in the mid-1830s when the dust was beginning to settle on the Reform Bill crisis.

In 1834 the **Duke of Wellington**, who had been Tory Prime Minister up to 1830, was replaced as leader by **Sir Robert Peel**. Peel, in seeking re-election to Parliament, wrote an address (known as the Tamworth Manifesto) to his **constituents** in the Staffordshire **borough** of Tamworth in which he outlined his proposed ideas. Peel made it clear that he accepted the 1832 Reform Act as an established fact and something that could not be reversed. He established the idea that the Tories would now accept change where it could be proved to be beneficial to the country. However, although he did not use the word, he indicated that *conservation* of what was worthwhile from the old system would have a high priority. He promised that the Tories (or Conservatives) would now undertake 'a *careful* review of all institutions civil and ecclesiastical . . . in a *friendly* temper for the maintenance of *established* rights' (author's italics).

The word 'Tory' never disappeared and still appears today as meaning essentially the same as Conservative, but it is clear that by 1846 the Conservative Party was now the most common term and it was already in frequent use when Peel succeeded in regaining real power for the Party in 1841, defeating the Whigs at a general election in that year. Peel had managed to modify the image of the Tories so that, while they could still be seen as a party primarily representing the landowning interest, they could also claim to govern for the interests of the country as a whole.

## Beliefs of the Conservatives
Parties at this time stood for broad principles rather than specific policies. At the start of Peel's Conservative ministry of the early 1840s it appeared clear what these were.

1 Conservatives greatly revered the position of the monarchy in the British political system. The monarch was entitled to exert real power and should do so when appropriate. Then there could be no dispute about the ultimate authority in the country. Queen Victoria was entitled to select her own ministers and the government was Her Majesty's Government.

2 Conservatives had a high regard for the British constitution and the workings of the traditional political system. Many Conservatives regretted the passing of the 1832 Great Reform Bill but they were prepared to accept its changes. They believed further adjustments were unlikely to be necessary. The place of the House of Lords was seen as equally significant as that of the House of Commons and democracy was associated with the USA and mob rule, both seen then as powerful disincentives to adopt it or anything remotely resembling it.

3 The landowning aristocracy were the given rulers of the country. Their background, education and wealth all entitled them to this status. The stability of the country depended upon a landowning class who had sufficient stake in the system to act in its best interests. The main desires of landowners would always take precedence over the manufacturing or commercial interest. The landed aristocracy and the House of Lords both depended on the hereditary system whereby titles and land were inherited in their entirety by the eldest sons.

**Constitutents** All the people who live in the constituency (area) represented by an MP.

**Borough** A town or village granted a Royal Charter giving it the privilege of electing its own two MPs.

**The old Tory and the new Conservative: Wellington (left) and Peel.**

Constitutional monarch? The young Queen Victoria.

4  The **Established Church of England** as a central plank in the social system was to be strongly maintained. The monarch was the earthly head of the Church and from the Church's Christian beliefs flowed the basis of society's organisation and principles. The senior bishops were members of the House of Lords. Since appointment of bishops tended to be political and the Tories had been in office for most of the period 1784–1830, the majority of the bishops were of that political persuasion for at least the first part of the nineteenth century and often beyond. Not for nothing was the Church of England described as 'the Conservative Party at prayer'.

All in all there was an admiration for the British constitution, a British Protestant monarch as head of a national Church and an English-based landowning aristocracy with numerous estates in Wales, Scotland and Ireland, all very much seen as part of one United Kingdom.

Some of these beliefs were not quite as rigid as they might sound. With a young Queen on the throne since 1837, it was expected that her ministers (the Ministers of the Crown) would now take more initiative. After the extension of the vote in 1832 the greater authority of the House of Commons was coming to be accepted. In contrast to the French aristocracy before the Revolution, the British landed classes were not totally opposed to some political role for the wealthy merchant middle class; indeed Peel himself was one of them. **Free trade** measures favouring the commercial middle classes had been passed by the Tories in the mid-1820s.

Whilst the privileges of the Church of England were to be stoutly maintained, there was to be religious toleration for other churches, although suspicion of Roman Catholics as foreign agents still lurked among the darker corridors of some of the great aristocratic houses. Nonetheless it had been a Tory government under Wellington and Peel that had passed **Catholic Emancipation** in 1829, albeit under threat of revolt in Ireland.

## THE BEGINNING OF THE LIBERALS

The displacement of Whigs by Liberals took a slightly different course and was longer in establishing its full effect. However, later in the century it was clear that the change had been complete and permanent. The label 'Whig', unlike the word 'Tory', was eventually to disappear completely from use but the word remained to describe particular political characteristics.

'Liberal' was a word used in the aftermath of the French Revolution of 1789; it was used to describe a political attitude in general rather than one party in particular. The term 'Whig' was always a fairly exclusive one that could be applied to a particular set of aristocratic families who, in the early nineteenth century, took a more 'liberal' view of the workings of the British political system than did the Tories. Whigs such as Earl Grey for instance, while not condoning the violent element in the French Revolution, admired its removal of **absolute monarchy** and regretted it had not been able to maintain the **constitutional monarchy** of its early days. When Grey was invited to form a ministry to govern the country in 1830 he was seen as the Whig most able to put through a reform of Parliament. This he achieved – though not without difficulty – and one of his principal arguments was that a liberal rather than rigid approach to the British political system was the one most likely to preserve its essentials. Liberals were not revolutionaries.

Although the use of the word remained vague and a little inconsistent 'Liberals' – now sometimes with a capital 'L' – were increasingly to be found on the Whig rather than Tory or Conservative side in the 1830s and the word was sometimes used interchangeably with **Radical**. By the time of the Corn Law Crisis in 1846 'liberal' was increasingly used to describe those who supported the move to free trade and their economic philosophy of **laissez-faire**.

### Beliefs of the Liberals

Whig-Liberal beliefs were not always as clear-cut as Conservative ones. However, there were some discernible trends.

1  A greater acceptance of reform and amendment of the political system than the Conservatives, as seen in 1832. Earl Grey, the Prime Minister of the time, argued that the Reform Act was 'the most aristocratic measure ever put before Parliament'. Whilst this was clearly a remark designed to win over waverers to the cause of parliamentary reform, it reflected his belief that change was necessary in order to preserve the essentials of the political system.

2  A greater suspicion of the monarch's use of power and a high regard for the 'liberties' of the ordinary Englishman. The restrictions on the powers of the monarch dating from the Bill of Rights of 1689 (see page 4) were seen as central to the political system. The British system was seen by Whigs such as Lord John Russell as superior both to the **despotisms** of continental Europe and the democratic 'excesses' of the United States. The system upheld the right of Parliament to be consulted on all major issues of policy including taxation. The **rule of law** was to be upheld in normal circumstances as was the right of free speech and a free press.

3  A more open attitude to allowing the middle classes into the heart of the political framework. The £10 householder (see page 14) to whom the Whigs gave the vote in 1832 was essentially the middle-class merchant and manufacturer as well as the small trader/shopkeeper who, henceforth, were all seen as natural political allies of the Liberals. This resulted in economic polices that were more inclined to freeing trade by removing **tariff barriers** and a general suspicion of unnecessary expense in government.

4  Less emphasis on the privileges of the Church of England and more attention to religious liberty. The Liberals showed greater sympathy towards **nonconformist denominations** and sometimes the Roman Catholics: they were beginning to believe in what today is called equality of opportunity for all, regardless of which Christian denomination a person belonged to. This was coupled with a concern to use the propertied wealth of the Church for the wider good, in such areas as education. The greater acceptance of the commercial industrial and urban changes through which Britain was going led to a concern with such issues.

## KEY TERMS

**Despotism** A system of government run by some form of dictator.

**Rule of law** The idea that everyone, whatever their status or position in society, must keep to the laws of the land.

**Tariff barriers** Limit put on the free movement of goods by a government-imposed duty on their importation. This could be either to increase government revenue or to restrict imports of goods that might compete with British-made ones.

**Nonconformist denominations**
Denomination: a particular religious grouping. Nonconformist: those Protestants who did not wish to conform to the beliefs and organisation of the Church of England. Among the most numerous and influential of these groups were Methodists, Presbyterians, Congregationalists, Baptists, Unitarians and Quakers.

What were Conservatism and Liberalism?

## Prime Ministers and their parties 1830–74

| Name | Party | Dates |
| --- | --- | --- |
| Grey | Whig | 1830–4 |
| Peel | Conservative | 1834–5 |
| Melbourne | Whig | 1835–41 |
| Peel | Conservative | 1841–6 |
| Russell | Whig | 1846–52 |
| Derby | Conservative | 1852 (Feb. to Dec.) |
| Aberdeen | Whig-Peelite Coalition | 1852–5 |
| Palmerston | Whig | 1855–8 |
| Derby | Conservative | 1858–9 |
| Palmerston | Liberal | 1859–65 |
| Russell | Liberal | 1865–6 |
| Derby | Conservative | 1866–8 |
| Disraeli | Conservative | 1868 |
| Gladstone | Liberal | 1868–74 |

5 Less emphasis on the role of government. Pre-1832 Tories were seen as having prosecuted an expensive war against France before 1815 and Liberals remained keen on low taxation and cheap government throughout the nineteenth century. In this respect they are more reminiscent of the late-twentieth-century Conservative Party than modern Liberal Democrats.

By 1846 the **organisation of the parties** was developing and the words 'Conservative' and 'Liberal' were being increasingly used in political circles: the events of 1846–66 were to produce changes that eventually brought them to the forefront of political talk.

## SUMMARY QUESTIONS

1 How were the names 'Tory' and 'Whig' replaced by the terms 'Conservative' and 'Liberal'?

2 What were the essential differences between the beliefs of the Conservatives and Liberals in the first half of the nineteenth century?

**Organisation of the parties**
The 1832 Reform Act was to encourage Whig-Liberals and Tory-Conservatives to employ Party Agents to try to maximise support. F.R. Bonham (Tory) and Joseph Parkes (Whig) became significant political figures. London clubs the Carlton (Tory) and the Reform (Whig) were used as places for meetings and discussions and attempts were made in Parliament to get party supporters out for controversial votes. However, party organisation remained much less significant than after the Second Reform Act of 1867.

# CHAPTER 2

# HOW WERE WHIGS TRANSFORMED INTO LIBERALS OVER THE PERIOD 1846–66?

## INTRODUCTION

A Whig ministry was formed in 1846 when **Lord John Russell** became Prime Minister after the downfall in the Commons of Sir Robert Peel's Conservative government. A year later in 1847 a general election was held which confirmed Russell in power, though with the party allegiance of many MPs uncertain his majority was difficult to calculate.

However, when Lord John (now Earl) Russell replaced **Lord Palmerston** nearly 20 years later in 1865, circumstances had altered. Russell was now clearly regarded as leading a Liberal government even though it may have contained some Whigs. A modern two-party system was in the process of developing and the change from Whig to Liberal appeared to symbolise it. How had this come about? Was it actually as clear-cut and complete a change as this seems to suggest? The real position is a little more complex and it was slightly later, in 1868, that the Liberal Party truly emerged under **William Gladstone**, who had never been a Whig but was most definitely now a Liberal.

This chapter will chart the move from Whig to Liberal. After a brief look at the formal change which occurred in 1859 it will delve more deeply to examine:

- the political situation in 1846;
- the composition of the Whig Party and its relationship on major issues with the Radicals and the Liberals;
- the extent to which the Whigs followed Liberal and Radical policies between 1846 and 1859;

- the moves towards the development of a strong Liberal Party between 1859 and 1866.

## LIBERAL REPLACES WHIG?

The word 'Liberal' took longer than 'Conservative' to establish itself as the name of one of the two main political parties. The formal change to Liberal did not come until 1859.

- Russell's ministry from 1846 to 1852 was usually regarded at the time as Whig, though individual members would have called themselves Liberal.
- Following a brief Conservative ministry under Lord Derby, the non-Conservative grouping that was formed by **Lord Aberdeen** in December 1852 was called a Whig-**Peelite** coalition. This lasted until January 1855.
- The government of Lord Palmerston between 1855 and 1858 was still seen as Whig, but when he re-formed his government in 1859, after another brief Conservative intermission of 16 months, it was now regarded as Liberal.

Thus, the formal start of the Liberal Party had been the meeting on 6 June 1859 in Willis's Rooms in London when MPs formally pledged themselves to unite to defeat Lord Derby's Conservative government and oppose his policy towards the **Italian Question**. However, we should not assign too much importance to this meeting in the history of the Liberal Party. This is because:

- many Liberal ideas were already formed well before this;
- Lord Palmerston's views after 1859 were no different from the ones he had held in his earlier ministry;
- it was left to Gladstone nearly ten years later in 1868 to become leader of a more coherent Liberal Party.

**The situation in 1846.** The issue of the repeal of the Corn Laws complicated the position of the main political parties in 1846. Up to this point the Whigs and Tories who had fought over the merits of the Reform Bills in 1830–2 had

KEY PEOPLE

**William Gladstone 1809–98** Son of a wealthy middle-class Liverpool merchant involved in the slave trade, Gladstone had a strongly Protestant upbringing but later accepted some Catholic – though never Roman Catholic – views and maintained a powerful religious faith. Educated at Oxford. Politically a Tory as a young man – he opposed the 1832 Reform Act – he was converted to free trade when first Vice-President and later President of the Board of Trade in Peel's 1841–6 government. Leading Peelite 1846–59; then a Liberal. Outstanding Chancellor of the Exchequer 1852–5 and 1859–66; Liberal Prime Minister 1869–74, 1880–5, 1886, 1892–4. He was noted for his intense seriousness of character, and possessed phenomenal energy.

**The Earl of Aberdeen 1784–1860** Scottish aristocrat who spent most of his life in England, Aberdeen was a Tory who stayed loyal to Peel in 1846 and became the leading Peelite after Peel's death. Foreign Secretary 1828–30 and 1841–6; Prime Minister 1852–5. An accomplished diplomat, his reputation was ruined (rather harshly) by the disasters of the Crimean War.

still been the principal groupings. The party position in the House of Commons at the end of 1846 was as follows.

**Conservatives.** Tory protectionists who had opposed repeal and did not favour free trade. They were led by the **Earl of Derby**, the most prominent of the Conservatives who split with Peel over repeal. They were the largest single group in the Commons but were outnumbered by others who all accepted free trade.

**Peelites.** A group of Conservatives who stayed loyal to their leader. Their number was distinguished rather than large. They included future Prime Ministers Aberdeen and Gladstone as well as a number of other ex-ministers of Peel's government. Peel steadfastly refused to ally with either Russell's Whigs or his old Conservative colleagues until his death in 1850.

**Whigs.** Led by Lord John Russell, now the party of government. The Whigs had increasingly come to accept the necessity of repeal of the Corn Laws, even though their previous leader, Lord Melbourne, had called it 'the wildest and maddest scheme' as late as 1839.

**Radicals.** Independent MPs who regarded themselves as Radicals. They had not formed themselves into a coherent party, but gave the Whigs broad support over free trade. Their numbers had fallen since the more reforming and exciting atmosphere of the mid-1830s.

After the election of 1847 the numbers of the parties in Parliament were about:

- 325 Whig-Liberal-Radical supporters;
- 230 Protectionist Conservatives;
- 100 Peelites.

These numbers did not vary enormously over the next 20 years though the Peelite vote was gradually absorbed by both Conservatives and Liberals.

**How far were the Whigs aristocratic rather than middle class?** In social background the Whigs were just as aristocratic as the Tories. Lord John Russell's **cabinet** in 1846 consisted of two marquesses, four earls, one viscount, two barons, three knights and just two untitled commoners. Many leading Whig aristocratic families like the Grosvenors, the Russells, the Spencers and the Cavendishes had intermarried and they were a closely-knit group though not numerous. To match the Tory-Conservative support in Parliament they had to rely on outside assistance and look to votes from more independent and radically minded members as well as **Irish support**.

Backing from these more radically minded members was certainly possible. By 1846, their tradition of supporting religious liberty had gained Whigs the support of a wide sector of the industrial middle classes: this included nonconformists who favoured religious liberty and who were now also attracted to the Whigs' free trade commitment. Only by cultivating this increasingly important sector of society could the Whigs hope to gain the support they needed to keep out the Tory-Conservative protectionists.

**What attracted liberal-thinking middle classes towards the Whigs?** The new political participation by the middle classes was an important feature of mid-century politics. The Whigs, for all their aristocratic attitudes, were the party the middle classes would naturally turn to. After all, why were the middle classes playing a more substantial role in the political affairs of the nation in the first place?

- They owed their opportunity for greater participation partly to the changes introduced by the Whigs in the 1830s. In the 1832 Reform Act the **£10 householder in the boroughs** was enfranchised (given the vote).
- The middle classes were playing the central role in the growth of local government. Although they may not have been actively seeking membership of the House of Commons in any significant numbers, they were increasingly being elected to local corporations thanks to the Whig **Municipal Corporations Act of 1835**. Alternatively they might seek election to the **Poor Law Board of Guardians** set up by the Poor Law

## KEY TERM

**Cabinet** The most important ministers in a government who meet regularly together and agree on important policy decisions.

## KEY CONCEPT

**Irish support** Members of the House of Commons elected in Ireland – about 100 – who sat in the English Parliament. In the period 1846–68 Irish nationalism was weakened severely by the famine of 1846. Many of these MPs were nationalistically inclined and wished to see major reforms in the way the country was run. They generally linked up with English Radicals and advanced Liberals, showing that, before 1870, some Irish MPs were quite well integrated into the British political system.

## KEY TERM

**£10 householder in the boroughs** The most important group of people given the vote by the 1832 Reform Act. Essentially the middle classes in the towns. Occupation of the property was enough to qualify for the vote; ownership was not necessary.

Amendment Act of 1834. The middle classes dominated such organisations and the aristocracy played little part in these urban developments.

- The middle-class factory owner may have been less keen on the Factory Act of 1833, which by restricting the hours of work for women and children in factories would also restrict his freedom of operation. But this was hardly a reason for supporting the Conservatives, who had extended the legislation in 1844. Even the 1833 Factory Act was supported by some Tories.
- The Whigs had not only passed political reform: they also seemed more likely to maintain and develop free trade and extend religious liberty. The Conservatives had opposed all three.

## WHAT WAS THE POSITION OF THE RADICALS?

One of the major changes in the process of moving from Whig to Liberal was that, whereas in 1846 middle-class Radicals in Parliament tended to operate separately from the established parties, by the late 1860s they were attaching themselves more formally to the newly emerging 'Liberal' Party. After 1832, middle-class Radicals had been elected in a number of seats though they did not form a tightly-knit group. Their number fell in the 1837 election and still further in 1841. After the repeal of the Corn Laws – partly attributable to the radical agitation of the Anti Corn Law League – their numbers revived but barely reached even at their peak more than 50 MPs. With the election of 1847, however, they optimistically anticipated further radical reform.

They were to be disappointed. The way that Corn Law repeal had been conceded was that Peel had raised the question as a statesmanlike-way of dealing with the Irish famine question. The decision was a parliamentary one with the powerful League merely onlookers at this crucial stage. The government had not caved in to the reformers through weakness, it seemed, but to an act of statesmanship by Peel. Russell did not feel obliged to let the middle classes into the government in large numbers. One member of the Anti-Corn Law League, Milner

Gibson, was given minor office but the administration was essentially a Whig one.

## What did the middle-class Radicals want?

- Further changes to the parliamentary system of representation throughout the country. The 1832 Reform Act had been a sound start but had not gone far enough.
- The extension of religious liberty so that there was not merely **toleration** for nonconformists but absolute equality.
- There was a need for more tariff reductions in order to develop free trade policies.
- Administrative reform leading to greater equality of opportunity. The aristocratic stranglehold on government had to be broken.

But in these areas the more radical middle-class Liberals felt unable to commit themselves fully to the Whig government led by a man such as Russell.

- Radicals wanted parliamentary reform to go further than it had with extensions of the franchise (to at least **household suffrage**), **redistribution of seats** and a **secret ballot**. Russell's proposals for reform were seen as inadequate and half-hearted.
- There were still major nonconformist grievances such as the compulsory payment of Church rates (see page 77) that the Russell government seemed unlikely to change.
- The Whigs' rather uninspiring Chancellor, Sir Charles Wood, did take action on free trade but was not seen to go far enough in reducing tariffs, and belief in free trade was central to middle-class Radicals, especially those of the **Manchester School**.
- Whig governments such as Russell's seemed to them far too dominated by the aristocracy and unwilling to let in new middle-class talent.

HEINEMANN ADVANCED HISTORY

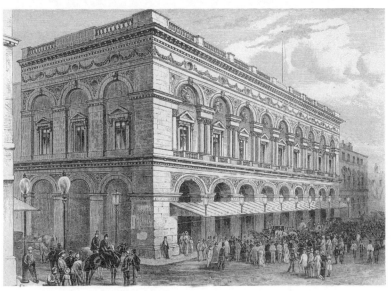

The only public building dedicated to a proposition? Free Trade Hall, Manchester, 1847.

KEY TERM

**Manchester School**
Originally a group who came from Manchester and industrial Lancashire who championed free trade and as little government interference with the workings of the British economy as possible. Cobden and Bright were leading representatives.

KEY EVENT

**Great Exhibition of 1851**
A special event held for several months in Hyde Park in the original Crystal Palace, designed by Joseph Paxton. It showed examples of the great variety of industrial products that were the fruits of modern technology.

KEY PERSON

**Prince Albert 1820–61**
Second son of the Duke of Saxe-Coburg-Gotha, a small German state. Cousin of Queen Victoria, who met him when he first visited England in 1836. They married in 1840. He became popular after initial anti-German prejudice. A major prop and support for the Queen, he guided her to a style of constitutional monarchy. Made Prince Consort 1857. Serious-minded and hard-working, he died of typhoid fever. Victoria was lost without him.

## THE POLICIES OF THE WHIGS BETWEEN 1846 AND 1859

### The Whigs and free trade

Russell's ministry from 1846 to 1852 was not a strong one. It lacked a clear majority and temporarily collapsed in 1851. But it did maintain free trade principles.

- It passed the Sugar Act in 1848 which removed the trading privileges of British West Indies sugar planters.
- It repealed the Navigation Laws in 1849. This meant that overseas traders could use any ships they wished to transport their goods abroad: they were not confined to the British Merchant Navy.

Also, the **Great Exhibition of 1851** advertised to the world the importance of British manufacture and international trading and significantly was only opposed by a few very traditional Conservative MPs. Although it was ironically the monarchy in the guise of **Prince Albert** that pushed for the exhibition, it helped the middle classes to feel that they were playing a full part in progress and change.

The Whigs – with the aid of the Peelites – maintained their reputation as the party of free trade in the early 1850s. The brief Conservative administration of Lord

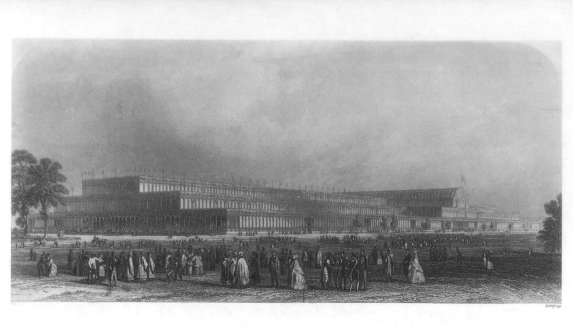

A VIEW OF THE GREAT INDUSTRIAL EXHIBITION IN HYDE PARK.

Derby in 1852 had been uncertain on the issue. When Lord Aberdeen formed a ministry at the end of 1852 he appointed Gladstone as his Chancellor of the Exchequer, an acknowledged financial expert now thoroughly committed to extending the principles of free trade and with the technical mastery to be able to accomplish his aims. Gladstone produced **budgets** that lowered tariff duties on a number of goods in order to encourage trade expansion. The budget of 1853 removed duties on 123 articles and reduced them on 133 more.

Such was the growing prosperity of the country that Gladstone felt he could introduce reductions without increasing the basic rate of **income tax**, despite the loss of government revenue the tariff reduction would bring. Trade would be encouraged so much by the change, argued Gladstone, that this would cancel out the need for any increases in income tax. Indeed, Gladstone forecast that if present trends continued the income tax itself could be abolished by 1860. This certainly pleased the commercial middle classes for two reasons:

- income tax was not popular and the prospect of its eventual abolition was encouraging news;
- not only this, the fact that Gladstone as Chancellor was planning ahead and actually bringing government

**A building to impress the nations: the Crystal Palace, opened 1851.**

### KEY TERMS

**Budgets** Annual financial statement by the Chancellor of the Exchequer. In the mid-nineteenth century the normal aim of these budgets was to ensure that government expenditure was matched by government income from taxation and trade.

**Income tax** Tax paid by individuals to the government in proportion to the size of their own income. First used in wartime 1797–1816; reintroduced as a temporary measure 1842. In the 1850s it had still not been established as a permanent tax.

financial policy in line with current economic trends sent a message to those same middle classes that government was now acting in their interests, and was not merely concerned with the well-being of the landed interest. The repeal of the Corn Laws had not been a one-off concession.

Gladstone had begun the process – by no means inevitable at this stage and some distance away – of becoming a friend of liberal-thinking people. However, in other important areas the Whigs (or Peelites in Gladstone's case) had not gone far enough to gain regular Radical support.

### The Whigs and political reform

On the question of further parliamentary reform there were some signs of movement after 1848 when the final **Chartist** demonstration had ended in heavy rain on Kennington Common. Russell had previously argued that there would be no more reform of Parliament after the changes of 1832. However, various ideas were put forward which never materialised.

- In 1851 he made a very modest proposal for reform of Parliament whereby the £10 household franchise would be reduced to £6. This never got to the vote.
- A similar proposal in 1852 bit the dust with the fall of the ministry
- And another one disappeared without trace in 1854 with the outbreak of the Crimean War.

### The Whigs and religious reform

On the question of religious liberty, the Whigs were seen as less dogmatic upholders of the privileges of the Church of England than the Tories but had not gained the support of the religious dissenters (nonconformists). What were the changes the more radical nonconformists wished to see?

- Abolition of compulsory Church rates.
- **Voluntarism** in education so that the Church of England schools did not have the advantage of state funding.

- The opportunity to attend Oxford and Cambridge universities on equal terms with Anglicans. For example, fellowships at these institutions were barred to them.
- They questioned the establishment of the Anglican Church in Ireland where the majority of people were Roman Catholic. They wished to see the wealth of the Church go elsewhere. Increasingly many were coming to the view that there should be no establishment in England either.

These were significant issues: religious questions were much discussed in mid-nineteenth century England and were central to the lives of many people.

The religious census of 1851 indicated that about half of total church attendance was not to the Established Church of England but to nonconformist churches, well supported by the industrial middle class. But the Whig governments of Russell, and later Palmerston, did not wish to move towards this degree of reform. The year of the religious census also saw Russell pass an Ecclesiastical Titles Bill, which was an illiberal measure. It prevented the English Roman Catholic bishops from taking up titles with the same name as their Church of England counterparts. Here, Russell may well have appealed to some of the Protestant

The growth of nonconformity: Pendre Congregational Chapel, South Wales, built in 1820.

nonconformist middle classes in a negative way, since their liberal attitude to differences in belief did not always extend at this time to Roman Catholics. But he did not impress more consistent Liberal thinkers such as John Bright who thought the measure 'absurd'.

## The Whigs and administrative reform

The desire of Liberals to enter the heart of the aristocratic establishment was as strong as ever. Although the middle classes had received the vote in 1832, the composition of Parliament did not reflect their proportion of the electorate. The kind of reforms desired included a widening of opportunity for the middle classes.

- Civil service appointments should no longer be reserved solely for those of upper-class backgrounds. Promotion on merit by competitive examination should be introduced.
- Top positions in the army should again be on merit and **commissions** should not only be available to those who could purchase them.
- More open government should be prepared to reveal details of departmental business, especially that of the Foreign Office.

But again, in this area there was little sign of concession from the Whigs. The Northcote-Trevelyan Report of 1854 did recommend competitive entry into the civil service. The **Crimean War** (1854–6) showed up some of these administrative inefficiencies in stark form: the uncertain generalship in the army and the lack of communication with government back home. For a time Radical demands for reform surfaced strongly with the founding of the Administrative Reform Association by figures such as Bright, in 1855, but the momentum did not last. Palmerston's government – strictly the last Whig one, between 1855 and 1858 – did not take up the challenge of administrative reform. It was only when Gladstone became Prime Minister in 1868 that action was taken, and it was the same with the question of the purchase of army commissions.

## KEY TERM °

**Purchase of commissions**
To attain officer rank in the army the commission (official authorisation of appointment as an officer) had to be bought. The higher the rank, the more expensive. Thus the top ranks of the army were confined to the wealthy landed classes (see also Chapter 5).

## KEY EVENT

**Crimean War 1854–6**
Started from a dispute between Russia and Turkey in which Britain intervened on the Turkish side. Britain had strong trading links with Turkey. The war was largely confined to the Crimea peninsula where British forces suffered heavy causalities and there was much criticism at home about how the conflict was conducted. It brought down Aberdeen's Whig-Peelite coalition early in 1855.

## Foreign policy and the importance of Palmerston's popularity

Palmerston was a surprisingly popular figure with the Radicals despite a reputation for being Conservative in many of his views and being a well-known opponent of further parliamentary reform. He managed to maintain the voting support of many of the Radicals with a popular foreign policy. The English middle classes were decidedly patriotic and Palmerston's vigorous foreign policy was already well known to them as he had been Foreign Secretary in Russell's ministry from 1846 to 1851 (see Chapter 7). In showing some sympathy with **1848 revolutionaries** and less concern for their governments on occasions, he gained a Liberal image. Whether this reputation was deserved is questionable. Arguably it was not so much his liberalism, as his general championing of English interests abroad, that endeared him to the Liberal middle classes.

The result was that at the age of 70 **Palmerston was reluctantly invited by Queen Victoria** to be Prime Minister in 1855. The Whig-Peelite coalition of Lord Aberdeen had fallen with the government's defeat in Parliament over its weak running of the Crimean War. When the Conservative Derby was unwilling to become Prime Minister, the fact that a number of other leading figures had been at least temporarily discredited by their involvement in the Aberdeen government allowed Palmerston to emerge.

The Radicals were disappointed. They did not even have the consolation of Gladstone as Chancellor since after at first accepting office he then decided he could not serve in the new ministry, disliking Palmerston's approach to government in general and his foreign policy in particular.

But there is no doubting the popularity of Palmerston's policy with the middle-class electorate. Even when he was defeated on a foreign-policy issue in Parliament in 1857, he immediately called a general election, and he and his supporters, Whigs and Liberals, were returned with a comfortable majority. Such was the uncertainty of party allegiance at this time, however, that Palmerston was again

### KEY THEME

**Palmerston and Queen Victoria** The Queen was reluctant to ask Palmerston to become Prime Minister because she disliked him intensely. Her joke name for him was 'Lord Pumicestone'.

**The dominant mid-nineteenth-century parliamentarian: Lord Palmerston addresses the House of Commons, 1863.**

defeated in Parliament the following year and Lord Derby formed the third of his brief administrations, only to fall at the polls in 1859 after another triumph for Palmerston's supporters.

The attitude to Palmerston's foreign policy among the Radicals was mixed, as were their views on the Crimean War. This division among them was not confined to foreign policy issues and helps to explain the lack of a properly organised Radical Party.

### WHY WERE RADICALS UNABLE TO FORM THEIR OWN PARTY?

Radicals were much too diverse a group and too divided to form their own party with any chance of lasting unity and effectiveness. They were interested in a number of different questions and different Radical members emphasised different issues as being of prime importance. On some of these matters – like foreign policy – Radicals took opposing sides and would never have possessed sufficient agreement to work together in one grouping. Only on free trade did there seem to be clear agreement. The differences can be grouped as follows.

1 **The range and degree of parliamentary reform.** Moderate Liberals favoured a lowering of the £10 household suffrage level to around £6 or £7. This would have included the very top end of the skilled working class. More **advanced Liberals**, now almost indistinguishable from Radicals, saw no objection to household suffrage with certain residence qualifications and up-to-date payment of poor rates. The most extreme Radicals favoured manhood suffrage. The Radicals John Stuart Mill and Henry Fawcett (see table) argued powerfully for female suffrage though on this point they were in a minority. Some felt a secret ballot was essential to overcome aristocratic influence while others regarded the secrecy involved as 'un-English'. Some, such as Mill, actually changed their views on the secret ballot question in the 1850s and decided the disadvantages of secrecy outweighed its advantages.

### Leading Radicals

| | Born | Background | Parliamentary career | Particular interests | Died |
|---|---|---|---|---|---|
| John Bright | 1811 | Owned mill in Rochdale | 1847–57 Manchester, 1857–85 Birmingham | Free trade, parliamentary reform, administrative reform, Ireland | 1889 |
| Richard Cobden | 1804 | Moved to Lancs when a child, manufacturer | 1841–7 Oldham, 1847–65 Manchester | Free trade, international peace | 1865 |
| John Stuart Mill | 1806 | Londoner, classical education | 1865–8 Westminster | Liberty and laissez-faire, votes for women | 1873 |
| Henry Fawcett | 1833 | Blinded in 1858, Cambridge professor in 1863 | 1865–84 Brighton | Parliamentary reform, votes for women | 1884 |
| Edward Miall | 1809 | Working-class Londoner, edited *The Nonconformist*, Congregationalist minister | 1852–7 Rochdale, 1869–74 Bradford | Disestablishment, church rates abolition, rights of nonconformists, education | 1881 |
| John Roebuck | 1802 (India) | Brought up in England and Canada | Bath 1832–47, Sheffield 1849–68, Sheffield 1874–9 (as Conservative) | Parliamentary reform, foreign affairs, education, free press | 1879 |

**Bright's anti-war speech**
'The angel of death has been abroad throughout the land: you can almost hear the beating of his wings … he takes his victims from the castle of the noble, the mansion of the wealthy and the cottage of the poor and lowly.' John Bright, House of Commons, 23 February 1855.

**George Jacob Holyoake 1817–1906** He founded the *Reasoner* magazine in 1846 questioning the value of religion. A keen social reformer. Secularists believed that society had no need for religious belief: it was out of date and impeded modern progress. Moral standards should be developed without regard for the Divine or an after life.

**American Civil War**
Fought between 1861 and 1865. The southern states in the Union wished to secede (leave) and the northern states wished to prevent them. Britain was officially neutral and opinion about whom to support was divided at first. But, as the war developed into a conflict about whether to retain slavery, support for the North grew, especially in more radical circles.

2 **Foreign policy.** Some Radicals such as John Arthur Roebuck were strong supporters of Palmerston's foreign policy and fully believed Britain to be championing the interests of small nations abroad against mighty despotisms like Russia. Others like Richard Cobden and John Bright were near **pacifists** who had strong moral and religious objections to any fighting that risked heavy casualties. They felt the spread of international free trade would make the world so interdependent economically that war would be suicidal. Bright, a great orator, delivered a powerful **anti-war speech** in the House of Commons in February 1855. Notwithstanding this eloquent plea, however, the peace-loving Radicals were in the distinct minority during the Crimean War and in Palmerston's subsequent foreign-policy adventures.

3 **Nonconformity and religious liberty.** Religious liberty was often a great unifying force for Radicals but there were major differences nonetheless. There were sharp divisions between nonconformist militants like Edward Miall and secularists like **George Jacob Holyoake**. While both might be agreed on disestablishment of the Church Miall wished to see temperance reform (see page 82) whereas Holyoake concentrated on founding secular societies to counter the influence of all religious institutions.

4 **Social reform.** Traditional laissez faire free traders such as Bright remained doubtful about the need for or desirability of government regulation of factories or even public health. Many Radicals, however, were becoming increasingly convinced of the need for such regulation even to the extent of modifying the rights of private property in the case of housing reform. The differences on social reform diminished as more and more Radicals came to acknowledge the need for government intervention in social questions.

However, many divisions remained as acute as ever in the 1860s. For instance, there was disagreement on who to support, if anyone, in the **American Civil War**. Should it be the southern states struggling to be free of northern domination, or the slave-abolitionists in the north? Radical division on the point was shown for instance by Roebuck backing the South and Bright rooting for the North (see also Chapter 4).

The social differences within the Radicals remained very wide. This meant many believed the establishment of a formal party would be extremely difficult. However, the coming-together of many different social groups to form a strong Liberal Party by 1868 showed it was not impossible. Between the formal formation of the Liberal Party in 1859 and its triumph at the 1868 election a number of factors combined to create unity in a way they had not for an earlier generation of Radicals.

## HOW FAR DID THE LIBERALS COME TOGETHER BETWEEN 1859 AND 1865?

This was an important period in the formation of the Liberal Party.

- Free trade policies continued under Gladstone whose reputation was rising rapidly.
- Gladstone also became politically more Liberal and a potential leader of a Liberal Party. Only the aged Palmerston, who continued to oppose it, stood in the way of more substantial parliamentary reform.
- John Bright emerged as a prominent leader for the more radical Liberals.
- The more complex European situation meant a vigorous Palmerstonian foreign policy was less appropriate. In future Liberal foreign policy would assume a distinctive character.

In addition:

- The middle-class provincial press was making a substantial impact on middle-class political opinion.
- The Liberals were also attracting the skilled working-class labour interest to a much greater extent than ever before.

**Free trade.** In Palmerston's ministry of 1859–65 and for a further year under Russell, Gladstone continued his free trade policies with fewer interruptions than he had had previously.

- The 1860 budget produced further major tariff reductions as only 48 items were left on the tariff.
- By 1865 income tax had been reduced from **10d to 4d** in the pound.
- Government expenditure was less in 1866 than it was in 1860 (£70 million down to £66 million).
- Sugar and tea duties were lowered in 1864 and 1865.
- The timber duty was abolished in 1866.

While technological change brought rapid developments on the railways and in ship-building which greatly cut costs, contemporaries saw free trade as the key to prosperity and viewed this as a 'Liberal' policy they could support.

**Gladstone and political reform.** Gladstone, an economic champion of the Liberal middle classes, was also becoming a political champion for a social group just below this: the skilled working class. During his second period as Chancellor he became increasingly convinced of their right to vote in elections. Deeply impressed with the way the Lancashire textile workers handled the cotton crisis of the American Civil War (see page 53) he asserted that the working man now had a moral right to vote. The 'people's William' had emerged. Gladstone seemed to be the Liberal leader of the future and the days of the 'two dreadful old men' (Queen Victoria's name for Palmerston and Russell in the early 1860s) seemed to be numbered. The Whigs had become merely a part of the Liberal Party.

**The emergence of Bright.** John Bright – a famous Radical figure because of his role in the Anti-Corn Law League – **lost much popularity** after his criticism of the Crimean War. Never an out-and-out democrat and uncertain about female suffrage he saw no reason why votes should not be extended to all male householders. His firm line on this question won over many Liberal MPs. The need for substantial parliamentary reform – even if there was still some disagreement on the details – now became a uniting more than a dividing factor for Liberals.

### KEY TERM

**10d to 4d** d was the symbol for (old) pennies. Two and a half old pennies make one new pence in current money.

### KEY IDEA

**Bright's loss of popularity**
He was defeated at the election in Manchester in 1857 and suffered health problems. However, he was re-elected to Parliament to represent Birmingham in 1857 and by the early 1860s he turned his considerable speaking powers to the cause of parliamentary reform.

Bright's long-standing colleague Cobden also played a significant Liberal role in the early 1860s and this would certainly have been greater but for his death in 1865. Though refusing Palmerston's offer of a cabinet post in 1859 he agreed to act as a government agent and negotiated an important free trade treaty with France in 1860.

**Changes in foreign policy.** The emergence of a powerful Prussia (Northern Germany) under its Prime Minister Bismarck in the 1860s and the unification of Italy at a similar time made the aggressive **Palmerstonian-style policy** look riskier than before.

**Death of Palmerston.** Another major factor here was the death of Lord Palmerston in October 1865 shortly after his Liberal grouping had been successful in another election. Palmerston was aware his passing would bring changes. His death led to Russell (now Earl Russell) succeeding as Prime Minister but Russell was 74 and in only moderate health. Gladstone would clearly be Liberal leader in the Commons and heir apparent. The 'strange doings' were about to begin. This led to a period between 1866 and 1868 of great political excitement and drama. It was only after this had unfolded that Gladstone emerged as the clear leader of a strong and relatively united Liberal Party.

**The role of the press.** During the 1850s and 1860s there was a substantial growth in the provincial middle-class press. Middle-class influence over public opinion in the industrial towns of Britain was substantial and that influence was frequently Liberal. The growth of the popularity of the newspapers was aided by:

- the repeal of the newspaper tax in 1854 and of the advertising tax in 1855;
- Gladstone's repeal of the duty on paper in 1861;
- the technological improvements brought about by the steam press in the 1850s;
- the rapid increase in communication caused by the railway and the telegraph.

**Leading nineteenth-century Radical: John Bright.**

### KEY CONCEPT

**The riskiness of a Palmerstonian-style foreign policy** A foreign policy that became too actively involved with Europe seemed now on reflection to be fraught with danger as large continental armies developed; too expensive and likely to disrupt the growth of the British economy – as had the Crimean War; in moral terms un-Christian, and impossible to justify unless the weak were clearly being severely oppressed, because of the suffering and death of innocent parties.

Liberal papers included:

- *Leeds Mercury*, run by the Baines family, strong nonconformist Liberals.
- *Leicester Mercury*, run by the vice-president of the Leicestershire Liberal Association.
- *Newcastle Chronicle*, run by Liberal Joseph Cowan.
- *Sheffield Independent*, run by the Leader family, also Liberals.

(List taken from John Vincent: *The Formation of the British Liberal Party, 1972*)

## KEY PERSON

**George Odger 1820–77** A shoemaker, Odger was an active trade unionist and took part in the large and widespread builders' strike 1859–60. Secretary of the newly formed **London Trades Council** (a group of leading trade union secretaries) in 1862–72, he had a very radical reputation in the 1850s and early 1860s. From 1868 onwards he identified more with advanced Liberals and Radicals giving broad support to Gladstone.

All these factors helped to make newspapers cheaply available everywhere and greatly encouraged the growth of more newspapers and of newspaper readers in the increasingly literate towns. Political knowledge and discussion were now less and less the preserve of the landed classes.

### Working-class involvement with the Liberals.

In the 1840s the political activities of the working class and middle class had tended to be separate. The radical demands of the Chartists were dominated by working-class people, and middle-class Radicalism was channelled into organisations like the Anti-Corn Law League. However, the Chartist movement faded badly after 1848. Even those who kept the Chartist flag flying were of the opinion by the 1860s that progress was only likely to be achieved in practice by an alliance of all Radicals under a broad Liberal umbrella.

In Birmingham class conflict was traditionally less because its workshop rather than large factory base meant less impersonal relations between employer and employee. Hence Bright was the acknowledged Radical leader for a wide social group. In London men like **George Odger**, Secretary of the **London Trades Council**, were working-class leaders with a Radical past who now developed close links with the Liberal middle classes. Odger supported the middle-class John Stuart Mill's successful bid to be elected for Westminster in 1865 as an advanced Liberal. With no effective socialist movement in sight many Liberals believed that an extension of the franchise into the skilled working class would benefit them rather than the Conservatives. They believed they had nothing to fear from respectable and increasingly moderate trade unionists.

Others, however, wondered whether the average working man would vote for the same person as his employer and in some areas working-class and middle-class organisations remained distinct with different demands. For instance, in 1864 the middle and working-class Reform Union was founded to campaign for household suffrage, but it went on to develop a middle-class membership. In 1865, those that wanted an exclusively working-class organisation to put forward more radical demands set up the Reform League which became committed to manhood suffrage.

**Survival of the Whigs.** Because Lord Palmerston had died in October 1865, soon after constructing his **new government**, Russell, his successor, made few changes. This meant, for instance, that the Liberal cabinet was still well stocked with aristocratic Whigs. Russell replaced himself as Foreign Secretary with the Earl of Clarendon. Six of the twelve members of the cabinet were peers from Whig families. Posts in government such as Foreign Secretary and Lord Chancellor – the head of the English legal system – were still positions traditionally reserved for the landed classes.

Thus the aristocratic Whigs (and Conservatives) were surviving remarkably well. Nonetheless, change was occurring. At each election a new influx of Radical MPs from non-landed backgrounds emerged. This was particularly true of the 1865 election when Henry Fawcett was elected for Brighton and John Stuart Mill for Westminster. Moreover, with Palmerston gone, the introduction of a parliamentary reform bill was much more likely. Over the next two years reform was to be the dominant issue and helped to continue the process of the transition from Whig to Liberal.

## CONCLUSION

To a large extent by 1866 the Whig Party had been transformed into a Liberal Party where Whigs were still prominent but where the liberal-minded middle classes – and a few working people – had been incorporated into a party with a much wider social and political base. What were the main factors behind this transformation?

- The inability of the Radical elements in Parliament to come together on an agreed programme and formally develop a party completely separate from the Whigs.
- An agreement on the development of free trade policies.

- The emergence of Gladstone and Bright as champions of the Liberal interest in the 1860s and their clear commitment to political and administrative reform.
- Strong nonconformist support from an increasingly powerful and politically literate middle class.
- The greater opportunities for a broad-based Liberal Party afforded by the death of Palmerston in 1865. This opened the way to a greater chance of agreement on foreign policy and further parliamentary reform.

## SUMMARY QUESTIONS

1  What was the relationship between Radicals and Whigs in the period 1846–59?

2  What were the main political issues that caused division in Radical ranks in the 1850s?

3  Why did the Liberal Party develop in the 1860s?

4  What was the importance of Gladstone in the emerging Liberal Party?

# CHAPTER 3

## WHY WAS THE CONSERVATIVE PARTY OUT OF OFFICE FOR SO LONG IN THE PERIOD 1846–66?

### INTRODUCTION

In the mid-nineteenth century the Conservatives had the largest support of any single party in the country. But:

- the disastrous split in 1846 over the repeal of the Corn Laws brought a long-lasting division between Peelites and protectionists that never fully healed;
- there were major problems concerning the leadership of the main group of Protectionist Conservatives;
- the unstable political climate but general economic stability of the period did not help in the quest to establish a more widely supported party – it was not always clear what the Conservatives stood for;
- the electoral appeal of Lord Palmerston, a near-Conservative Whig, did not assist the cause of the Conservative Party.

This chapter will investigate the factors that kept them out of office for so long.

### ORIGINS OF THE SPLIT

The Conservative Party recovered well from its heavy defeat by the Whigs after the passing of the 1832 Reform Bill. Under Peel, the Tories – often now referred to as Conservatives – had re-assumed office in 1841 with a strong effective ministry. The recovery involved a change in direction. Conservatives had accepted parliamentary reform and for the moment the Whigs intended no more. So the two issues which seemed to separate the parties were that:

---

**KEY EVENT**

**The Maynooth Grant**
Maynooth was a college near Dublin for training Irish Roman Catholic priests. It had received a government grant of £900 a year since 1795. It is said that some students attended without any inclination towards the priesthood in order to take advantage of general educational opportunities rarely found elsewhere. They would then leave before their final vows. In 1845 Peel proposed to treble the grant. Many Conservatives voted against the grant and Peel was embarrassingly forced to rely on Whig support to get the measure through.

---

- the Conservatives were the stronger defenders of the landed interest in general and the Corn Laws and protectionist principles in particular;
- the Conservatives were also keen not to undermine the position and privileges of the Church of England in any way.

### The Maynooth Grant and repeal of the Corn Laws

Peel now proceeded to take two decisions which seemed to undermine these basic principles. Both issues had an Irish link.

Peel believed that he had acted in the national interest on both these issues but his actions were very damaging for the Conservatives as a party.

- By increasing the **Maynooth Grant** in 1845 he offended many Conservatives who objected on principle to a measure which to their eyes undermined the Established Church. Roman Catholicism was not generally looked upon sympathetically by the majority of the landed interest. No matter that the grant was merely being increased and used for general educational purposes, the objection was still strong.
- Peel's decision to **repeal the Corn Laws** in 1846, while partly inspired by strong humanitarian feeling, proved the breaking point for many Conservative landowners who saw this as a betrayal of their interests and principles. Agriculture was still felt to be economically the largest single industry, and to fail to protect the farming community was seen as undermining the strength of the country in an unacceptable way. A pledge of 1841 to maintain the Corn Laws in the next Parliament had been broken. Repeal was seen to be taking away the main form of protection for the landed interest.

The most eloquent and successful speech in attacking Peel was by **Benjamin Disraeli** who in a powerful performance in the Commons accused Peel of betraying his party. And this, argued Disraeli, was disastrous:

'For it is only by maintaining the independence of party

**Benjamin Disraeli**
**1804–81** Born in London, son of Jewish writer, Disraeli had a modest but not poor upbringing and was educated privately. He studied law, became a writer, especially of novels, entered Parliament in 1837 as a Conservative. Not given office by Peel in 1841 to his great disappointment. Early reputation as an elaborate speaker, fancy dresser with a fondness for gambling and society ladies. His speeches in 1846 against Peel made his reputation overnight. Leader of the Conservatives in the Commons 1846–68. Chancellor of the Exchequer 1852, 1858–9, 1866–8; Prime Minister 1868 and 1874–80. Created Earl of Beaconsfield 1876.

that you can maintain the integrity of public men, and the power and influence of Parliament itself.'

The repeal of the Corn Laws was passed by a majority of 97 in the Commons with Whig support; the influence of the Duke of Wellington – loyal to Peel – ensured it also passed through the House of Lords.

---

### The voting figures in the Commons were:

For repeal:      339    112 Conservatives (Peelites), 227 Whigs, Liberals and Radicals

Against repeal:   242    all protectionist Conservatives

Majority:        97

This shows the serious nature of the Conservative split.

---

## Results of the split

The day after the repeal of the Corn Laws was passed by the House of Lords, Peel's government was defeated on a routine bill concerning the maintaining of law and order in Ireland. **Protectionist Conservatives** were bitter about what they regarded as Peel's betrayal. Never before had Conservatives voted against an **Irish Coercion Act**. In doing so they ensured the political defeat of Peel and a spell of government for the Whigs and their Liberal allies. Peel and his loyal colleagues – Peelites, and prominent among them was Gladstone – went for the time being into the political wilderness, refusing to attach themselves to either the Tory/Conservatives led by Lord Derby or the Whig/Liberals led by Lord John Russell. But they cannot have imagined that in the next 20 years Conservatives would have only been in power for two very short spells barely amounting to two years.

### KEY TERMS

**Protectionist Conservatives** Name given to those Conservatives who refused to support the repeal of the Corn Laws and remained general supporters of the principle of protection for a few more years.

**Irish Coercion Act**
Coercion in general terms means force. In this context the Act would remove the Rule of Law in Ireland and allow the authorities to arrest nationalists on mere suspicion of violent revolutionary activities. Such Acts were passed almost as a routine in the early nineteenth century and were normally supported by the Conservatives without question.

## THE SPLIT CONTINUES 1846–52

### Party problems

**The Peelites.** The minority of Conservatives who had supported repeal stuck to the name Peelites, claimed to be the true Conservatives and refused for the moment to link up with any other grouping. Senior politicians such as Peel's ex-Chancellor of the Exchequer, Henry Goulburn were not likely to attach themselves to any other party and he maintained, like all the other senior Peelites, a fierce loyalty to Peel. But Peel's actions hardly helped the cause of re-union. He could not bring himself to realign with those who had failed to support him in his hour of need. It would, as he put it, 'be inconsistent with my sense of honour' even to discuss tactics with the protectionists on how to organise opposition to Russell's Whig government. Since Peel would not stand down as leader either, the Conservatives remained an embarrassingly divided party.

This was particularly apparent in the general election of 1847 when the chief Conservative agent F.R. Bonham used what few central funds the party had at that time in favour of Peelite candidates. Matters would have been even worse if Peelite and protectionist Conservative had frequently fought each other in the election in the same constituency. Fortunately for them this only happened on about ten occasions. Parliamentary constituencies were usually two-member seats and in 1847 there was generally an arrangement whereby either a Peelite or a protectionist would contest the seat, whichever had the best chance of winning. Despite this, the result of the election was a definite victory for those who supported repeal (see table on page 39) and therefore free trade. True, Russell would only have a parliamentary majority if he could rely on the support of all the non-Conservative elements in Parliament and it was not a strong government; but it was the only one possible if Peel stayed aloof from all other groups. So, Russell's government continued and the Conservatives remained out of office.

### Leadership problems

**The protectionist leadership: Lord Derby.** Who would lead the protectionist Conservatives? In the nineteenth century parties not in government frequently had two leaders, one in the Commons and one in the Lords. Leadership in the Lords was a straightforward matter. The **most suitable Conservative leader** was Lord Stanley who became the Earl of Derby in 1851 (referred to throughout this book as Derby).

But Derby was reluctant to take on the full responsibilities of leadership. He was in the aristocratic tradition that saw political service as an important duty to one's country but one that was essentially a part-time occupation. Some of his other interests were equally important to him. Like one of his beloved horses faced with too large a jump, his reaction to being overall party leader of the protectionist Conservatives was to shy away. His reluctance to take over was increased by the fact that the outlook for the Conservatives seemed bleak.

One major problem was the lack of politicians who had previously been ministers. With the exception of Derby those with experience and ability had stayed with Peel.

**The protectionist leadership: Disraeli** Derby might be the obvious leader in the Lords, but leadership in the Commons was not so clear. If Benjamin Disraeli was regarded as a prominent contender it was for very different reasons from Derby. Passed over for office by Peel in 1841 – which might help to account for the tone of his attack on the Prime Minister later – he had sprung to the forefront in 1846, leading the protectionist charge in the Commons against Peel with his series of brilliant speeches. But parliamentary fame was one thing, leadership quite another. While his parliamentary abilities were widely acknowledged – he was the best debater the Conservative protectionists possessed – other factors would count against him. Disraeli's background was not as humble as he sometimes liked to imply, but it was certainly not a landed aristocratic one. His Jewish origins, unusual style, more radical past, racy lifestyle and transparent ambition were all seen to prejudice traditional Conservatives against him. Protectionist Conservative **Chief Whip** William Beresford revealed his feelings about Disraeli in a letter to Lord Derby in 1847: 'As to Disraeli, I would not trust him any more than I would a convicted felon' (criminal).

### Leading ministers who stayed loyal to Peel

| Name | Position in Peel's government |
|---|---|
| Aberdeen | Foreign Secretary |
| Graham | Home Secretary |
| Goulburn | Chancellor of the Exchequer |
| Herbert | War Secretary |
| Gladstone | President of the Board of Trade (then succeeded Derby as Colonial Secretary) |
| Dalhousie | Succeeded Gladstone at the Board of Trade |

These were all regarded as able administrators and capable speakers and without them the remaining Conservatives felt lost. More junior able ministers such as Edward Cardwell (see Chapter 5, page 78) also stayed loyal to Peel. On the **backbenches** there were protectionist Tories in overwhelming numbers, but they lacked the experience, confidence or inclination to take a leading role.

**Leadership confusion.** The result was that the Commons leader of the party was **Lord George Bentinck** but he was not a success. His fiery temperament was hardly what was required for healing wounds in the party. Moreover, while having passionate feelings about protecting the landed interest he did not feel so strongly about the Church. When he voted against the removal of **Jewish disabilities** at the end of 1847 he was criticised and decided to resign.

Disraeli was the obvious successor but the party could not stomach the idea. Lord Granby held the position briefly for three weeks but then decided to be one of a triumvirate (group of three) who would lead the party between them. These were Granby, J.C. Herries and Disraeli. In practice this meant that, eventually, Disraeli emerged as the effective leader of the protectionist Conservatives in the Commons.

## Policy arguments – the question of protection and free trade

Disraeli and Derby faced another major difficulty. Did they cling to the principle of protection? Or should the party accept the moves that had been made towards free trade? Officially, up to 1852, the party remained a protectionist one and in theory would, if returned to power, reimpose the Corn Laws. These did not end suddenly in 1846 but gradually over a period of three years up to 1849. For a time it would be hard to admit that free trade did not appear to have damaged English agriculture which showed more signs of prosperity by 1850 (see page 47). After all, they called themselves the protectionists. But the longer Russell stayed in office and the more other free trade measures were introduced, such as the repeal of the Navigation Laws in 1849 (see page 17), the less likely it appeared that a reversion to protection would occur. The electorate was now predominantly middle class. The growing prosperity of the country meant:

- more people were becoming £10 householders in the boroughs and so were entitled to a vote;
- free trade was associated with prosperity and a re-imposition of protection looked like a vote loser.

Disraeli seems to have had doubts as to whether protection could be retained forever as a policy. Not a member of the landed gentry, he was less committed to it emotionally and he was never a person to stay with a cause that was clearly lost. His attacks on Peel had been personal, and he accused Sir Robert of deserting his party's principles. He did not defend protection rigidly as a matter of principle. The landed interests were entitled to special privileges to maintain their position in the English countryside but these did not have to be founded upon protection. Derby and his fellow Conservative peers might need more convincing but even Derby realised that there was no real alternative policy to repeal to offer.

## Election results 1847–65

These figures are based on the estimates of Rubenstein (1998): without modern party discipline it is hard to be certain about exact numbers. There were 658 MPs, almost all of whom loosely associated with one or other of the major groups.

| Year | Protectionist Conservatives | Whigs/Liberals | Peelites |
|------|------|------|------|
| 1847 | 225 | 330 | 100 |
| 1852 | 290 | 323 | 40 |
| 1857 | 281 | 348 | 26 |
| 1859 | 307 | 347 | n/a |
| 1865 | 298 | 360 | n/a |

The Peelites gradually faded out as a separate party: in the early days some returned to the Conservatives. Some remained independent until they died, like Aberdeen, but many of the more distinguished ones became Liberal supporters eventually.

KEY EVENT

**The resignation of the Russell ministry** Russell's government was defeated in Parliament when Palmerston, who had been sacked in 1851, combined with the protectionist Conservatives to vote against it. The shifting political alliances and the importance of personal feelings in political fortunes is well illustrated by this event.

## LOST OPPORTUNITIES 1852–9

**The Who Who ministry 1852.** With the resignation of the Russell ministry in February 1852 Derby formed the first Conservative administration since the split on repeal. However, the Peelites refused to join and the weaknesses of the Conservatives without them were exposed even more clearly now they were in office. They lacked sufficient people of the right calibre and experience to take senior office. As the names of Derby's ministers were read out in the House of Lords the increasingly aged and deaf Duke of Wellington shouted out after each name 'Who? Who?' The nickname stuck, for out of all the ministers only three had previous experience of government.

The government was a minority one and Derby felt he must call an election in the summer of 1852 to try to establish a majority. The result was not entirely discouraging for the Conservatives, since a few Peelites returned to the fold, but this did not include the most prominent ones, and other parties still outnumbered the protectionists (see table on page 39). The question was did they still believe in protection? Derby was rumoured to be keener on having a corn duty than Disraeli, who spoke of the benefits of free trade. Even before the days of a **parliamentary mandate** it was a strangely uncertain position for the party to be in.

**Disraeli as Chancellor.** Disraeli felt somewhat out of his depth as Chancellor of the Exchequer. When he protested to Derby about his unsuitability for the post his chief replied 'They (the civil servants) give you the figures.' It was Disraeli's budget that brought the brief ministry to a close. Though not intending to reimpose the Corn Laws he did take measures to aid the landed interest.

- The **malt tax** and taxes on sugar were reduced.
- To make up for this, income tax was extended to cover those on lower incomes than before.

Disraeli called this 'compensation instead of protection' since the lower middle class was effectively paying more to make up for the tax reductions for the landed interest.

Speaking for the opposition of Whigs and Peelites, Gladstone weighed in with a comprehensive demolition of the economics behind Disraeli's budget. Comparing Disraeli unfavourably with Peel he cast doubt upon Disraeli's figures and theories and convinced the House to vote against the budget by a majority of nineteen votes, and Derby resigned. The Conservatives were to remain in opposition until 1858. The tense relations between Gladstone and Disraeli date from this time.

**The Whig-Peelite coalition 1852–5.** Since it seemed that no government could now be formed without the Peelites a Whig-Peelite coalition was formed with:

- a Peelite Prime Minister in Aberdeen;
- a Peelite Chancellor in Gladstone;
- a Whig Home Secretary in Palmerston;
- a Whig Foreign Secretary in Lord John Russell.

**Parliamentary mandate** A twentieth-century political concept whereby, if a party is elected into power at a general election having set out its policies to the electorate, it is seen to have obtained a mandate (permission) to carry those policies through. Occasionally in the nineteenth century, as with the Great Reform Act of 1832, a party elected to government was expected to introduce a certain measure.

KEY TERM

**The malt tax** A tax on barley – or other grain – used for brewing beer or distilling whisky. It was never popular among the landed classes (the tax not the whisky).

It appeared that though a few Peelites had returned to the Conservative fold, the most important seemed to be identifying with the other side. This further weakened the Conservative position. Whigs and Peelites shared positions equally in the cabinet with one Radical, Sir William Molesworth.

**The effects of the Crimean War.** It might be thought that the disasters of the Crimean War (see page 21), which brought down the government at the end of January 1855, might have brought the Conservatives back to office. For a very short time this appeared likely. The Queen asked Derby to form a ministry but he declined to do so. He suspected, probably rightly, that public opinion was clamouring for Lord Palmerston to be given the post. Palmerston had resigned from the previous government complaining they had not taken a sufficiently strong line against the Russians before the outbreak of the war; now he seemed to be vindicated. Only Palmerston, it was believed, had the experience, expertise and will to bring the war to a successful conclusion.

Derby's refusal of office was therefore shrewd if timid. He correctly saw in Palmerston a person who, though in many ways an old-fashioned politician of a past generation – he was 70 and had first held government office back in 1809 – was in one crucial way very modern: politicians now had to take into account an expanding electorate and

**The Charge of the Light Brigade at the Battle of Balaclava during the Crimean War, October 1854.**

Palmerston had the personality, policies and willingness to appeal to and exploit public opinion in his favour. His vigorously anti-Russian policy was well received by a middle-class public who saw the maintenance of a Turkish Empire freed from Russian influence as vital to British trading interests in India and the Far East. What Derby could hardly have foreseen was that Palmerston was not a stop-gap Prime Minister who would quit office at the end of the war: he would be Prime Minister for most of the next ten years and only allow the Conservatives a brief period of government in that time.

## The importance of Palmerston

Palmerston's aggressive foreign policy was not confined to the Crimean War. For this he counted on a good deal of support in Parliament and from the electorate. If he overstepped the mark with MPs he could appeal to the voters. In 1857 his aggressive tactics went too far for many tastes. It united Gladstone and Disraeli against him.

Palmerston, however, was not to be outdone. He decided on a dissolution of Parliament and the election of 1857 (see table on page 39) was a triumph for him and his supporters.

**Palmerston's views.** Now it was apparent that Palmerston was likely to remain in office for longer than anyone had expected and this was again bad news for the prospect of the Conservatives regaining office. For Palmerston was the most cautious of Whigs and indeed had been a moderate Tory in his younger days in office before 1830. It is true that some Whigs and Radicals disliked him and that some of the big names in Parliament opposed some of his activities in foreign policy, as the *Arrow* incident in China had just showed. Yet he could muster support from a wide range of MPs. His foreign policy appealed to:

- his fellow Whigs such as Russell;
- quite a number of Conservatives such as Lord Malmesbury;
- some of the Radicals (though not Cobden and Bright) such as Roebuck;

(see table on page 39)

## KEY EVENT

***Arrow* incident** There was a dispute over the seizure by China of a Chinese-owned vessel, *The Arrow*, dubiously flying the British flag in the Canton river adjacent to Hong Kong. It was almost certainly involved in smuggling and piracy but no proof was found. Though the Chinese released the crew who had been arrested, they refused to apologise and so a squadron of the Royal Navy shelled Canton causing many casualties. Palmerston, though he had not known about the bombardment, expressed his full approval. This high-handed action brought condemnation in Parliament and Cobden's vote of censure (condemnation) was carried by 263 votes to 247.

## KEY TERM

**Indian Mutiny 1857–8** An Indian uprising protesting against British imperial control, it was centred on the army in Bengal. Both sides were guilty of brutality at first but though Palmerston acted firmly he powerfully backed the Governor-General of India, Lord Canning, who some had accused of following a relatively lenient policy towards the rebels.

- the liberally minded middle classes who liked his general image of championing British interests and standing up to despots abroad.

In short, Palmerston was all things to all people. As Home Secretary in the Aberdeen Whig-Peelite coalition he had shown himself capable of Liberal reform: he abolished transportation of prisoners abroad and introduced special institutions to deal with young offenders. But he was seen as someone the Conservatives would find hard to oppose. This was because:

- he consistently opposed further parliamentary reform;
- he refused to consider many of the demands for change after the Crimean War such as the administrative reform of the civil service;
- they were impressed with his handling of the **Indian Mutiny** in 1857–8;
- though not a particularly religious man he showed no sign of attacking the position of the Church of England.

For his **Prime Ministerial ecclesiastical appointments** he relied on the advice of his son-in-law Lord Shaftesbury who recommended **evangelical** clergymen who would not be sympathetic to Roman Catholicism.

Even the royal family had come round to liking Palmerston. Victoria and Albert had earlier disapproved of what they saw as his **low moral tone**. They found his conduct of foreign policy high-handed and Victoria and Albert were responsible for his sacking in 1851, vowing he would never be Foreign Secretary again. (He wasn't, but he did become Prime Minister.) In this respect the Conservatives were not seen as any better. Derby's racing companions excited suspicion and Disraeli's high reputation with the Queen remained in the future. Prince Albert had been appalled by the tone of his attack on Peel.

**The mid-Victorian political situation.** The attitude of the Queen to the leaders of the different parties was not as significant for those seeking to gain office as it had been, it was soon to become of little importance at all. But, between 1846 and 1866 when party loyalties were fluid,

## KEY TERMS

**Prime Ministerial ecclesiastical appointments** By the mid-nineteenth century the Prime Minister rather than the monarch had the greater say in church appointments, such as bishops. **Evangelicals**, a group within the Church of England, stressed the importance of individual faith and the authority of the Bible and preaching, rather than the Catholic emphasis on the authority of the Church as a body and the importance of sacraments.

**Low moral tone** Victoria and Albert set high standards of morality for personal conduct. They took a dislike to Palmerston's occasionally flippant manner and less-than-serious conversation. In particular Palmerston was a well-known ladies' man. He never satisfactorily explained why, when staying at Windsor Castle in 1839 as the guest of the Queen, he was found one night entering the bedroom of one of the Queen's Ladies-in-Waiting.

royal influence enjoyed a final opportunity. With the parties evenly balanced and party allegiance muddled and variable, Queen Victoria could exercise her own discretion in choosing the man she could invite to form the next government – though whether he would necessarily accept was another matter.

This fluidity and uncertainty certainly counted against the Conservatives. Though they dropped the policy of protection after the 1852 election the Whig-Peelite-Liberal-Radical-Irish grouping continued to work against them. True it was not a united group and the more nationalist Irish members despaired of Palmerston – who owned land in Ireland – doing anything constructive to repair the ravages of the country caused by the famine of 1846 – for Peel's gesture in repealing the Corn Laws had not averted disaster. But it meant that though the Conservatives were generally the largest single group in Parliament they could never command a clear majority in this period. This difficulty is shown in their next brief period of office in 1858–9. Palmerston was again defeated in Parliament – though this time strangely for not being nationalistic enough – in the **Orsini Affair**. Palmerston did not feel he could ask for another dissolution and so Derby and Disraeli had another opportunity to form a Conservative government. It lasted just 15 months and was destined to be another minority administration.

## The Conservative government of 1858–9

The formation of a Conservative government proved almost as difficult as in 1852. Such was the uncertainty of party allegiance – not least among the remaining Peelites – and the continued absence of talent in the Conservative ranks that Derby invited Gladstone to join his government; but he declined. It was clear that dislike of the Conservatives by other groups was still strong and, above all, Disraeli was still regarded with a good deal of suspicion. Gladstone could not bring himself to be in the same government as Disraeli.

**Disraeli and reform.** The feeling that Disraeli was motivated by power rather than principle was enhanced by his introduction of a reform bill in 1859. It met

**The Orsini Affair** Orsini was an Italian nationalist who attempted unsuccessfully to assassinate the French Emperor Napoleon III in 1858. The plot was hatched in England and Napoleon III complained that no existing English law could restrain such an activity. Palmerston then brought in a Conspiracy to Murder Bill. This was defeated in Parliament. For once, Palmerston stood accused of giving in to foreign interference in British affairs.

considerable resistance: this was not merely from the opposition but also from his own side where distaste of any parliamentary reform was still strong. In the short run at least it was not a success. The terms of the Bill, which included a redistribution of seats (see Chapter 4), were seen as an attempt to gain political advantage for his own side. Disraeli was strongly opposed even by those traditionally associated with reform such as Russell. As a result it was Russell's motion opposing the Bill that was carried by 39 votes and the government was weakened as a result.

**The downfall of Derby's government.** But it was on an issue of foreign policy that Derby was finally brought down. Outside Conservative ranks Palmerston was at his strongest and most popular when he supported liberal causes in foreign policy, and support for the Italian nationalists struggling to be free of the rigid rule of the Austrians was one such. It was this that produced the meeting at Willis's Rooms as Whigs, Peelites and Radicals agreed to a 'Liberal' coalition to defeat Derby. A motion of no-confidence was passed by thirteen votes. Although the Conservatives made up some ground at the ensuing election, the more united nature of the opposition meant that Palmerston was able to form another government. The Conservatives would have to wait just as long as before for another opportunity – over six years – and even then they formed yet another minority administration.

### 1859–65: Still in the shadow of Palmerston

In the early 1860s Conservative prospects for office looked no better than ten years previously:

- Derby was in despair about the likelihood of forming a strong Conservative administration.
- Many Conservatives found Palmerston's cautious policies at home very much to their liking. Quite a number of Conservative MPs were prepared to give what they described as 'independent support' to Lord Palmerston.
- Disraeli was still regarded with suspicion both inside and outside the party as an unprincipled opportunist.
- The newly found Liberal unity looked as if it was going to last.

- The Peelite grouping had steadily declined and, while a few had gone back to the Conservatives, many men of talent had now moved over to the Liberal side.

The most notable of these was Gladstone. Despite the fact that he had voted against the motion of no-confidence that brought down Derby, he now made arguably the most fateful political decision of his career. Swallowing his reservations about Palmerston he joined the new government in 1859 as Chancellor, the post he had held with such success in 1852–5. Moreover, the Conservatives were now to find it difficult to oppose his free trade policies when they were seen to operate so effectively.

## Economic prosperity and Conservative fortunes

In the Palmerston government of 1859–65 Gladstone proved a very successful Chancellor of the Exchequer. He was able to pick up the threads of his free trade policy from the early 1850s (see Chapter 2) and this time there was no Crimean War to interrupt him. The obvious achievement of Gladstone as a Liberal Chancellor was another blow to the Conservatives. Indeed, the general mood of economic confidence in the country between 1848 and 1866 – punctured only momentarily with a brief crisis in 1857 – had tended to favour the fortunes of the government in office and this was rarely the Conservatives. Some significant features of the prosperity related to the increasing fortunes of the Liberal middle classes, which derived from a variety of developments:

- the prosperous manufacturing of textiles, coal and iron and (in the 1850s) steel;
- the **invisible exports** of merchant shipping, international banking and insurance;
- large-scale **capital investment** abroad;
- the development of prosperous new industries such as the manufacture of rubber goods and Portland cement along with considerable growth in metal trades and engineering;
- the continued growth of the railway network.

The overall prosperity of the country was seen as intimately bound up with these developments and they in

### KEY TERMS

**Invisible exports** The provision of services to a foreign country rather than the selling of actual goods which can be seen.

**Capital investment** British money put into developments overseas. The profits then returned to their British owners in this country.

turn relied on the free trade policies that were more strongly associated with the Liberals and their allies. Although the Conservatives no longer officially supported protection after 1852, it was their opponents who benefited from their earlier commitment to the free trade cause.

The Conservatives were not helped by their doom-and-gloom predictions with regard to British agriculture after the repeal of the Corn Laws. In fact the next 20 years were seen as the **Golden Age of British agriculture**. With the landed community prospering it was difficult for the Conservatives to attract support and portray Palmerston as someone who was acting against their interests.

**The end of Palmerston.** When Palmerston's Liberal coalition increased its majority in the general election of 1865 it seemed the Conservatives would be out of power for even longer – but Palmerston was over 80 and he was mortal. When he died in October 1865 he was replaced by Lord John – now Earl – Russell. But without Palmerston the issue of parliamentary reform was likely to rear its head once again.

## KEY THEME

**Golden Age of British agriculture** While a few small and ineffective producers were forced out of business, many learned to farm more efficiently using the new mechanical improvements, including steam-driven machinery. Moreover, the landed interest benefited directly or indirectly from industrial development. Some received income from mineral rights and others from urban development. The railways, initially regarded with suspicion by many landowners, were now cutting their costs and widening their range of markets.

## CONCLUSION

- The Conservative Party had been the largest single party in the House of Commons during the mid-century period.
- It had two men of great talent in Derby and Disraeli.
- On the two occasions when it had been briefly in government it had improved its performance at the subsequent general election.
- It had shown it could govern and managed to drop the embarrassing issue of protection.

However:

- The split over repeal had been a damaging and long-lasting one: many Peelites moved eventually to the Whig-Liberal side, and with few exceptions the Conservatives lacked experience and talent.

- Derby was very wary about forming a minority government and refused the chance of government in 1855.
- Disraeli was viewed with great suspicion both by his own side and opponents such as Gladstone.
- Palmerston adopted such a moderate but non-Conservative pose between 1855 and 1865 that it was difficult to oppose him effectively.
- The economic prosperity of the period confirmed the triumph of free trade and the need to govern more in the interest of the middle classes.

## SUMMARY QUESTIONS

1  Why was the split of 1846 so damaging to the Conservative Party?

2  What was the role of Palmerston in keeping the Conservatives out of office in this period?

3  What role did the Peelites play in this period?

# CHAPTER 4

## What was the significance of parliamentary reform for the Liberal and Conservative parties?

### INTRODUCTION

After the 1832 Reform Act, further reform of Parliament was not really an issue until the 1850s. In 1832 the Whigs had been the party of cautious parliamentary reform while the Tories had strongly opposed any change. Once Peel had accepted that reform had come to stay in the mid-1830s, however, it no longer seemed an issue to divide the parties. Both were united in their desire to oppose the Chartists' demands (1838–48) and resist universal male suffrage or equal electoral districts, as well as payment of MPs and a secret ballot. Whigs were just as adamant as the Conservatives. Lord John Russell had called the 1832 Reform Act a final adjustment to a well-nigh perfect British constitution.

### THE 1850S: REFORM BECOMES AN ISSUE AGAIN

By 1850, however, Russell had changed his mind. The franchise might be extended further quite safely. Though it was not to become a central issue again until the late 1860s the different party attitudes towards it now had to be considered once more. Why?

- The near collapse of the Chartists and the absence of revolution in Britain in 1848 – in contrast to the 1848 revolutions abroad (see Chapter 2, page 22) – suggested that extension of the vote to lower down the social scale would be safe.
- More men were acquiring the vote anyway: the **growth in population** and greater prosperity of the skilled working classes had produced an increase in the

**KEY CONCEPT**

**Growth in population**
The population of England and Wales grew from 14 million in 1831 to nearly 23 million in 1871. In the United Kingdom as a whole the increase was 25 million to 31.5 million. Ireland's population dropped as a result of the famine in 1846 through both death and emigration.

electorate from 717,000 in 1833, to 1,364,000 on the eve of the next Reform Bill in 1866.

- To grant the franchise to the skilled working-class man just below the £10 limit would be safer than continuing to stop them voting and possibly driving them into the arms of extreme Radicals.
- Given therefore that further reform might come anyway, party politicians felt that their party could gain an electoral advantage by being the party to introduce such a change.

**The 'respectability' of the skilled working man.** The economic boom which lasted almost uninterrupted from about 1843 to 1873 benefited the literate and skilled worker who was now thought 'respectable' by the middle class and whose revolutionary mood of earlier in the century was now much less evident. The suitability of this skilled male worker for the franchise was becoming generally accepted.

For this group, wages generally rose while prices remained steady or fell, employment was regular and there was more incentive to accept the norms of the society in which they lived. Many were becoming literate and joined increasingly influential and expanding trade unions such as those that got together to form the **Amalgamated Union of Engineers** in 1851. The skilled working classes appeared patriotic, often applauding Palmerston's foreign policy, religious (if not always Anglican) and loyal to the monarchy. To political leaders they appeared generally sober, sensible and **thrifty**, forming Friendly Societies (see page 94) and putting away savings for old age or a time when work might not be so abundant. Many had become £10 householders and appeared to have used the privilege of the vote with care and thought. Surely, more could be safely admitted to the franchise?

In contrast, contemporaries made a sharp distinction between the upper and lower working class. The unskilled working class did not share in this prosperity or general advance and were not seen as fit for the 'privilege' of voting. Even Radicals such as John Bright spoke of a 'residuum' who would not ever be fit to vote.

**KEY ORGANISATION**

**Amalgamated Union of Engineers** Union founded by William Allen of Crewe and William Newton of London who brought together the different engineering groups that had developed in the early nineteenth century as a result of the industrial revolution. Like other large unions of skilled workers of the time it demanded high subscriptions from its members but provided generous sickness and funeral benefits.

**KEY CONCEPT**

**Victorian thrift** To be 'thrifty' is to look after your money very carefully and spend it cautiously and effectively, not on gambling and drink for instance. In an era when the financial resources of many were adequate but not enormous, thrift and saving were seen as major virtues.

*Work* by Ford Maddox Brown, painted in 1863. The painting shows a mid-nineteenth-century artist's rose-coloured view of working life: but the skilled working classes *were* becoming more prosperous.

**The extension of borough boundaries** Boundaries would be redrawn so as to take in the surrounding countryside. Disraeli's idea was that the predominance of the independent-minded urban £10 householder (usually Liberal) would be counterbalanced by more conservatively minded rural voters.

**KEY TERM**

**Lodger vote** Voting in boroughs was based on occupancy not ownership of a house. At this time, lodgers in a house, especially common in the larger cities, were not qualified to vote at all.

**Reform again?** At first it was the Whig-Liberal-Radical grouping that considered further change, but interest within and without Parliament was very limited in the 1850s. The attempts to raise the question in the early 1850s were to come to nothing (see Chapter 2, page 19). However, the decision by Derby and Disraeli to introduce reform in their brief ministry in 1859 was more significant, if not more successful. For it indicated that the Conservatives were no longer totally opposed to parliamentary reform of any kind. The idea of looking at reform from the point of view of party advantage had begun. Disraeli himself would have disputed this last sentence. He felt the Whigs had constructed a bill in their own interest back in 1832 and the Conservatives were now entitled to do the same.

## Disraeli's proposals in 1859

- The £10 borough franchise limit to be extended to the counties.
- The **extension of borough boundaries** to include more rural voters.
- A £20 **lodger vote** for both county and borough seats.
- A second vote was to be given to those who owned at least £60 in a savings bank and had an income of at least £10 a year from investments in government funds or a pension from the government of at least £20 a year.

- A limited redistribution of seats: the smaller boroughs would lose 70, most of which (52) would be given to the more populous counties and the remainder to larger boroughs.

This Bill would clearly favour the Conservative county vote and was opposed by Liberals. Bright sarcastically gave the name 'fancy franchises' to the idea of extra votes targeted at the respectable and thrifty working classes. In fact the idea was not Disraeli's, but came from one of Russell's earlier efforts at reform. The Bill was defeated when Russell proposed a **resolution** calling for an extension to the borough vote which passed the House of Commons by 330 votes to 291: Derby resigned. Because of their resolution Palmerston and Russell were now honour-bound to bring forward their own reform proposals. They duly did this in 1860 suggesting a lowering of the borough franchise, but their hearts were not in it. Faced with hostility and apathy in the country they soon dropped the idea. In truth, Palmerston had never liked it and there was little apparent demand for reform in the country at large.

## FACTORS FAVOURING PARLIAMENTARY REFORM IN THE 1860s

**The advances of the skilled, urban working class.** Though the issue now faded for a few years, parliamentary reform was established as something that could be introduced at any time. No longer were working men considered as necessarily unworthy of the vote. They were rapidly developing the education, political knowledge, experience and economic stability to do justice to the 'gift' of the vote. Their efforts had made Britain the workshop of the world and the leading industrial nation. Had they not earned the franchise?

> ### KEY TERM
>
> **Resolution in the House of Commons** An expression of opinion by the Commons on any issue: it does not go before the Lords and so does not have the force of law.

The continued increase in political knowledge can be explained by:

- the spread of education to the skilled working classes;
- the cheaper press encouraged by the abolition of the stamp duty in 1855 and the paper duty in 1861;
- the growing number of appearances of national politicians who used the railway to travel around the country.

Even Palmerston felt obliged to move with the times. Visiting Bradford in 1864 he was surprised to find the advanced Liberal MP W.E. Forster criticising him for not introducing parliamentary reform. This stirred up considerable local political excitement.

**Gladstone supports reform.** Gladstone was another political figure who made use of the increased opportunities to go travelling and speaking. But unlike Palmerston he was well received. He was impressed with the advances of the working people and particularly so with the Lancashire cotton workers. Between 1861 and 1865 it would have been in their self-interest to condemn the northern states in the American Civil War for blockading southern state ports. This blockade prevented raw cotton leaving for Lancashire and thus was ruining the workers' livelihood. However, their support for the northern states on the principle of opposing slavery made a deep impression on Gladstone, doubly so because of his own family's previous involvement in the slave trade. Gladstone created quite a stir in a speech in Parliament in May 1864 which was reported as suggesting that all working men had the '**moral right**' to a vote. No matter that he had hedged round the comment with numerous qualifications: Palmerston as Prime Minister was taken aback and predicted that if Gladstone succeeded him there would be 'strange doings'. There were. When Palmerston died in October 1865 and the aging Russell became Prime Minister, Gladstone in the House of Commons was seen as the vital figure in the government. Reformers' hopes were raised.

**Other effects of the American Civil War.** It was not only Gladstone on whom the American Civil War had a significant effect. Reformers saw the triumph of the Union as a victory for freedom and democracy. It could act as a spur for reform in Britain. The eloquence of supporters of reform such as John Bright – listened to with renewed respect after the Crimean War and the recovery of his health – would also raise the profile of the issue. According to Bright the victory of the North in the Civil War was 'the event of our age and future ages will confess it'.

**Visit of Garibaldi.** Nor was America the only place to find democratic heroes. The Italian **Garibaldi**, on his visit to England in 1864, was treated as one such – if somewhat inaccurately. His visit caused such excitement in Radical circles that Palmerston's government cut short his speaking tour lest it stirred too much agitation for reform. Garibaldi unexpectedly went home – early – but his impact continued. A protest committee formed to complain about his early departure developed into a permanent organisation campaigning for manhood suffrage – the Reform League.

**Role of the trade unions: economic problems.** One area of support for the Reform League was from the trade unions, now busy passing reform resolutions at their meetings. Their demands for change were soon to become more insistent. This was because of:

- the unexpected collapse of a major finance company – Overend and Gurney – in May 1866;
- a poor harvest after a wet summer;
- cattle plague epidemic;
- a major cholera outbreak;
- a temporary depression and unemployment in the winter of 1866–7.

**Guiseppe Garibaldi 1808–82** Italian nationalist and soldier who played a central role in the 1848 revolutions in central Italy. In 1860 he undertook a sensationally successful military campaign throughout southern Italy which was crucial to the unification of the country. Refusing all powers, rewards and honours, he retired to his farm and became a romantic liberal and nationalist hero.

## THE REFORM BILL OF 1866

All this meant that the introduction of what might have been regarded as another routine effort at reform in 1866 produced more excitement than all the last few attempts put together. It was not surprising that Russell, freed from Palmerston's influence, should introduce a bill. Its terms were mild.

- A lowering of the borough franchise from £10 to £7.
- An extension in the counties to those paying an overall rent of £14 or more.
- A 'fancy franchise' for those with over £50 in a savings bank deposit.
- Very modest redistribution, grouping small boroughs into large constituencies rather than abolishing them altogether.

But the changed circumstances in the country brought two major differences.

- Opposition to the Bill was vigorous and partly from the Liberal side.
- The reaction in the country when the Bill was defeated was far more excited.

Robert Lowe, Liberal MP for Calne in Witshire, made an especially powerful speech against the Bill. His time spent in Australia had convinced him of the perils of democracy and he spoke passionately against working-class involvement in the political process. In one passage he argued that this inclusion would bring '**venality**', 'drunkenness' and 'violent feeling'. His speech achieved two things:

- It persuaded enough Liberal members to reject the measure and so cause the government's resignation.
- It inflamed working-class opinion and produced meetings of protest organised by the Reform League.

John Bright's eloquence in favour of reform matched Lowe's eloquence against it. Speaking in large cities such as Birmingham and Manchester, Bright attacked those who had opposed this modest reform as being 'out of touch'. They had retreated into a political **Cave of Adullum**. Ironically, Lowe's attitude had stirred up the supporters of reform and increased the pressure for it. Reformers were dismayed at the resignation of the Russell government and the coming to power of yet another Derby–Disraeli government whose supporters had helped to reject the recent Bill. Would reform now be lost? By no means.

**Why did Disraeli decide on Reform?**  Russell's Liberal government was replaced by a **minority administration** of the Conservatives. It may seem strange that this new government should introduce and eventually carry through a substantial Reform Bill when they had helped Lowe's Adullamites to reject a more modest one. The new Prime Minister Lord Derby would probably not have done so had he been acting alone; but he was elderly and in failing health and the real power lay with Disraeli in the Commons. What influenced Disraeli?

- He was anxious to score political points off Gladstone and reach a successful settlement of the reform question where the Liberals had failed.
- A major bill could provide electoral advantage, especially if the Conservatives could determine the terms and also the details of the redistribution of seats.
- By granting a large franchise extension Disraeli could satisfy the Radicals demanding change such as the members of the Reform League. Although he was not prepared to meet their demand for manhood suffrage, he was prepared to consider household suffrage, with safeguards. This would, he hoped, quieten down agitation.

This last point was not a trivial one. On the rejection of Russell's and Gladstone's bill in June 1866 there were angry protests that Parliament appeared to be rejecting even modest reform. In July, the Reform League planned a major demonstration for **Hyde Park**. When the new Home Secretary, the Conservative Spencer Walpole, tried to ban it, he was unsuccessful. Although the gates were locked, the force of the large crowd was so great that the railings collapsed and thousands surged into Hyde Park

## KEY TERMS

**Cave of Adullam: Adullamites**  A cave in an Old Testament biblical story (First Book of Samuel) where the followers of King David hid from their Philistine opponents. Bright's speeches were full of biblical references such as these; this comparison of David's followers with those of Lowe was particularly apt as the opponents of even moderate reform were indeed 'distressed and discontented'.

**Minority administration**  A government that did not have majority support in the House of Commons. Since the Conservatives won no election between 1841 and 1874, the three brief administrations of Lord Derby 1852, 1858–9 and 1866–8 were all minority ones.

## KEY PLACE

**Hyde Park**  The largest London park (138 hectares), Hyde Park has been a public park since the seventeenth century. Used for many different purposes, including large political meetings, its north-west corner is traditionally the home of public speakers on all topics asserting the absolute right to free speech.

and held their meeting anyway. Nor was this an isolated incident. John Bright and other Radical speakers were drawing large crowds in the north of England at reform rallies. Later, when amendments to Disraeli's bill were being debated, a further demonstration was held in Hyde Park in May 1867.

**Disraeli, reform and the Conservative Party.** How did Disraeli persuade naturally anti-reform Conservatives to pass the Bill? He seems to have convinced them of both the advantages and necessity of reform. The Liberals were dominant in the borough seats. By granting the vote to all borough householders it would in effect give the vote to the skilled working-class man in the towns. They might not vote for the same candidates as their (frequently) Liberal employers. Moreover, Disraeli 'sold' the package of household suffrage because it included many safeguards:

- personal payment of rates: this would exclude a substantial number of **compound householders;**
- a two-year residence qualification before being allowed to register to vote. It was believed this would exclude large numbers of workmen who travelled from job to job;
- 'fancy franchises', such as those with at least £50 in a savings account,

These safeguards, combined with the kind of electoral influence (which could be a mild hint, outright bribery or a threat that a wrongly directed vote could lead to the end of employment prospects) that was possible with an open ballot, seemed to convince many of the doubtful Conservatives. Derby was a convert if not a very enthusiastic one. He called it a 'leap in the dark'. Significantly, it was a leap he persuaded many of his fellow peers to make later when the Bill, having passed through the Commons, came to the Lords.

Another factor that helped Disraeli was the ineffectiveness of the Conservative opponents. Though there were quite a number, they resisted from their own individual positions rather than from an Adullamite-like grouping. They included three cabinet members – Lord Carnarvon, General Jonathan Peel (brother of the former Prime

## KEY TERM

**Compound householders**
Householders (around 400,000 of them) who paid their rent to their landlord and then added on (compounded) their rate – local tax – which was sent in by the landlord. Thus 'compounders' did not qualify for the vote as they did not pay rates personally, one of Disraeli's supposed conditions for voting. In practice, many ex-compounders were still prevented from voting before legal cases and subsequent legislation established their right beyond doubt.

Minister Sir Robert) and Lord Cranborne (the future **Marquess of Salisbury**). Cranborne was the most formidable of the opponents but even he did not stop to organise a concerted opposition to the Bill's terms. Like the other two, he contented himself with resigning. But Disraeli simply replaced the three men and continued. The contrast with the previous Liberal collapse is considerable, and testimony to Disraeli's powers of persuasion and political skill.

**Amendments to the Bill.** Things did not turn out quite as Disraeli had anticipated. His original proposals were subject to a number of important amendments which passed the Commons.

- The two-year residence qualification was reduced to one despite Disraeli's opposition.
- A £10 lodger franchise undermined the household-only principle. This time Disraeli accepted the change without a vote.
- He also accepted **Hodgkinson's amendment** which effectively gave the vote to the compound householder.
- The 'fancy franchises' were removed.

Why did Disraeli accept most of these changes that altered the nature of the Bill?

- Party advantage: Disraeli opposed all amendments coming from Gladstone and his supporters but accepted ones from Liberals (more often Radicals) who were not close to Gladstone.
- A desire to settle the reform question with a substantial bill and so put a stop to the growing public agitation such as the Hyde Park protests.

**Party advantage?** Did Disraeli gain the political initiative he was seeking for the Conservatives at the expense of Gladstone's Liberals? In the short run yes, but not for long. Gladstone was outmanoeuvred over the Bill itself. Disraeli had the pleasure of seeing Radical Liberals such as Henry Fawcett revolt against Gladstone's authority in a protest originating in the House of Commons' tea room. Fawcett and his colleagues would vote for or against each

### KEY PERSON

**Marquess of Salisbury 1830–1903** A strong opponent of parliamentary reform, though reluctantly accepting its necessity in 1884, Salisbury was a firm defender of landed interest and the Church of England. Like Gladstone, he had a strong, personal religious faith. Always pessimistic about the way British society was going. A formidable political operator, and a long-serving Foreign Secretary and Prime Minister.

### KEY TERM

**Hodgkinson's amendment** Grosvenor Hodgkinson, the otherwise largely unknown MP for Newark, came up with the simple but clever idea of abolishing the compounding of rates with rent to the landlord. Thus they would have to pay their rates personally and so qualify for voting.

amendment on its merits: this generally meant supporting the more radical ones. But if Disraeli thought Liberal disunity would last long enough for the Conservatives to triumph over the Liberals in the first election under the new franchise in 1868, he was to be disappointed.

In February Lord Derby finally retired and Disraeli briefly became Prime Minister. However, Gladstone had also replaced Russell as Liberal leader and soon brought about Liberal recovery from lost unity over reform with a master stoke. In March he successfully introduced into the Commons resolutions calling for the disestablishment of the Anglican Church in Ireland. This move delighted nonconformists and struck a chord with many in the country at large. The working man did not proceed to show his gratitude for the franchise to Disraeli and the Liberals were elected with a majority of 112 in the election of November 1868.

## THE EFFECTS OF THE 1867 REFORM ACT

### Bribery and corruption

The 1867 Reform Act helped to bring in what we would recognise as the modern British political system in a number of ways. Firstly, the old system that was often dominated by bribery and corruption took a severe blow. What had been the main features of this system?

- Many voters were prepared to accept money for casting their vote for a particular candidate.
- If someone's voting decision was personal it was based more on his position in society than on his own political opinions.
- Landed influence over voting was seen as a legitimate use of privilege.
- Many seats were left uncontested: this was partly because of deals done by the parties in **two-member seats** to avoid the excessive expense of campaigning.
- Elections were often unruly and drunken, even violent affairs.

**KEY TERM**

**Two-member seats** Before 1885 many, though not all, parliamentary seats were represented by two MPs. Quite often a close and potentially expensive contest could be avoided by an agreement for each side to share the representation.

With the increase in the electorate of about 1 million people, the attempts to continue these features led to ruinous expense, violent conduct and extensive corruption at the 1868 election with **election petitions** at record levels. Gladstone's Liberal government after 1868 therefore decided on the introduction of a secret ballot for voting: a long-standing Radical demand. The Ballot Act was passed in 1872. Perhaps the Liberals felt this move would aid them as they saw the landed interest in the Conservative Party as having most to lose by such a restriction. In fact, influence, **treating** and outright bribery were at their worst in small boroughs, many of them Liberal. Even after the 1867 Act there were a number of small boroughs with just over 10,000 people where corruption was rife. Nor did the Act have a sudden or dramatic effect; bribery continued in other ways such as offering money for the supporters of one side to abstain from voting. In any event the move did not benefit the Liberals directly in 1874 because the Conservatives won the election in that year.

### KEY TERMS

**Election petitions** If a candidate defeated in an election felt his successful opponent had used illegal tactics to acquire votes, he could petition Parliament to look into the circumstances of the election. Parliament had the power to overturn the result if it considered the complaint justified.

**Treating** The giving of generous amounts of free food and drink by prospective candidates to potential voters shortly before an election.

## THE VOTE AUCTION !

**Corruption and violence: nineteenth-century electioneering. This cartoon appeared in *Punch* in March 1853.**

When the Liberals were returned to power in 1880 there were demands for further legislation, especially after a Royal Commission on election petitions found abundant evidence of bribery, corruption and violence. In the election in Gloucester in 1880 it was established that over half the borough's 5000 voters had accepted bribes. There was also serious violence in Leamington and wholesale corruption in Macclesfield and Worcester. The Corrupt Practices Act of 1883 was even more significant in clearing up elections.

- It defined unlawful practices very clearly and so made legal action against them more straightforward. The new definition of illegality included impersonation, undue influence, bribery, treating, payment for conveyances to the polls, assault, abduction and perjury (lying on oath).
- In addition, financial restrictions were placed on candidates' **election expenses**.
- **Party agents** would have to account for their expenses very precisely.
- Election workers were paid a fee for their services to lessen their chances of accepting a bribe.

## Party organisation

Because of the gradually changing nature of political activity and the growing numbers of voters, both Liberals and Conservatives were forced to change their approach. They would now need to seek support from the wider electorate on the merit of their policies, and organise themselves to project these more effectively. The Liberals were first to do this. In the 1868 election campaign, Bright appeared in widely separated places in the British Isles speaking at Limerick, Edinburgh and Birmingham. Gladstone made a series of speeches in Lancashire industrial towns, by all accounts some of his very finest. In contrast Disraeli made only one speech, at Aylesbury in his Buckinghamshire constituency midway through the campaign (voting was still spread over several weeks) and otherwise merely wrote a letter outlining his ideas to the same constituents.

**Election expenses** In borough seats with over 200 electors candidates could spend £380 plus £30 for every extra 1000 people; in counties the equivalent figures were £710 and £60.

**Party agent** The person who is employed to help a parliamentary candidate win the election. Agents were responsible for organising the finances of the campaign and until 1883 possessed considerable freedom of action.

By 1874, however, the Conservatives had made up for lost ground in party organisation. Thanks to the work of **John Gorst** they were now, like the Liberals, establishing a party presence all over the country. In sharp contrast to 1868, Disraeli issued a 'manifesto' outlining Conservative ideas although it tended to be a general promise to defend the major institutions of the country and concentrated on attacking the 'mistaken' policies of Gladstone's government. Gladstone for his part promised the electorate the abolition of the income tax if the Liberals were elected. This was his long-cherished ambition, but never before had it been dangled as a carrot to the voters. Gladstone lost the election and so his promise was never put to the test. All of this, however, suggested a recognisably modern era of party politics.

## How did the parties go about trying to win mass support?

- The development of local constituency associations. These would enrol members, look for funding, and try to maximise the vote at both national and local elections – for elections to the municipal corporations (councils) were becoming more party political. Many constituency associations had begun in the years before 1868 but they now met more regularly and encouraged a wider social range of members.
- Linked to these associations would be clubs, Conservative and Liberal, of a more social nature where a drink and a game of billiards with like-minded friends could be enjoyed in pleasant surroundings and where, occasionally, more serious political discussion, talks and meetings could take place. Again, some of these had already developed in the 1850s and 1860s but now there was a rapid growth
- National party institutions were also set up. The National Union of Conservative Associations was set up in 1869 to co-ordinate activities and helped to make up some of the ground lost to the Liberals. Gorst was the first to see that the new middle classes in the **suburbs** were potentially Conservative and he wanted to work on getting support from **Villa Tories**. After their defeat in 1874 the Liberals set up the National Liberal Federation

### KEY PERSON

**John Gorst 1835–1916**
Conservative Party organiser and MP, Gorst was asked to help with party organisation in the post-1867 reform era, a task he accomplished with great success. When re-elected in 1875 he directed his efforts to his own political career and also fell out with the Chief Whip Sir William Hart-Dyke. He was disappointed to see his successors lose many of the advantages he had established over the Liberals.

### KEY TERM

**Villa Tories in the suburbs**
The railways were making it possible for the middle classes to live away from their place of work in the city centres. The suburb was born and the first commuters came into existence. The Conservatives, especially Gorst and then Salisbury, saw potential Conservative voters in these people, among whom the richest lived in large detached houses, sometimes called 'villas'.

in 1877 (see below) which went even further in organising support for the Liberal Party.

Despite this central interest, however, the emphasis on the local area to organise its own affairs and find its own candidates was still strong. With the Conservatives, professional and regional agents that linked the local and national organisations more effectively were not to develop until after 1885 with the appointment of a new Chief Agent, 'Captain' Middleton. Liberals, however had gone further.

**National Liberal Federation.** By the late 1870s the Liberal organisations had rapidly made up for the lost ground of the early 1870s when Gorst had been so active for the Conservatives. One of the terms of the 1867 Act encouraged further organisation. For the large cities of Birmingham, Manchester, Glasgow and Liverpool a third MP had been created, but the qualified electorate still only had two votes.

- Only **Liverpool** of these cities was likely to return a Conservative. The Conservative idea behind this clause was that in the other cities with this arrangement, the third candidate elected was normally likely to be the top Conservative. This would give the Tories valuable minority representation.
- The Liberals countered this idea but developed a particular approach to voting in these areas. Supporters in different parts of the town would be told to vote for a different pair of candidates with the idea that all three Liberals would then get enough votes to be elected and continue to exclude the Conservatives. But of course this involved a great deal of organisation not to say compulsion. This was one of the tasks of the National Liberal Federation (NLF).

The NLF was set up in 1877 and originated in the Birmingham of **Joseph Chamberlain**. In that year almost 50 Liberal associations in different boroughs affiliated to the NLF. Members would elect a general council which would make decisions about party organisation and tactics. Conservatives (and often the remaining Whigs in the

Conservative city: nineteenth-century Liverpool. This photograph was taken in 1890.

Liberal Party) complained about this development. It was seen as dictatorial and at worst (inaccurately) similar to the American **caucus**.

* It did give ordinary Liberal members a say in electing management committees.
* In a city such as Birmingham members of these management committees or 'councils' were often skilled working men, actively involved in the political process for the first time.
* It helped the Liberals in their election performances in 1880 and 1885.

### The two-party system and political personalities

One important effect of the 1867 Act had been to end the rather confused party state of the 1850s and early 1860s. Liberal and Conservative were now the two clearly established groupings, and this helped to increase party organisation. Peelites such as Aberdeen, Goulburn, Sir James Graham and Sidney Herbert had died or had, like Gladstone and Edward Cardwell, eventually drifted over to the Liberals. Radicals were less independent than before and generally associated themselves with Liberal policy. Conservatives now accepted free trade, and the bitter days of division were long behind them. There can be more confidence about the precise party allegiance of most MPs as 'Independent' was now rarely a name they gave

---

**KEY TERM**

**Caucus** Originally one who advises or encourages. In Britain the caucus tried to co-ordinate political activity and decision-making in a constituency, whereas in the United States it was (and still can be) a preliminary meeting of members of a party to select candidates for office.

---

## KEY PERSON

**Sir Stafford Northcote
1818–87** Baronet 1851.
Helped draw up the Civil
Service Report 1853.
Conservative MP from 1855.
Held office under Lord
Derby. Chancellor of the
Exchequer under Disraeli
1874–80. Leader of the party
in the Commons 1880–5.
Created Earl of Iddesleigh
1885. Foreign Secretary
1886.

themselves. At the elections of 1868, 1874, 1880 and 1885 the electorate had a clear choice: only the Irish grouping remained partly – and increasingly – separate.

For the first time voters might wish to consider party policies as a whole when casting their vote, a far cry from the local and sometimes corrupt factors that dominated nineteenth-century elections so frequently. Moreover, it was also clear who was to become Prime Minister if his chosen party was successful in 1868, 1874 or 1880: Gladstone if the Liberals succeeded or Disraeli if the Conservatives were triumphant. Only after Disraeli died in 1881 was there uncertainty about a future Conservative Prime Minister, Salisbury from the Lords or **Sir Stafford Northcote** from the Commons, soon resolved in favour of Salisbury. It was clear that Queen Victoria, however much she detested Gladstone, would eventually agree to ask him to form an administration if he was electorally successful as in 1880. In 1880 she asked Lord Hartington to be Prime Minister but he declined and she had to ask Gladstone.

The Liberal success in 1880 was partly owing to Gladstone's Midlothian campaign. This was a dramatic tour of the Scottish constituency of Midlothian in late November–early December 1879. A Conservative seat, Gladstone had decided to contest it and made a series of brilliant speeches in Edinburgh and other Midlothian towns such as Dalkeith and West Calder. He ruthlessly attacked the foreign and economic policies of Disraeli's government. With the election looming Gladstone undertook a second campaign in March 1880 and was himself elected for his adopted constituency. His speeches had produced cheering crowds of many thousands; personalities had become both an important part of the political process and a factor in aiding the decision of the electorate.

## THE 1884 REFORM ACT

**Background.** The rather haphazard passing of the 1867 Reform Act with its extensive increase in the borough rather than the county franchise was always likely to lead to a demand for a further reform act. One aspect of the 1867 Act had been to extend the boundaries of many small boroughs out into the countryside. The Conservative thinking behind this had been that rural Tory votes might then outweigh Liberal town votes. However, it led to **anomalies**. Neighbours would find themselves in one case as a borough householder and thus entitled to vote, while down the road just outside the borough boundary, a county dweller was still denied the franchise.

By the early 1880s the improving educational standard of the rural working classes, especially after the Education Act of 1870 (see page 74), also helped to remove objections to their enfranchisement though opponents claimed they had not 'earned' the vote as their more sophisticated town cousins had done. Still, many Liberals were keen to go ahead. After the Secret Ballot Act and the Corrupt Practices Act they hoped for an independent rural vote in their favour rather than the workers opting for the Conservatism of their landowning masters. However, the remaining Whigs had reservations about this move towards more democracy in the countryside.

**Terms of the Act.** Gladstone had no great difficulty in passing the Bill of 1884 through the Commons. Its main terms were that the householder vote in the counties would be granted on the same terms as the boroughs.

However, the Lords provided resistance to the proposals. This was not surprising.

- The Conservative-dominated Lords feared the decline of the landed aristocratic influence if the Bill were to be passed.
- A Liberal-Radical government always had more difficulty in passing major reform through the Lords (e.g. in 1832) than did a Conservative administration, which could argue that if it considered it necessary the Lords should agree (e.g. in 1867).

Nevertheless the Bill eventually became law as follows:

### Redistribution Act 1885

Boroughs with fewer than 15,000 people lost both MPs.

Boroughs with fewer than 50,000 people lost one MP.

Of 670 constituencies all but 23 were now single-member seats.

- The Bill passed the Commons without difficulty at the end of February 1884 by a comfortable majority of 130.
- In June the Lords voted for Salisbury's motion of outright rejection of the Bill by a majority of 59. They refused to budge unless there was also a redistribution bill passing at the same time as the Reform Bill.
- Until October there was a tense atmosphere. There was talk of the **creation of peers** to get the Bill through the Lords and Radical Liberals such as **John Morley** were hostile. Of the Lords, his verdict was 'Mend 'em or end 'em'. Reform disturbances occurred in Aston, Birmingham, and a Liberal rally for reform was held near Chatsworth, the stately home of the Duke of Devonshire, a leading Whig opponent of further reform. The atmosphere was very briefly reminiscent of 1866–7 though never as serious or as prolonged.
- Then, after talks in October and November, Gladstone and Salisbury reached a compromise. The Lords would let the Bill through as long as it was accompanied by a separate redistribution bill.

The Redistribution Bill was of real advantage to the Conservatives. This was because of the decision to go for single-member rather than the double-member constituencies that had remained the common if not universal method of election. In the boroughs, this created a single member for the more prosperous area of town or suburb and thus gave the Conservatives an opportunity to gain representation in urban areas previously dominated by the Liberals. For the Whigs, however, it was not good news. They frequently had an arrangement with more Radical Liberals in the two-member seats whereby they would have one candidate each. This would no longer be possible and Whigs such as **Hartington** feared that they would lose out badly in the new single-member seats. It seems that Salisbury's calculation that the Conservatives would gain seats was more accurate than that of the Liberal Sir Charles Dilke, who calculated that the Liberals would benefit from the single-member constituencies more than they did. But complications over Ireland were to change the whole political scene and render these calculations of little effect.

- After the political uncertainty of the mid-century years, parliamentary reform had again become both a major national question and a party political issue in the 1860s. Disraeli played a significant part in accepting the possibility of reform from Conservatives as well as Liberals although Salisbury continued to oppose it at least until 1885.
- The Act of 1867 heralded a political era which could be termed modern in that:
  - a clearer two-party system emerged
  - Gladstone and Disraeli became well-known personalities who received national coverage to an extent previously unknown.
- After 1868, electoral corruption declined with the larger electorate, thanks to changing public attitudes and the Secret Ballot and Corrupt Practices Acts.
- Improved party organisation was essential to recruit and maintain the support of the new electorate and at different times, and in slightly different ways, both parties went about the task.
- The legislation of 1884–5 confirmed the era of mass politics now accepted by both parties. The Radicals were increasingly prominent in the Liberal Party at the expense of the Whigs. Among the Conservatives, even Salisbury and his supporters had now accepted the necessity of reform.

## SUMMARY QUESTIONS

1 Why did parliamentary reform become such a prominent issue in the mid-1860s?

2 Why did the Conservative Disraeli pass such a substantial Reform Act?

3 What were the main political effects of the 1867 Act?

4 Why did the House of Lords accept the third Reform Act?

# CHAPTER 5

## Political and social issues of Gladstone's ministries 1868–85

### INTRODUCTION

Gladstone held office as Liberal Prime Minister for two periods of just over five years:

- December 1868 – February 1874;
- April 1880 – June 1885.

During this time Ireland came to dominate English politics in a way it had not since the famine of 1845–6 and Gladstone devoted a good deal of attention to it. 'My mission is to pacify Ireland' he had remarked in December 1868 on hearing that the Queen had asked him to form a ministry.

Political reform continued with acts passed in both ministries: in the first ministry to help reduce bribery and corruption at election time and in the second another instalment of parliamentary reform with a further extension of the franchise and a separate act to redistribute seats more evenly according to population.

### GLADSTONE'S FIRST MINISTRY 1868–74

The greatest run of reform came in the first two and a half years of Gladstone's first ministry. This period produced a series of major changes concerning not only Ireland and the introduction of the secret ballot, but also education, social reform and public houses, and the passing of legislation concerning prominent institutions in the country such as the army, the law, the universities, the civil service, local government and burgeoning trade unions.

## Why was 1869–72 such an important time for reforms?

Some of Gladstone's reforms such as in education (partly) and the secret ballot (largely) could be seen as a natural result of the 1867 Reform Act. Action over trade unions could be attributed to a specific legal difficulty over the safety of their funds which arose in 1866. However, the need for change in many of these areas had been apparent for some time.

- The Crimean War in the 1850s revealed a number of inefficiencies in the army, and in the civil service. Bodies such as the Administrative Reform Association, set up in 1855, called for greater openness in appointments in these areas.
- Palmerston, however, deflected many of these requests for change by using his popularity in other areas, especially foreign policy: by the mid-1860s many reformers felt it better to wait for new measures until after his retirement or death.
- Although lip service was still paid to the doctrine of laissez-faire, the greater complexities of an increasingly urban society meant state intervention concerning social questions such as public health and the problems of alcoholism was increasingly seen as justified.
- Nonconformists, on whose vote the Liberals relied, were an increasingly numerous and powerful element in society and were putting heavy pressure for changes not only for regulating sales of alcohol but also regarding admission to, and privileges at, **Oxford and Cambridge universities**. Having failed to raise sufficient funds to finance many of their own schools, they had come to the conclusion by the late 1860s that state financing of non-denominational schools was the answer.
- The need for action on Ireland had been highlighted by Irish nationalist **Fenian** activity in 1867. Their activities were linked to attempts to get Fenian prisoners released including an attempt to seize Chester Castle in February, the killing of a police officer in Manchester in September (for which three Fenians were hanged) and an explosion at Clerkenwell Jail in London in December.

### KEY TERMS

**Oxford and Cambridge universities** The only two ancient English universities. For long seen as the preserve of the Anglican aristocracy and without rivals. In the 1830s collegiate universities had begun in Durham and London, and Oxbridge was raising its academic standard by the middle of the century.

**Fenian Brotherhood** An Irish nationalist group of American origin founded in 1858. Its members sought a military solution to the problem of English control of Ireland. Some saw service in the American Civil War, and when this ended in 1865 many returned to Ireland well supplied with money.

**Why was Gladstone's government able to deal with these issues?** Gladstone's ministry of 1868–74 saw the Liberal Party stronger and more united than it had ever been. It had:

- a comfortable majority in Parliament: the Liberals had a majority of 112 over the Conservatives;
- a forceful leader, Gladstone, who had united the Liberals under his leadership with divisions over the 1867 Reform Bill largely forgotten;
- a definite sense of direction to remove unjustified privilege, reform a number of existing institutions and to open up opportunities to a wider range of people within society.

By 1872, however, the reforming impulse had blown itself out; as Disraeli pointed out, the Liberal front bench reminded him of a 'range of exhausted volcanoes'. Nonetheless the catalogue of achievement was considerable and the character of nineteenth-century Liberalism is clearly shown in the various issues tackled.

## THE DISESTABLISHMENT OF THE ANGLICAN CHURCH IN IRELAND 1869

**Background.** After the comparative confusion in Liberal ranks in 1867 as a result of Disraeli's passing of the Reform Bill, the Liberals recovered swiftly. This was due to Gladstone's shrewd choice of a subject that could bring the party back together. Since Russell had, like the Conservative Derby, now retired from active politics, Gladstone was free to select the debating ground that he wanted. He chose the Irish Church. This proved effective because:

- religious liberalism united the party more firmly than most other issues;
- the Irish Church was an establishment that was difficult to defend. Only 12 per cent of the population of the country were Anglican by **religious belief**;
- as champions of the Established Church, the Conservatives would feel obliged to defend the institution.

In March 1868 Gladstone moved resolutions in the House of Commons on the Irish Church, calling for its disestablishment: these were passed by a majority of 60. This was not surprising. After all, the Parliament was the one elected in 1865 in the last days of Palmerston and on paper had a Liberal majority. Only parliamentary reform had clouded the issue for a time. Now, Disraeli's days were numbered and another election inevitable, especially since the newly enfranchised voters would be anxious to exercise their freshly acquired privilege. Once Gladstone was installed in office the disestablishment of the Irish Church was likely to be his first undertaking.

**The terms and the passing of the Act.** In 1869 the Anglican Church was **disestablished and partially disendowed**.

The measure was opposed by the Conservatives. Disraeli argued that it 'licensed confiscation' but it passed by the comfortable majority of 118. The Commons accepted Gladstone's argument that the Irish Church Establishment was one that could not be justified. Its passage through the House of Lords was more difficult but the Irish Church had never been the most popular part of the Anglican Establishment and few were prepared to fight to the last ditch to defend it when a newly elected government had been so clearly committed to the proposed change. It passed by a majority of 33.

**Effects of the Act.** This was the most successful piece of Gladstone's Irish legislation in that it removed a major Irish grievance and extended the principle of religious freedom to Ireland. It did not lead to the disestablishment of the Church of England as many of its opponents feared, though it did encourage the strongly nonconformist Welsh to a similar campaign later in the century. But in going on to tackle the land question in Ireland, Gladstone was less successful.

## IRISH LAND ACT 1870

**Background.** After an exhaustive study of the intricate legal problem of **Irish land tenure** Gladstone produced his **Irish**

**Land Bill** to reform the landlord–tenant relationship. The central complaint had been the relative ease of eviction of tenants by their landlords. Tenants frequently had to pay for their own improvements on their holdings. In Ulster, but rarely elsewhere, it had been the custom to pay compensation for these improvements when the tenant quitted the holding. With the property value enhanced, landlords could now charge a higher rent to the incoming tenant.

**The passing of the Act and its effects.** The result was less satisfactory than the 1869 Disestablishment Act. The Lords, sensitive to property rights, made it far less likely that the courts would indeed judge that rent was pitched too high by amending 'excessive' rent to 'exorbitant'. Arguably, the land system required complete overhaul but Gladstone had done his best to reform it. Within a few years it was seen that his best was not good enough. Gladstone's policy had again been liberal – the wholesale raising of rent and failure to compensate for improvements was an abuse of privilege – but Irish nationalists did not see it as radical enough: they wished to do away with the English landlord class altogether.

Nineteenth-century Ireland: rural poverty. This photograph, taken in Co. Donegal in 1885, shows a tenant and his family being evicted for failing to pay rent. Their furniture was removed and the thatch roof destroyed to prevent it from being re-tenanted.

# IRISH UNIVERSITIES BILL 1873

**Background.** Along with the English Established Church and a foreign absentee landowning system, Gladstone saw Irish educational grievances as fundamental to solving the problem of poor relations between the two countries. **Trinity College, Dublin** was a university of high repute but its whole atmosphere was Protestant and although Catholics could attend they could not hold official positions there and few wished to attend.

**The failure of the Bill.** Gladstone proposed to set up a new university for Roman Catholics. But in his anxiety to cater for all viewpoints he introduced aspects of the Bill which pleased no one. In particular, the fact that three controversial subjects would not be taught – theology, philosophy and modern history – pleased neither the Catholic bishops nor more secular reformers. The Bill was defeated by nine votes in the Commons and Gladstone offered to resign and let Disraeli form a government. Disraeli, however, shrewdly refused and let what he correctly saw to be an increasingly weakening government stagger on for a little longer.

# EDUCATION ACT 1870

**Background.** Gladstone was not only concerned with Irish education. Given Robert Lowe's (see page 55) sour comment 'we must educate our masters', it is hardly surprising that one of Gladstone's first priorities should be education. Greater numbers of people in society now exercised political choice and it needed to be a considered one. But the impact of the 1867 Reform Act was only the immediate cause of the change. Barely half the 5–13 age group (elementary) were attending school with any degree of regularity. Nonconformists ministers aided by Birmingham politician Joseph Chamberlain had formed a National Education League which demanded state-aided **non-denominational education**.

**The struggle to pass the Bill.** Concern over the religious clauses in the Bill was the greatest challenge for W.E.

(see page 55)

**Trinity College, Dublin**
University founded in 1591. Trinity was to be the first of a number of colleges for a University of Dublin but it turned out to be the only one. It had (and still has) a high academic reputation.

**KEY TERM**

**Non-denominational education** Education that did not teach the views of one religious denomination (meaning the views of, for example, the Church of England, or, alternatively, Roman Catholicism) to the exclusion of others.

Forster, the Vice-President of the Board of Education, whose tricky job it was to pilot the Bill through the House of Commons. The struggle illustrates the central and still controversial role that religion played in domestic politics. Forster had to please both nonconformists and Anglicans. The Established Church was anxious to keep the educational initiative: it already controlled about 80 per cent of the existing elementary schools of religious foundation, which in turn formed about 80 per cent of all elementary schools. But nonconformists in the country as a whole were almost as numerous as Anglicans. So they were determined to stop a similar Anglican domination in the new board schools set up by the 1870 Act. What would the religious education be in these schools? The question was 'solved' by an amendment put forward by a Liberal MP, William Cowper-Temple, who proposed that religious teaching should not be 'distinctive of any denomination'.

**Main terms of the Education Act.**
- Children between 5 and 13 were to attend an elementary school.
- Where Church of England schools and other voluntary schools (those funded by voluntary contributions) existed they would remain, but in areas where Church provision was not sufficient a specially created school board would be established.
- This board, elected by ratepayers, male and female, would raise money locally and organise the supply of buildings, equipment and teachers.
- The boards had discretion to excuse fees for children of poor parents or to decide whether to make attendance compulsory. The fees were on average about £1.50 per year per child.
- Religious teaching was not to be distinctly in favour of one church, and parents could ask for their children to be withdrawn from Scripture lessons.

**Effects of the Act.** The Act passed was immensely significant: it led to the mass elementary education of the English and Welsh populations. In fact, the long-term importance of this Act would be hard to exaggerate:

- It produced a largely literate generation by the end of the century.

- It therefore encouraged the development of a popular press and, subsequently, lead to widespread media power and influence.
- It vastly increased educational opportunities for girls, who soon proceeded to learn to read and write at the same level (or better) than boys.
- Although the Act was purely educational and administrative, later educational legislation widened the state role to the physical well-being of the children, with schools meals and medical inspections shortly after the turn of the century.

## TRADE UNION ACT 1871

**Background.** The action on education was not the only one clearly influenced by events around 1866–7. Trade union legislation was passed to clear up doubts about their legal status suggested by the verdict in the courts in 1866 of Hornby versus Close. Close was the treasurer of the Bradford branch of the Boilermakers Union and had run off with £24 of union funds. The union officials thought that the Friendly Societies had protected them from such a loss. It was ruled by the judges that the union was technically an illegal organisation, being 'in restraint of trade', and so could not recover the money.

**Terms and effects.** The new Act made it clear that actions **in restraint of trade** would be lawful and funds secure. Legal recognition was secure providing trade unions officially registered their funds. Significantly perhaps, the legislation benefited precisely the class given the vote in 1867 – the skilled, male, urban working class. Was Gladstone trying to win its support? If so, one aspect of the legislation did not help. The Liberals also imposed an unwelcome restriction on the unions. A re-statement of the 1825 Criminal Law Amendment Act outlawed **peaceful picketing**. Unions felt that the size and nature of their activities made some form of picketing essential if strikes were to be effective. This was one of Gladstone's less liberal moves and trade unions campaigned for change; Disraeli was later to oblige them (see page 97).

**Action in restraint of trade** Any activity that prevented normal business or production in a firm but usually referring in legal terms to a strike by workers.

**Peaceful picketing** An attempt by organisers of a strike to draw attention to it by assembling outside the workplace and informing all workers of the reason for the dispute. Peaceful persuasion would be used to attempt to prevent employees from continuing to enter the factory while the strike continued.

While for the Trade Union Act Gladstone's attention was turned to the working classes, much of his other legislation concerned more traditional institutions. One of the major Liberal principles enacted in this government was the removal of unjustified privilege. This had influenced the Irish legislation and was now also to be applied to England and Wales.

## RELIGIOUS EQUALITY AND THE UNIVERSITY TESTS ACT 1871

**Background.** Issues of religious equality of opportunity are apparent in a significant reform of Gladstone's ministry and one with which he was personally involved. The Prime Minister's strong Anglican Christian faith was not diminished but his view of nonconformists had become more tolerant. No longer did he believe, as in his younger days, that the state had a duty to distinguish in precise terms between truth and error in religious belief. In 1868 he had not only successfully moved the Irish Church resolutions but also steered through the abolition of **compulsory Church rates**. Now he turned his attention to one of the few remaining grievances of nonconformists that prevented them from feeling that true **religious equality**, rather then mere toleration, had been achieved. Although non-Anglicans could enter Oxford and Cambridge without a religious test after reforms of 1854 and 1856 they still could not hold any kind of official position in the universities or be fellows (teachers) of any college.

**Terms and effects of the Act.** Gladstone's Act meant all academic appointments at Oxford and Cambridge (except for a few theological positions) were now open to those of any religious belief or none. So, for example, a nonconformist could now become Professor or be Master (in charge) of a college.

This was a significant change, all the more so coming from the devoutly Anglican Gladstone who had been opposed to it only a few years previously; it was a truly Liberal measure. It did not have a dramatic or immediate effect, although a college like Queen's College, Oxford did take more students from the north of England including quite a number of nonconformists. The general atmosphere, however, remained Anglican for some years yet.

## ARMY REFORMS

The army reforms of **Edward Cardwell** in 1869–71 bring out clearly the humanitarian side of Gladstonian Liberalism as well as its concern for administrative and operational efficiency and, once again, the removal of unjustified privilege.

**Background: personnel.**  Recruits into the ranks of the army had traditionally been regarded as coming from the 'lower' sectors of society and army officers believed that severe discipline such as flogging was the only language they understood. However, attitudes towards severe corporal punishment had changed and had become more hostile. Officers in the army were originally commissioned (authorised) by the monarch and commissions could now only be obtained by purchase. This reserved for the landed classes a useful occupation (like the Church and the legal profession) for younger sons who would not inherit the family property. By 1870, however, ideas in favour of promotion on merit and equality of opportunity were widespread and made the continuance of the system far less acceptable.

**Background: administrative.**  No changes of any substance had been made since the Crimean War. The army was in need of a simplified organisation and more up-to-date equipment. The success of the slick and well-organised Prussian troops against the French in 1870–1 did not cause the reforms but certainly hastened them.

### Terms of the reforms.
- **Humanitarian:** the abolition of peace-time flogging in the army.
- **Administrative and operational efficiency:** infantry regiments were reorganised on a territorial basis so that 69 new county areas each contained two battalions of

the old regulars. The local militia and volunteers were now attached to and trained by the regulars. The battalions took it in turns to serve abroad, which meant that recruits could be properly trained at home.

- The staff structure of the army was completely reformed.
- The minimum period of service of twelve years was reduced to six with six further years in the reserves. This meant that enlistment was encouraged and the military authorities could build up reserves.
- The infantry was re-armed with the breech-loading Henry Martini rifle used by the Prussians in 1870–1.
- **Removal of unjustified privilege:** this involved the radical and controversial abolition of purchase of commissions. Although originally included as part of the Army Enlistment Act of 1871 it was opposed by the House of Lords and had to become law by a special Royal Warrant from the Queen who had the authority to override the rejection of the Bill by the House of Lords.

The British army, reformed by Edward Cardwell in Gladstone's first ministry. This painting shows a squadron leader of the Royal Horse Guards, halting his men after a charge.

**Effects of the reforms.** Although the Duke of Cambridge, cousin of the Queen and Commander-in-Chief of the army, opposed further reforms such as the introduction of a proper **General Staff**, the changes had a lasting impact. On the one hand, the efficiency of the army was greatly increased, on the other, Gladstone's popularity with the landed classes was seriously damaged. In 1880 flogging was also abolished for men in active service. The reforms made possible rapid and large-scale campaigns such as the one in Egypt in 1882 (see page 122). The improved reputation of the British army after the reforms gave strength to the arguments of Foreign Secretaries and other diplomats who had to conduct diplomatic negotiations.

## CIVIL SERVICE ACT 1870

**Background.** Another institution whose shortcomings had been apparent in the Crimean War was the **civil service**. Ironically, a report advocating its reform had been produced just before Britain entered that war, in 1854. The calling of the inquiry in the first place indicated a feeling that civil servants were too often lazy, inefficient and lacking in initiative. The report, produced by Sir Charles Trevelyan (Assistant Secretary to the Treasury) and Sir Stafford Northcote MP, recommended amongst other administrative changes the introduction of competitive examinations for appointments to the service, and indeed suggested that the civil service was the resting place for those 'whose abilities [would not] succeed in the open professions'. But Palmerston had not acted on the suggestion.

**Terms and effects of the Act.** Gladstone's measure opened the examination to all those who wished to sit for it. In combining ideas of greater efficiency and fairer competition it was a typical measure of the ministry right down to the last Gladstonian characteristic. Because men of high social standing were still thought essential for the Foreign Office that particular department was exempt from the change. Again the move was so strongly opposed that an **Order in Council** was required to make it law. The civil service was gradually to change from a hiding place for the lazier younger sons of the landed classes to a solid middle-class profession.

# LOCAL GOVERNMENT AND SOCIAL AND LEGAL REFORMS

**Introduction.** The Liberal Party of Gladstone clearly stood for political reform but the changes of Gladstone's first ministry were more restricted in this area. The Ballot Act of 1872 (see page 60) needed the more substantial Corrupt Practices Act of 1883 (see page 61) to make it effective. A further extension of the franchise at parliamentary level, or a redistribution of seats, was unlikely after Disraeli's achievement in 1867: developments in this area again had to wait for the 1880s.

**Background.** A more likely possibility for reform was local government. Powers of local authorities had been growing steadily since the **municipal corporations** had been established in 1834, taking on numerous responsibilities in the areas of sewerage, water supply, street paving and lighting. The argument that all ratepayers should have a say in how their money was spent had grown ever stronger. In 1869 female householders were granted the vote in municipal elections, the first time they had been allowed to vote in any kind of election.

**Terms and effects of the reforms.** As frequently occurred in Gladstone's Liberal ministries, reorganisation was a principal theme. All that **George Goschen** was able to do was set up a Local Government Board which planned, none too successfully, to co-ordinate poor relief and public health measures: but it was a long way from a modern Ministry of Health.

**Social reform.** Unlike Disraeli later in the decade, the Liberals did not have a reputation for wide-ranging social reform, as this was supposed to offend their laissez-faire principles. However, the temper of the times frequently demanded measures in this area, as even the cautious Palmerston had earlier acknowledged, as shown by his Divorce Act of 1857 which liberalised the law in this area. When Gladstone's measures ran directly counter to the enabling of freedom, they tended to be ineffective and led to Disraeli having to develop further the legislation (see pages 96–9). Alternatively, they caused offence. The best example of this was the Licensing Act of 1872.

# LICENSING ACT 1872

**Background.** Alcoholism was seen as a major social problem, a destroyer of families and a major cause of poverty, crime and violence. In the country there was a strong teetotal movement spearheaded by the **temperance organisation**, the **United Kingdom Alliance**. The subject was first brought before Parliament in 1871 but this bill was so unpopular that it had been withdrawn.

**Controversial passage and terms of the Act.** In a genuine attempt to deal with these issues, Home Secretary Bruce's Bill proposed to restrict the opening hours of public houses, but it ran into opposition. The debate aroused strong passions on both sides. 'An England free better than an England sober' was a common cry, literally so in the case of Bishop Magee of Peterborough in one of the House of Lords' debates on the subject. Perhaps Gladstone had run into trouble here because this was not typical Liberal legislation: in his desire to please his nonconformist supporters from whose ranks many of the teetotallers were drawn, the government had produced an untypical and illiberal measure. It provided for:

- licensing hours to be determined by the local authorities;
- penalties against tampering with the contents of the beer;
- enforcement of the above regulations by police.

**Effects.** Opening hours of many public houses were restricted to lunch times and evenings only, and a movement grew for a local option, where boroughs or counties could choose to become dry altogether or at least ban sales on Sundays. These ideas had considerable support and some success in Wales, a number of counties opting to remain dry.

Gladstone's ministry did address some other social questions such as river pollution, merchant shipping and public health. Yet the Prime Minister's parting shot in the 1874 election campaign – the proposal to abolish the income tax in the next parliament – hardly suggests that the Liberals were planning major state social intervention on social questions in subsequent years.

## JUDICATURE ACT 1873

**Background.** This was the Gladstone administration's last major piece of legislation in its weaker days of 1873. It was a largely administrative measure introduced by the **Lord Chancellor**, Lord Selbourne.

The slowness, the complexities and the cost of English law had long been complained of and satirised by writers such as Charles Dickens. When Attorney General in the 1860s, Roundell Palmer, later the first Lord Selbourne, had spoken in favour of simplifying and consolidating centuries of these complicated laws. A Royal Commission was set up and reported in 1869. After an earlier bill had failed in 1871 Palmer was appointed Lord Chancellor in 1872 and produced his own proposals which were much praised on all sides and passed without difficulty.

- **Common law and equity were fused.**
- The complex court system was reorganised so that there was just one supreme court of judicature.
- The appeals' system was transformed and a final Court of Appeal established.

**Effects.** This Act represented a considerable act of administrative achievement. Further reorganisation of the court system followed in 1880 but the Act of 1873 still forms the basis of much of the legal system of England and Wales to this day. Initially, a final appeal to the House of Lords was removed but it was reintroduced by an amendment in 1876.

### KEY TERM

**Lord Chancellor** The head of the British legal profession and effectively responsible for senior legal appointments and the overall running of the legal service. He was always a peer and always in the cabinet.

### KEY CONCEPT

**Fusion of common law and equity** The complexities of the law were increased by some courts running on the principle of common law – based on judges' previous decisions – and equity – based on principles of fairness. The two systems were now combined into one and, where they clashed, equity would prevail.

## GLADSTONE'S SECOND MINISTRY 1880–5

When Gladstone was re-elected in 1880 to form his second ministry there was less of the far-reaching domestic legislation which had been apparent between 1868 and 1874. The main issues were:

- foreign policy (see page 118) where Gladstone's previous stance of non-intervention was now much less apparent;
- parliamentary reform (see page 65) for the third Reform Act of 1884 and the Redistribution Act of 1885;
- the growing Radical element in the Liberal Party led by Joseph Chamberlain (see page 85);
- Ireland, where nationalist activity was a far more serious threat than before 1880 (see page 86).

### The growth of Radical Liberalism: the position of the Whigs

Given its very diverse nature, the Liberal Party of Gladstone's first ministry had been a relatively united one. Gladstone had:

- placed many Whigs in his cabinet (such as **Earl Granville**, the Duke of Argyll, the Earl of Kimberley and the Marquess of Ripon);
- pushed through substantial legislation that the more radical element in the party found acceptable, especially with regard to the removal of unjustified privilege;
- exerted strong leadership himself which was almost universally accepted.

By 1880, however, conflicting tensions in the party were more apparent. The changes begun with the second Reform Act back in 1867 were beginning to work themselves out. The composition of Parliament was changing as aristocratic elements were no longer so dominant.

Although 151 Liberal members of the Commons were still those with landed interests they were now outnumbered for the first time by the combination of lawyers and those with business and commercial dealings. The latter would naturally expect the party to look after their interests.

| Liberal Members in 1880 | |
| --- | --- |
| Total Members | 358 |
| About 80 of these were aristocratic, and 71 more were 'great landowners' | 151 (43.6%) |
| Middle-class industrialists and merchants | 114 (32.6%) |
| Lawyers | 93 (26.9%) |

## KEY CONCEPT

**Aristocratic talent for government** A widely held belief (among aristocrats) that their well-educated upbringing, coupled with the practice of management of estates and workers, and their financial independence, made them ideally suited to exercise the responsibilities, and cope with the demands of, governing the country and the Empire.

## KEY TERM

**Junior ministerial experience** At this time junior ministers were generally assistants to more senior ministers in charge of departments. It was normal to occupy one of these posts as a first step on the political ladder unless the party in question came into government after a long period in opposition. To be put straight into the cabinet by being immediately given a very senior post suggested Chamberlain was regarded as exceptionally able.

Landowners were now outnumbered by those from other backgrounds in the Liberal Party but were sufficiently numerous to be able to resist measures they felt to be too radical. The landed influence of the Whigs was still crucial in getting electoral support and financing candidates. A Whig-Liberal supporter in one county remarked that if the leading Whigs in the area deserted to the Conservatives then 'a Liberal candidate might as well stand for the moon' because of all the help, financial and otherwise, that would be lost. Since these Whigs contributed so much they in turn would also assume that the Liberal Party would follow their lines of thought.

Gladstone was anxious to use Whig talent.

- He held the traditional belief that aristocrats had a **natural talent** for government.
- The landowning Whigs contributed more to the Liberal election effort in 1880 than they did in 1874 and the party had done much better.
- The House of Lords was still significant in political debate and decision-making. Without Whig aristocratic peers in this Upper House the Liberals would be very weak indeed in the Upper Chamber, which had a large Conservative majority anyway.

### The growth of Radical Liberalism: Joseph Chamberlain

In 1880 Gladstone clearly signalled the importance of Joseph Chamberlain by putting him – without **junior ministerial experience** – straight into the cabinet as President of the Board of Trade. But the two never got on and regarded each other with mutual suspicion. Gladstone never confided in Chamberlain as he did in some of his more Whiggish colleagues such as Lord Granville. For his part Chamberlain felt Gladstone to be insufficiently radical and gradually developed his own ideas for a new direction in Liberal policy. His social reforms in Birmingham had showed him keener on the role of government than Gladstone and he was more positive than the **GOM** about further political reform.

Chamberlain's position in the Liberal Party in the 1880s bore some resemblance to Gladstone's himself 20 years before in the 1860s. As a senior cabinet minister Gladstone seemed at that time to be striking out on his own in advocating parliamentary reform and finding the Prime Minister Palmerston old and out of touch. Now in the mid-1880s it was Chamberlain's turn to suggest new radical policies not yet officially approved by the Liberal Party. This took the form of his Unauthorised Programme. The principal elements were:

- free elementary education for all;
- the extension of house building and public sanitation by local authorities paid for by rate increases;
- higher taxation of the wealthy and the landed in particular;
- Church disestablishment in England and Wales;
- more democratic local government;
- manhood (though not female) suffrage;
- payment of MPs.

The programme was unauthorised in the sense that Chamberlain was a cabinet minister and yet his ideas had been put forward without reference to his cabinet colleagues. The tension between advanced Chambelainite Liberals and traditional Gladstonian supporters was widening all the time. It was on Ireland that the break was to come but the nature of the party's split was hardly predictable.

## IRELAND

Gladstone's legislation concerning Ireland had not altogether worked and nationalist feeling was growing.

- The Secret Ballot Act of 1872 had helped the nationalist cause by enabling many of the Irish electorate to defy their landlords.
- **Charles Stewart Parnell** had taken over from Isaac Butt as leader of the Irish Home Rule Party in 1877 and proved a much more aggressive leader of the Irish nationalist MPs.

KEY TERM

**GOM** Grand Old Man: a term frequently used to describe Gladstone in his later years after about 1880.

KEY PERSON

**Charles Stewart Parnell 1845–91** Irish landowner of Protestant background from County Wicklow. MP 1875; leader of Home Rule Party 1877. Controlled 61 nationalist Members after 1880 and led them in vigorous obstruction to English legislation on Ireland. Continued to campaign after the failure of the Home Rule Bill. Politically ruined by unfavourable publicity after being cited as co-respondent in divorce case 1889–90.

HEINEMANN ADVANCED HISTORY

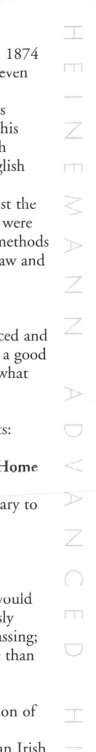

- Disraeli had given Ireland little attention between 1874 and 1880 and opposition to English policies and even English presence was growing.
- Above all, however, the poor harvests of the 1870s produced the kind of crisis Gladstone had hoped his legislation would avert: wholesale evictions of Irish tenants from the land, frequently by absentee English landlords.
- The **Land League** activities which protested against the whole concept of English ownership of Irish land were leading Irish nationalists to much more extreme methods of protest and creating a major crisis in terms of law and order.

## The second Irish Land Act 1881

At first Gladstone responded positively. He introduced and passed a second Irish Land Act in 1881 which went a good deal further than the one of 1870. It gave the Irish what many had demanded, the '**three Fs**'.

But the Irish had gone further in two crucial respects:

- many nationalists now wanted nothing less than **Home Rule**;
- many were now prepared to use violence if necessary to get it.

This resulted in:

- obstruction in Parliament where Irish Members would talk for hours on end in order to prevent previously routine measures like Irish Coercion Acts from passing;
- terrorist activities in Ireland itself on a wider scale than those seen before.

In 1882 Gladstone found himself in the weak position of having to do a deal with the Irish leader Parnell. Imprisoned in Kilmainham Jail under the terms of an Irish Coercion Act for calling for renewed violence in Ireland, Parnell was let out on the understanding that he would use his influence to stop that very violence from getting out of hand. Unfortunately soon after this the new Chief Secretary for Ireland, Gladstone's nephew Lord Frederick

### KEY TERMS

**Land League** A militant, nationalist organisation in Ireland which campaigned for a transformation of the Irish land system by attacks on unpopular landlords. Parnell was elected its President but its main inspiration came from Michael Davitt.

**Home Rule for Ireland** The idea of giving back to Ireland its own Parliament (abolished in 1800) and making the Irish responsible for running their own domestic affairs. Defence and foreign policy would be left in the hands of the Westminster government.

### The second Irish Land Act (the 'three Fs')

- Fixity of tenure so that tenants could not be removed save for non-payment of rent or serious violations of their contract.
- Fair rent now to be fixed by an independent tribunal.
- Free sale of the land of which they were tenants without the need for landlord permission.

Cavendish, and his Under-secretary T. H. Burke, were murdered in **Phoenix Park** soon after taking up the posts. No matter that it was the work of an extremist fringe, nationalist group, the 'Invincibles', it soured Anglo-Irish relations and made further political negotiation difficult.

### Home Rule crisis 1885–6

By 1885 Gladstone appears to have been converted to the idea of Home Rule for Ireland. Apparently Gladstone had reconsidered the issue in the summer when on holiday in Norway; but the timing of his conversion looked to many to be based more on political calculation than principle. Moreover, at this stage the position of the two major parties on the issue was uncertain. There followed a complex series of events.

* The Irish Nationalists helped defeat the Liberals in Parliament believing at this point that the Conservatives might do more for them.
* Lord Salisbury then became Conservative Prime Minister.
* When a general election was held later in the year the Liberals had a majority over the Conservatives of 86.
* This was, however, exactly the number of Parnell's Irish Nationalist MPs who could now hold the **political balance of power.**
* Gladstone's conversion to Home Rule meant the Irish Nationalists now switched their support to him which brought Gladstone back into office early in 1886. However, his Home Rule Bill terms were unpopular; the Bill split the Liberals and was defeated in the Commons by 30 votes.
* At the subsequent election the Conservatives were returned with a comfortable majority.
* The Liberal Party remained divided and **Liberal Unionists** gave support to the Conservatives on maintaining the Union with Ireland.

The more traditional landowning Whigs like Lord Hartington could not accept Home Rule and had voted against it. Intriguingly, they were joined by more Radical Liberals such as Joseph Chamberlain, who felt it was the

Westminster government's responsibility to deal with Irish problems. The defection of Chamberlain made the Liberal split a complex one from which they only ever partially recovered. The unity of the earlier days of Gladstone's leadership had gone forever.

## CONCLUSION

Gladstone's first ministry was one of substantial reform which in many ways established a new outlook and direction for governments yet to come.

What did the first ministry achieve?

- It removed a good deal of what Gladstone considered to be unjustified privilege.
- It completed the programme of religious liberalism that gave non-Anglicans virtually full legal equality.
- It set a radical new direction in education.
- It began the process of cleaning up the corrupt electoral system.
- It reformed some of the country's major institutions such as the army, civil service and universities, and set trade unions on a secure legal footing.
- It tackled the problems in Ireland with the utmost seriousness and thoroughness.

In his second ministry what did Gladstone achieve and face?

- He continued and substantially extended his policy of Irish measures and electoral reform.
- He had greater difficulty than in the first ministry in holding together the Liberal coalition of Whigs and Radicals.
- He found that the Irish legislation did not produce the desired result of quietening down Irish discontent.
- He produced a fatal split in the Liberal Party in 1885–6 when taking on the cause of Irish Home Rule.

## SUMMARY QUESTIONS

1 What were Gladstone's most important achievements in his first ministry, 1868–74?

2 What were the major difficulties which Gladstone ran into in his second ministry, 1880–5?

# CHAPTER 6

## Political and social issues of Disraeli's government 1874–80

### INTRODUCTION

Disraeli had first become Prime Minister in February 1868 when Lord Derby resigned on grounds of ill-health. 'At last I have reached to the top of the greasy pole' he remarked. Indeed, he was soon to slither down as Gladstone's Liberals comfortably won the election of 1868. However, this election result was reversed in 1874 when the Conservative majority was 105 over the Liberals, and 48 overall when the **Irish Home Rule Party** supporters are taken into account: Disraeli had finally achieved real power. The fact that there was a comfortable Conservative victory at all was significant. It was the first time this had occurred since Peel's triumph in 1841.

Whether Disraeli would take full advantage of this opportunity, however, was another matter. He was 70 years old and on his own admission lacked the drive and energy he had possessed just a few years previously. 'It has come too late' he admitted when he was congratulated on becoming Prime Minister again. In truth he had never possessed the forcefulness and zest of a man like Gladstone and had a much hazier idea than the Liberal Prime Minister of what policies he would introduce. In these last years of his life (he died in 1881) he apparently suffered from asthma, gout, bronchitis and, towards the end, kidney disease.

### HOW POPULAR WERE THE CONSERVATIVES?

**The victory of 1874.** The election victory in 1874 had not necessarily come for positive reasons. True, party organisation had played a part thanks to the work of the National Union and the administrative skills of John Gorst

---

**KEY TERM**

**Irish Home Rule Party** The Irish nationalist party that wished to see a Parliament in Dublin once again as it had been in the eighteenth century. It was founded by Isaac Butt, a conservatively minded Protestant lawyer whose views had become more nationalistic after defending Fenian prisoners in the late 1860s. The party was successful at the 1874 election with 56 MPs elected.

(see page 62), and the Liberals were not to catch up in this field until the election of 1880. But a good deal of Conservative support came from those upset by Gladstone's reforms which had undoubtedly ruffled many feathers. The formerly Liberal middle classes increasingly saw the Conservatives as the party most likely to maintain and consolidate the position in society that they had recently won. Measures such as throwing open the army and civil service to all comers no longer seemed so attractive to those now well-established in society and no longer on its fringes. The drink trade had been offended by the restrictions of the Licensing Act and some publicans had allowed only Conservative election meetings and not Liberal ones on their premises.

**Middle-class Conservatism.**  But though specific factors may have been important in the Conservative victory, the most significant element seems to have been a general feeling of unease in middle-class suburbia about what the Liberals might get up to if re-elected. In 1865 three out of four City of London MPs were Liberal and one Conservative: in 1874 the situation was reversed. Suburban seats also changed hands in areas such as Middlesex and the London end of Kent, Surrey and Essex. This trend continued, and by 1885, when Middlesex, Kent and Surrey were made up of 21 constituencies, all elected Conservatives. The Conservatives were becoming a party increasingly associated with the prosperous middle classes.

Whether Disraeli anticipated or wanted this is another matter. After the 1867 Reform Act he seems to have hoped that the newly enfranchised working class would support the Conservatives. A significant minority of working men (and later, women) did proceed to vote for the party or they would not have got elected so frequently in the next 130 years; but they were not the mainstay of Conservative support.

**What was Disraelian Conservatism?**  Could Disraeli take any of the credit for this popularity? After his defeat in 1868 there had been moves to depose him as leader, but he held on to make two significant public speeches – something he did much less often than Gladstone – in

## KEY PLACES

**Free Trade Hall, Manchester** Built in 1847 as a celebration of the victory of the principle of free trade with the repeal of the Corn Laws in 1846. Possibly the only building named after a proposition rather than a person or a place.

**Crystal Palace** A huge glass building designed and built for the Great Exhibition in Hyde Park in 1851 to show off the world's – but especially Britain's – industrial and technological advances. Removed to a permanent site in south London, it burnt down in 1936.

## KEY TERMS

**National Party** Disraeli saw the Conservatives as appealing to all groups and classes in society and the nation, and believed that the party's policies would unite them all. At various times in the twentieth century, much was made of this 'One Nation Conservatism'.

**Imperial** Until Disraeli's speech when he used this word, it had been regarded as a continental term referring to foreign emperors such as the French or Russian rulers. Disraeli's opponents criticised him for using it, especially as he had criticised the Liberals for being too continental. They sarcastically referred to his 'imperialism' as a term of insult. However, the word stuck and became used for those who gloried in the size and strength of the British Empire.

1872 at the **Free Trade Hall** in Manchester in April and at the **Crystal Palace** in south London in June. In them he outlined his interpretation of Conservatism. At Manchester in a long address fortified by brandy (special white brandy so it would look like water) he promised to:

- be proud of Britain and to uphold the institutions of the country such as the monarchy and the Church and the landed aristocracy, and to maintain the British constitution;
- stand up for British interests abroad – with a side-swipe at what he saw as a weak Liberal foreign policy;
- act on the need for sanitary reform – this was only a tiny fraction of the speech but has been made much of since, in view of later reforms.

At the Crystal Palace he emphasised similar themes:

- the Conservatives were the '**National Party**' rejecting the 'continental' ideas of the Liberals. They were the party to appeal to all classes and unite the nation;
- the working classes would be proud to belong to an '**imperial**' country;
- social reform rather than political reform was now required – again a minor part of the speech.

Disraeli was certainly aware of the much enlarged working-class electorate from his own reform in 1867 and sensed they would be attracted by a firmly nationalistic policy abroad and improvements to their own quality of life at home. To simplify his message considerably, the Conservatives would stand for tradition, imperialism and social reform. This did indeed prove popular, though not always with the people Disraeli intended.

## BACKGROUND TO DISRAELI'S SOCIAL REFORM

The frenzy of legislative activity in Gladstone's first ministry was not repeated in Disraeli's second. Nevertheless, in the field of social reform the ministry was very active. In an era when national politics, national issues and national parties were all developing, national solutions were demanded. It is true to say that Gladstone's government had tackled these issues but, as Disraeli had sensed in his speeches, public opinion was looking for further action in certain areas.

## Firstly, in areas which Gladstone's government had not fully addressed

- **Housing.** Poor-quality building of back-to-back, ill-ventilated and cramped housing in the larger industrial towns was a major handicap to a satisfactory quality of life for many working people. There had been a Housing Act proposed by a Liberal MP which became law in Disraeli's first ministry in 1868 but it had not been effective.
- **Merchant shipping.** There had been an increase in shipping disasters due to overloading with cargo.
- The growth of **Friendly Societies** required regulation. This had been recognised by the Liberals who had set up a Royal Commission to investigate the issue in 1870 but there had been no legislation.

## Secondly, where Gladstone's changes had not been seen to settle the question

- **Food adulteration.** As an increasingly urban society grew less and less food for themselves and bought more and more, problems of hygiene and inaccurate labelling had became a major issue. Also, some supposed medical remedies were very dubious. A Liberal Act of 1872 had been seen as ineffective in this area.
- **Labour relations.** Trade unions had objected to Gladstone's ban on peaceful picketing and also complained that the law punished workers who broke their contract more severely than employers who did the same.
- **Licensing of public houses.** Gladstone's restrictions had been regarded as too severe.

## Thirdly, where previous legislation needed to be consolidated and/or developed

- **Public health.** There had been a mass of **legislation from the 1840s** to the Liberal Act of 1872. Regulations were

### KEY TERMS

**Friendly Societies**
Associations whose members paid fixed contributions to ensure help in sickness and old age and ensure provision for their families in the event of death.

**Food adulteration** Mixing harmful, unwanted or unmentioned ingredients into food. Salt in beer to make the drinker more thirsty or watering-down milk to save expense involved unwanted ingredients, but more harmful substances could also be inserted.

**Public health legislation from the 1840s** The most important measure was the Public Health Act of 1848 which set up a Central Board of Health, but the provisions were not compulsory for local authorities to take up. After 1854 it was disbanded and its functions taken over by another government department, the Home Office.

**Maximum number of hours worked** The first effective restrictions on the hours worked in textile factories by women and children were introduced in 1833. There had been further restrictions on hours in 1844 and 1847 and a widening of the provisions to workshops in 1867.

becoming complex and contradictory. River pollution was now a serious concern.

- **Factories.** Administrative complexity was again an issue and public opinion now favoured a further reduction in the **maximum number of hours worked**. This had been recommended by a Liberal inquiry which had reported in 1873.
- **Education.** The provisions from the trail-blazing Act of 1870 were to be amended.

Though Disraeli was not a good administrator himself a strong group of ministers in his cabinet was able to produce substantial reforms in these areas. The most active

PUNCH, OR THE LONDON CHARIVARI.—March 6, 1875.

**INJURED INNOCENTS.**

Bung (*to* Bumble, *Vestryman and Owner of Unwholesome Dwellings*). "TALK OV 'ARASSING LEGISLATION! IT WAS OUR TURN LAST SESSION; NOW IT'S YOUR'N!"
Bumble. "A REGULAR CROSS, I CALL IT. MIGHT JUST AS WELL 'AVE THE T'OTHER LOT BACK AGIN!"

**A cartoon from *Punch*, March 1875. Whether passed by Gladstone's or Disraeli's ministry, social reform always upset someone.**

figures were the Home Secretary, **Richard Cross**, and the President of the Local Government Board, George Sclater-Booth. As a result of their efforts, eleven major acts of social reform were passed in the two years 1875 and 1876.

## THE LEGISLATION

| | |
|---|---|
| *Title* | **Artisans Dwelling Act 1875** |
| *Minister responsible* | Cross |
| *Main terms* | Local authorities, if they wished, could purchase slum property and organise the building of new, cheap properties to be let at favourable rents to urban workers. |
| *Significance* | The first-ever substantial piece of legislation with regard to housing; prepared to interfere with property rights in exceptional cases with the idea of compulsory purchase. |
| *Effects* | Considerable in Birmingham where Joseph Chamberlain used the Act to transform the city's housing. Overall, however, because the Act was **permissive** and not compulsory many authorities, shy of expense, did little. Only ten authorities had taken advantage of it by the end of the 1870s though, later, Liverpool was more active in its implementation. In London it could even create a housing problem as properties of the very poor were demolished without being replaced with dwellings these people could afford. |

| | |
|---|---|
| *Title* | **Merchant Shipping Act 1876** |
| *Minister responsible* | Viscount Adderley (President of the Board of Trade) |
| *Main terms* | Shipowners were made to draw a line (the Plimsoll line) around a vessel to indicate the maximum load that could be taken. |
| *Significance* | Backbench pressure. The Act owed its existence to Samuel Plimsoll, Liberal MP for Derby, who had made a scene in the House of Commons the previous year when an earlier bill had been dropped. It was a compulsory act and one of a number that increased state regulation. |

| | |
|---|---|
| *Effects* | Not totally effective since the line could be drawn by the owners of the vessels, but an important step towards greater regulation. |

| | |
|---|---|
| *Title* | **Friendly Societies Act 1875** |
| *Minister responsible* | Sir Stafford Northcote (Chancellor of the Exchequer) |
| *Main terms* | A degree of regulation of the societies was introduced. The societies could be given **actuarial advice** by the government and their funds would be safeguarded. |
| *Significance* | The idea was to ensure the societies could continue their work even more effectively in providing insurance for the better-off working class. |
| *Effects* | Friendly Society funds continued to grow. By 1891 they had 4.2 million people investing in them a total of £22.7 million. By 1901 the equivalent figures were 6.2 million and £48.2 million. |

| | |
|---|---|
| *Title* | **Sale of Food and Drugs Act 1875** |
| *Minister responsible* | Sclater-Booth |
| *Main terms* | Ingredients harmful to health were forbidden in foods. Certain drugs were forbidden from general sale. |
| *Significance* | Another major step in state regulation and the main piece of legislation in this field until 1928. |
| *Effects* | Fairly successful but limited to prohibition of harmful substances. Thus, adding salt to beer or water to milk was not covered. |

| | |
|---|---|
| *Title* | **Conspiracy and Protection of Property Act 1875** |
| *Minister responsible* | Cross |
| *Main terms* | Legalised peaceful picketing. |
| *Significance* | Pleased the trade union leaders and removed a major grievance. |
| *Effects* | Ensured the moderate and peaceful development of the trade union movement. |

| | |
|---|---|
| *Title* | **Employers and Workmen Act 1876** |
| *Minister responsible* | Cross |
| *Main terms* | Replaced the **Master and Servant Act** with more |

## KEY TERMS

**Actuarial advice** An actuary is an official in an insurance office who estimates the best rates of premium to charge for insurance based on rates of probability.

**Master and Servant Act** In the 1860s, particularly in Scotland, magistrates could still threaten strikers with prison for breach of contract when a strike began. After 1876 'aggravated cases' could still result in a criminal prosecution.

sensitive names implying greater equality. Before the Act employees could be sued in the criminal courts as well as the civil courts, but this did not apply to employers. All cases regarding conditions of employment and possible breach of contract would now be dealt with in the civil courts.

| | |
|---|---|
| *Significance* | The law would now treat all classes equally on legal questions. |
| *Effects* | Disraeli now felt all major problems regarding the relations between labour and capital had been settled. The Secretary of the **Trades Union Congress**, George Howell, also expressed himself satisfied. |

| | |
|---|---|
| *Title* | **Licensing Act 1874** |
| *Minister responsible* | Cross |
| *Main terms* | Amended Bruce's Licensing Act. Drinking time was increased by 30 minutes, police rights of search reduced and **magistrates**' discretion on interfering with hours of opening removed. |
| *Significance* | A good example of Disraeli's government amending an unpopular Gladstone act in a popular direction. |
| *Effects* | Government intervention in this area was now accepted. Some publicans favoured the Conservatives as a result, though this can be exaggerated. |

| | |
|---|---|
| *Title* | **Public Health Act 1875** |
| *Minister responsible* | Sclater-Booth |
| *Main terms* | Consolidatory measure (bringing together and simplifying a mass of different and possibly contradictory existing laws). In 1872 the Liberals had put into practice the recommendations of a Sanitary Commission Report set up when Disraeli was first Prime Minister in 1868. **Medical officers of health** had been appointed in large towns and sanitary authorities established. What Sclater-Booth's Act did was to consolidate the measure and define the powers of the new authorities more clearly. |
| *Significance* | Seen as a triumph for administrative efficiency and more effective than the Liberal legislation of 1872. |

| | |
|---|---|
| *Effects* | Coupled with the Pollution of Rivers Act of 1874, it remained the basis of Public Health law until the 1920s. |
| *Title* | **Factory Acts of 1874 and 1878** |
| *Minister responsible* | Cross |
| *Main terms* | 1874: Hours in textile factories reduced from 60 hours a week to $56\frac{1}{2}$ for women and young people. The ban on half-time employment for children was raised to 10 years and full-time to 14. 1878: Consolidated all previous legislation and abolished the distinction between factories and workshops (smaller than factories, employing not more than a few dozen people). |
| *Significance* | A great achievement for Cross whose praises were literally sung to the words: 'For he's a jolly good fellow, whatever the Radicals think, For he has shortened the hours of work and lengthened the hours of drink.' |
| *Effects* | Reducing the hours of essential female and young workers often meant hours were effectively reduced for adult men as well. Laissez-faire beliefs were hanging on sufficiently well to make direct restrictions on adult male labour more difficult to pass. |
| *Title* | **Education Act 1876** |
| *Minister responsible* | Viscount Sandon (Vice-president of the Committee of the Council for Education) |
| *Main terms* | Children between 10 and 14 could only leave school if they had a certificate indicating minimum levels of attainment. Parliamentary grants of money for voluntary schools could exceed what the schools themselves had raised. |
| *Significance* | Conservatives hoped to encourage more voluntary (usually Anglican) schools as these seemed to be expanding at a slower rate than the newly established board schools. |
| *Effects* | Elementary education up to the age of 10 was now effectively compulsory as long as local authorities were prepared to enforce attendance. Moreover, more and more of them were exempting the poorer families from school fees. |

Disraeli's ministry is remembered especially for its social reform but his Conservative high regard for the great institutions of the country, the monarchy, the landed interest and the Church featured prominently in his activities. Moreover, in Disraeli's time the Empire came to be added to this important list.

## DISRAELI AND THE QUEEN

One of the revealing developments of Disraeli's second ministry was the partial return to public life of Queen Victoria. Widowed by the death of Prince Albert at the end of 1861 she had become something of a recluse, being only rarely seen in public and spending a good deal of time at her Scottish retreat of Balmoral, or at Osborne on the Isle of Wight. Disraeli, generally at ease in women's company, handled her more sensitively than Gladstone. 'Mr Gladstone addresses me as if I were a public meeting' complained the Queen, whereas Disraeli knew how to flatter her. Although Disraeli's **skill with the pen** was much greater than the Queen's he was tactful enough to make comments such as 'We authors, Ma'am'. Nor were Gladstone's letters as enjoyable as Disraeli's who could, as the Queen's Secretary remarked, write 'in an amusing tone while seizing the points of an argument'.

**The widower and the widowed.** When Disraeli's wife Mary Anne died in 1872, Victoria's condolences were profound, sincere and doubtless made with her own widowhood in mind. Both may have been a comfort to each other, but, while Victoria may have helped Disraeli overcome his loss on a purely personal basis, Disraeli's aid to the Queen had wider consequences. The monarchy had become unpopular around 1870 because of the Queen's reluctance to show herself in public since Albert's death and because of the behaviour of the Prince of Wales, a known womaniser and gambler. However, after the Prince almost died of typhoid fever (the illness which had killed his father ten years before) at the end of 1871, public sympathies changed.

Disraeli's encouragement to the Queen to appear more in

**Disraeli's skill with the pen** Disraeli wrote novels on and off throughout his life. Two, *Coningsby* and *Sybil*, written in the 1840s, are still highly regarded today. *Coningsby* provides an insight into the political activities of the day and *Sybil* is famous for its portrayal of social problems, including the idea of the 'two nations' of rich and poor.

**Royal constitutional duty** Although, theoretically, the Queen invited someone of her own choice to form a government, in practice by the mid-nineteenth century it was understood that the person would normally be the leader of the majority party in Parliament – though there might be two leaders, one in the Commons and one in the Lords, from which to choose the Prime Minister.

public was an important element in the recovery of her popularity. Moreover, the contrast in her relations with Gladstone was marked. This did not usually mean, however, that the Queen overstepped the mark in terms of exercising her power. When Disraeli lost the election of 1880 she knew that she would have to perform her **royal constitutional duty** which meant accepting his resignation and asking the Liberals to form a ministry.

**Empress of India.** After a visit to India in 1875–6 by **Edward, Prince of Wales**, the Queen let it be known to Disraeli that she would like to add to her royal titles and become Empress of India. It appears to have been her own idea and Disraeli may not have approved. Certainly he did not feel the timing was right but he went along with the suggestion and a Royal Titles Bill was introduced into Parliament in 1876. Opposition was considerable, with the leading Liberal peer Lord Granville speaking strongly against it in the House of Lords. The Prince of Wales returned from India annoyed that he had not been informed of the development previously. Disraeli had two main justifications for the Bill:

- It would emphasise that British authority in India was much more welcomed than at the time of the Indian Mutiny in 1857.
- It would indicate to the Russians that an **expansion of the Russian Empire** near India would not be welcomed.

Once passed it was clear that the monarchy was assuming the role of head of the British Empire and not just the British Isles. The whole incident associated the Conservatives with both monarchy and Empire.

## DISRAELI AND THE CHURCH

Disraeli, a man of Jewish origin and baptised into the Christian faith at the age of 13 on the orders of his **sceptical father**, never possessed the devout faith of someone like Gladstone. However, finding himself at the head of the Conservative Party, he was prepared stoutly to defend the privileges of the Church of England. He had

### KEY PERSON

**Edward, Prince of Wales 1841–1910** The eldest son of Victoria and Albert. Reacted against his strict upbringing and worried his parents with his tastes for fine food, women, gambling and shooting parties. Only his severe illness at the end of 1871, and dramatic recovery, brought an end to growing republican feelings.

### KEY TERM

**Expanding Russian Empire** Russia was expanding its borders to the south and east in the mid- to late nineteenth century so that by the 1870s only Afghanistan stood between it and the British Empire in India (see Chapter 7, pages 119–21).

### KEY CONCEPT

**Disraeli's sceptical father** Isaac D'Israeli (his son Benjamin dropped the apostrophe) was a substantial man of letters in his own right. He had fallen out with members of his Jewish Synagogue in London, lost his religious faith and had his children baptised as Christians so they could get on in the world.

opposed Gladstone's disestablishment of the Irish Church and took a considerable interest in **church appointments** as Prime Minister, preferring not to recommend known Liberals. He sensed that the very high churchmen were not generally popular in the country as a whole and their ritualistic practices were far too close to the Roman Catholic tradition for many Protestants. The Queen agreed, and in fact wished to go further than Disraeli in stopping them.

**Public Worship Act.** The result was the Public Worship Regulation Bill of 1874 which provoked a lively discussion in Parliament. Certain rituals would be banned and the idea that clergy defying the ban could ultimately end up in jail on a point of conviction troubled many. Gladstone spoke against the Bill on the grounds of religious liberty but it passed both Lords and Commons. After all the controversy that had resulted, Disraeli tried to avoid controversial Church issues for the rest of his period of office.

KEY TERM

**Church appointments**
Senior clergy were officially appointed by the Queen, but by this time the Prime Minister was also consulted. Sometimes there was quite a battle between Victoria and Disraeli, as when in 1868 she persuaded him to accept her own choice for Archbishop of Canterbury, Archibald Tait, whose Liberal leanings were distrusted by Disraeli.

## DISRAELI AND THE LANDED INTEREST

As with the Church, Disraeli was an outsider when it came to the English aristocracy, but he took to the idea of a landed life enthusiastically after his father acquired a modest house at Bradenham in Buckinghamshire in 1828. Disraeli himself became the squire of Hughenden, near High Wycombe in 1848. He enjoyed the conversations and lifestyle of the aristocratic country houses where he was frequently regarded as good company. Whereas Gladstone, a man of great energy, chopped down trees, Disraeli preferred to watch others. But, on the desirability of having the advantage of landed aristocrats in government, the two men, for once, agreed.

However, the landed interest went through a difficult time in the late 1870s, a time that coincided with Disraeli's premiership.

- A series of cool wet summers brought very poor harvests.
- Cheap foreign corn imports were now made possible by steam-powered ships.

- Free trade was far too popular and far too important for the commercial and industrial interest in the country to consider a change of policy. It was a revealing moment.

## DISRAELI AND IRELAND

The agricultural depression also had a major impact in Ireland. Because of it many tenants were evicted and Gladstone's first Land Act of 1870 was now seen as inadequate. By 1879 the activities of the Irish Land League included violent attacks on landlords and their property.

**Disraeli's analysis.** Back in 1844 Disraeli had accurately summarised the Irish Question as 'a starving population, an absentee aristocracy, and an alien Church and in addition the weakest executive in the world'. By this he was describing the system whereby the Irish were governed on a day-to-day basis by an English-dominated executive (government). This executive had a Viceroy (monarch's deputy) residing in Dublin Castle and a Chief Secretary for Ireland, an English MP who was also a member of the English government, travelling backwards and forwards between the two countries. This hardly made for efficient government. Moreover, the Dublin Castle executive was firmly subordinated to the English government.

However, in office Disraeli showed little sign of turning his analysis into action and developing a programme similar to the one Gladstone had proposed in order to deal with the question. Clear-sighted but short-sighted, as Lord Salisbury once remarked of him in a general context, he appears not to have appreciated fully the growing discontent and nationalist feeling in Ireland until near the end of his premiership.

**Disraeli's lack of action.** The Irish Home Rule Party led by Isaac Butt had made substantial gains at the 1874 election, but all Disraeli had to offer were Coercion Acts to try to control law and order. Perhaps he was aware of the political reputations Ireland had broken in the past, like that of Peel, and how the politicians who had avoided the question as much as possible, such as Palmerston, seemed to have prospered. After the terrible harvest in 1877 economic grievances were increasingly translated into militant political action as Parnell took over the Home Rule Party leadership from Isaac Butt. As a result, Gladstone was to inherit a difficult situation in 1880.

## DISRAELI AND THE LIBERAL OPPOSITION

**Success.** After Disraeli's victory in the 1874 election Gladstone temporarily retired from party politics and the Liberal leader in the Commons was Lord Hartington. Disraeli found him a much easier man to deal with than Gladstone. 'Harty Tarty', as he was referred to by Disraeli and others, was a conscientious statesman but he did not possess the debating prowess of Gladstone. Disraeli was therefore in a strong position, and the first two years of government showed a strong ministry capable of passing major reform.

**Problems.** But when Gladstone returned to the fray to attack Disraeli's foreign policy in 1876 (see Chapter 7, page 120, for the Bulgarian Horrors), the Prime Minister had a much tougher time. It was at this point that the Queen offered a peerage which would allow him – as the Earl of Beaconsfield – to sit in the quieter pastures of the House of Lords for the remainder of his political career. His later years in office, 1876–80, were much harder for Disraeli than the first two.

- His health was not good.
- Foreign difficulties (see pages 119–22) predominated.
- Gladstone was back with a vengeance attacking Beaconsfieldism. His Midlothian campaign (see page 65) won the Liberals considerable popularity.
- The government lost a number of **by-elections** as Liberal Party organisation rapidly improved and the government's foreign policy was unpopular in a number of quarters.
- The earlier achievements in social reform were in the past and there was little in the way of further domestic achievement.

## The defeat

When a Liberal parliamentary seat was won by the
Conservatives in a by-election at Southwark (London) early
in 1880, Disraeli mistakenly assumed the tide had turned
and asked the Queen for a **dissolution of Parliament.**
However, the election in April proved a triumph for the
Liberals who returned with a majority of 115 over the
Conservatives. Irish Home Rulers again did well with 63
seats. Although the Queen tried to avoid having Gladstone
as her Prime Minister by sending for Lord Hartington, it
was known that he would refuse the offer and she would
eventually have to ask Gladstone. The latter had made a
comeback from his defeat in 1874. Disraeli knew the same
would not happen to him. Now aged 77 and suffering
from kidney disease he sensed he had not long left. Of his
defeat, Disraeli remarked to the 19-year-old son of his
Foreign Secretary Lord Salisbury 'for you this is an event,
for me it is the end'. A year later, on 19 April 1881,
Disraeli died of bronchitis and asthma.

## CONCLUSION

What had Disraeli's government achieved?

* It formed the first strong Conservative administration
  since 1841.
* It attracted increasing numbers of middle-class voters
  into the Conservative camp.
* It had shown administrative competence or better –
  Cross was one of the most outstanding Home Secretaries
  of the century.
* It achieved a great deal of reform and clarity in social
  reform and its regulations.
* It had been active abroad and developed the imperial
  idea.
* It eased the Queen back into public life.
* It continued the Conservative Party's identification with
  the Church of England and the landed interest.

Where did Disraeli's government fall down?

* It failed to deal with the question of Ireland as the
  Home Rule movement grew.

- It ran out of steam on domestic policy after 1876.
- It had a leader whose health was increasingly frail.
- It found itself under strong attack after Gladstone's political recovery in 1876, especially for its foreign policy.
- It saw increasing division in the Church of England and the start of a decline in landed prosperity.
- It suffered a comprehensive election defeat at the end of its period of office.

## SUMMARY QUESTIONS

1 What were the main achievements of Disraeli's ministry in the field of social reform?

2 What contribution did Disraeli make to the recovery of the monarchy's reputation?

**Timeline of Disraeli's life**

| | |
|---|---|
| 1804 | Born in London |
| 1813 | Baptised into Church of England |
| 1837 | Became an MP |
| 1846 | Made the crucial speech attacking Peel over Corn Law repeal |
| 1849 | Became leader of Conservatives in House of Commons under Lord Derby |
| 1852 | Chancellor of the Exchequer in Derby's first ministry |
| 1858–9 | Chancellor in Derby's second ministry |
| 1858 | Supported removal of Jewish disabilities |
| 1866–8 | Chancellor in Derby's third ministry |
| 1867 | Piloted second Reform Bill through Parliament |
| 1868 | (February–December) Prime Minister when Derby resigned through ill-health, first ministry |
| 1868–74 | Leader of Conservative opposition to Gladstone's Liberal government |
| 1872 | Major speeches in Manchester and London |
| 1874–80 | Prime Minister, second ministry |
| 1876 | Created Earl of Beaconsfield |
| 1881 | Died |

# CHAPTER 7

# What were the main principles of British foreign policy 1846–1902?

## INTRODUCTION

During this time Britain's overseas interests became increasingly wide-ranging and the commitments of the British Empire played a major part in foreign policy. However, this would hardly have been apparent at the start of the period.

Before the 1840s, British colonial control was to be found principally in parts of India, Canada (recently united under British rule), the southern tip of Africa, the West Indies and, for convict purposes, parts of Australia. By 1902, however, there was a substantial amount of additional territory in the Indian sub-continent and Burma, Africa (north, south, east and west), Australia, New Zealand, as well as trading posts on the Chinese coast such as Hong Kong.

In India and Canada there were the problems on the frontiers with the Russians and the United States in the 1840s. In 1902, in the face of the growing Russian Empire, the Indian tensions were just as great, but relations with the United States had improved. In 1846 the overseas possessions were referred to as 'colonies' but in 1902 they were seen as part of the 'British Empire'.

**Sea power and trade: the Congress of Vienna.** In both 1846 and 1902 British sea power was of the first importance, the British army often playing what was regarded as a secondary role to the British navy. Throughout the period around the world there were a number of vital British naval bases established to maintain British interests, and frequently also linked with trade. In fact, Britain's maritime reputation in Europe had been a strong one since the sixteenth century. More recently, the naval defeats of Napoleon in the first decade of the

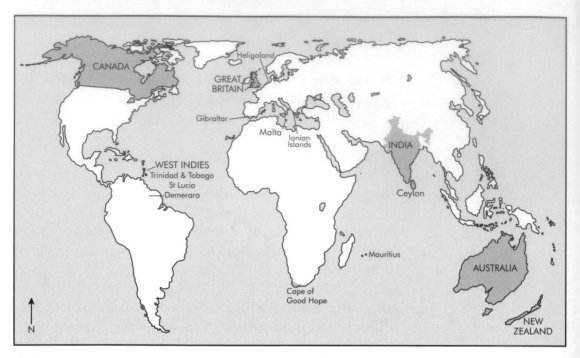

**British-held possessions in the mid-nineteenth century reflecting the country's trading interests.**

nineteenth century in battles such as Trafalgar had emphasised British strength on the oceans.

Great Britain had established a reputation as a commercial, trading and maritime nation and the wide extent of its interests and possessions was evident as far back as 1815 at the **Congress of Vienna** when British ownership of islands and naval bases around the world was confirmed. Although gaining Malta Britain gained no mainland European territory, but was guaranteed continued possession of well-distributed naval bases. These areas included the Cape of Good Hope, Gibraltar, Heligoland, Malta, Ceylon, the Ionian Islands, Mauritius and the West Indian islands such as Trinidad and Tobago and St Lucia, and Demerara.

### KEY TERM

**Congress of Vienna 1815**
A large meeting of European powers to re-draw the map of Europe – and sometimes beyond – because of the downfall of the Napoleonic Empire.

## WHAT WERE THE MAIN AIMS OF BRITISH FOREIGN POLICY?

The broad aims of British foreign policy were closely linked to the protection of Britain's overseas possessions.

## Important sources of raw materials for Britain

| | |
|---|---|
| West Indies | sugar, bananas |
| North Atlantic | fish |
| India and the Far East | cotton, silks, spices and tea |
| Europe | wines, naval stores and timber |
| Australia and New Zealand | wool |

**Eastern Question** The question of what should be done about the declining Turkish Empire, since friendly relations with its rulers were so vital to British trading interests. Should it be propped up? Reformed? Abandoned? How should Russian aggression against it be treated?

**Opium trade** Opium was widely used as a narcotic drug in the nineteenth century; there were rooms in Britain and elsewhere known as opium dens. British traders were widely involved in its trade in the Far East.

- Maintenance of British naval supremacy which was so successfully confirmed at Vienna. The numerous if scattered possessions were useful naval staging posts that would provide harbour facilities and vital supplies.
- The use of the strength of this naval tradition to keep an eye on and protect British trading interests in different parts of the world.
- Attending to British possessions in India and the 'white colonies' where British people had settled, especially Canada, Australia, New Zealand and South Africa.

This meant that there were areas around the world of significance to foreign policy and with regard to Empire.

- The Ottoman (Turkish) Empire at the eastern end of the Mediterranean, where it was regarded as vital to preserve the overland trade route to India. This involved much more trouble in this period, for example the Crimean War of the 1850s and the **Eastern Question** of the 1870s. Maintaining Turkey's strength was arguably Britain's largest single priority in foreign policy.
- The Far East, where relations with China hinged around trade – the **opium trade**.
- The borders with India where Afghanistan was seen as a particularly sensitive area since the expanding Russian Empire was regarded as potentially dangerous.

## EUROPEAN DIPLOMACY

Its international interests were so far flung that in this period Britain tended to avoid too much involvement with continental Europe. Relations were most difficult with France and Russia:

- France because of its past history of European expansion and domination which had disrupted British trade through Europe.
- Russia because of its intermittent interest in expanding south and east towards British trading interests in India and the Turkish Empire.

British involvement in war and European entanglements, however, was generally regarded as best avoided. To maintain both the wider British interest and the general peace in this period was on the whole agreed, but there were different schools of thought as to how to approach the various problems, which emphasised different principles. There were three broad and overlapping traditions.

1  **The Concert of Europe** was steadily pursued by Castlereagh (Foreign Secretary 1812–22) and Peel in former times, and Aberdeen as Foreign Secretary in the early 1840s and also 1852–5 when, because of the Crimean War, he was singularly unsuccessful. Britain would take a detached interest in European affairs and hope that the major powers of Europe, of which it was seen as one, would co-operate on important matters of stability and security. There would be an attempt to secure the **balance of power**, and ensure that no one country became too powerful in Europe, as Napoleonic France had done before 1815.

   Any danger of this kind of domination would necessitate British intervention, but otherwise the country could stay out of direct action in European affairs. It was the fear that the Russians were upsetting the balance of power that caused the conflict in the Crimea (see page 113).

2  **The second belief was to keep out of European affairs as much as possible** and pursue policies relating to British trade and possessions, while avoiding wars at all costs. This was the view of the smallest group, led by Cobden and Bright, who might be described as international Radicals – the Manchester School – who shared other Radicals' distaste for absolutist governments, but went along with non-intervention as a general rule. They believed that international harmony and peace would grow as countries became more and more dependent on each other in trading terms. They strongly opposed the Crimean War, for instance, and generally were critical of Palmerston's foreign policy and the more aggressive approach of some of their fellow Radicals such as Roebuck.

3  **Support for constitutional states or constitutional movements in states.** This became apparent in the revolutions of 1848 which tended to have nationalistic

**Concert of Europe** The idea that the major powers of Europe should act in concert – together – as much as possible to prevent minor disputes becoming serious wars. It was a popular idea in the nineteenth century from the end of the Napoleonic Wars.

**Balance of power** The idea of ensuring that no one country in Europe – or the wider world – should exert too much influence over events. Palmerston accepted the idea, but it was challenged by Cobden who saw it as a deceptively tame phrase. The application of the principle of the balance of power, he argued, could get Britain involved in disputes all over the world in order to maintain a mythical 'balance'.

**Constitutional states** Countries governed by a set of laws and a constitution to restrict powers of a ruler and prevent an absolute monarchy or a dictatorship arising.

and/or politically liberal demands. In Italy in 1859 there was British support for liberal nationalism against absolute monarchies trying to suppress unification though some agreed that support for continued Austrian control of parts of northern Italy was the best means to ensure the balance of power.

Palmerston was seen to sympathise with several such movements, much to the delight of the British Radicals who had previously wished to see Britain play a more prominent role on the continent in supporting these developments. However, this approach was not shared by many other occupants of the Foreign Office and even Palmerston's attachment to it can be exaggerated. It was most evident in his period as Foreign Secretary between 1846 and 1851.

### Foreign Secretaries 1846–1902

Although the office actually changed hands nineteen times there were only eight people who occupied the post in nearly 60 years. Most were members of the House of Lords. The exceptions were Palmerston, whose Irish peerage only entitled him to sit in the Commons, and the first short periods of occupation of the post by Russell (made an earl in 1861) and Lord Stanley (who succeeded to the earldom of Derby on the death of his father – the former Conservative PM – in 1869). All were landed aristocrats.

| | | | |
|---|---|---|---|
| Palmerston | 1846–51 | | |
| Granville | 1851–2 | 1870–4 | 1880–5 |
| Malmesbury | 1852 Feb.–Dec. | | 1858–9 |
| Russell | 1852–3 | 1859–65 | |
| Clarendon | 1853–8 | 1865–6 | 1868–70 |
| Derby | 1866–8 | 1874–8 | |
| Salisbury | 1878–80 | 1885–6 | 1887–92 |
| | 1895–1900 | | |
| Rosebery | 1886 Feb.–Aug. | | 1892–4 |

## Lord Palmerston

This period was dominated by Lord Palmerston. He was Foreign Secretary 1846–51, and Prime Minister 1855–8 and 1859–65 when, although **Clarendon** and Russell respectively were his Foreign Secretaries, Palmerston was clearly very influential indeed in helping to formulate and follow through policy.

The Palmerston approach saw Britain playing a part, if possible, in upholding constitutional states, but regarded the prime factor in foreign policy as upholding British trading interests abroad. This policy, inherited from Canning (Foreign Secretary 1822–7), was a forceful one. Palmerston had the advantage that some of the Radicals in Parliament supported his policy and particularly liked his sideswipes at absolutist states such as his approach to **General Haynau** and **Louis Kossuth** in the aftermath of the 1848 revolutions in Europe.

Palmerston's forceful attitude towards maintaining the interests of British citizens abroad is seen in the extreme case of **Don Pacifico**. Palmerston's support for him was much criticised since both Don Pacifico's very slight British connection and very dubious complaint against the Greeks were not considered weighty enough to warrant action.

As far as Europe was concerned one of the most significant relationships was with France. This was a delicate relationship, marked as it was by what one historian has called 'past conflicts, present mistrusts and future fears'. This was apparent in 1846, the early 1860s, and over Africa in the 1890s with war between the two countries almost breaking out in 1898. It could be argued that Britain in general and Palmerston in particular considerably exaggerated the French 'threat'.

Palmerston wished to prevent any kind of expansion of French influence.

- In Spain, there had been a royal marriage linking the French and Spanish royal families in 1846. However, the fear of extended French influence was greatly reduced by

KEY PEOPLE

**Earl of Clarendon 1800–70** An important and underrated Whig diplomat. The first Foreign Secretary to have served as an ambassador (at Madrid in the 1830s). During his first time as Foreign Secretary (1853–8), he survived the change of government. Not one of the Queen's favourite Foreign Secretaries. Frequently worked 14 hours a day and spoke many European languages. Lord Lieutenant of Ireland in the famine years. Died in office.

**Haynau and Kossuth** The Austrian General Haynau, nicknamed Hyena, had been notoriously violent in suppressing rebels in Italy and Hungary in 1848–9. When he visited England in September 1850, protestors attacked him at a brewery in Southwark, outraged at reports of his ordering the flogging of women. Palmerston annoyed Queen Victoria by sending only a very mild apology for his treatment in England. In contrast, Palmerston made it clear, when the Hungarian nationalist Kossuth came to England, that he reserved the right (which he never actually exercised) to invite him to his own home despite clear royal disapproval of the visit.

## KEY EVENT

**Don Pacifico** In 1850 Palmerston ordered the shelling of Athens when a Portuguese moneylender Don Pacifico, having been born in the British territory of Gibraltar, claimed the help of Britain over a financial dispute with the Greek government.

## KEY CONCEPT

**Belgian independence and neutrality** When Belgium staged a revolt against the Netherlands and gained its independence in 1830, powers such as Russia and Austria considered invading to crush what was seen as a dangerous liberal and nationalist revolt. However, Palmerston, newly appointed as Foreign Secretary, made clear his support of the Belgians. A friendly Belgium would be a great boost for the easy and safe movement of British goods. After a belated attempt by the Netherlands to regain the territory in 1839, Britain formally guaranteed Belgium's independence and neutrality. It was the German invasion of France through Belgium in 1914, rather than French aggression, which brought about a British response to defend Belgium and the widening of the conflict that became the First World War.

the downfall of the French monarchy in the revolutions of 1848.

- Belgium and the Netherlands were sensitive areas because of the vast quantity of British exports that went through these two countries. There had been earlier French attempts to increase French influence in this area and Palmerston was anxious to maintain the independence of these two countries. However, this was achieved throughout the period from 1839 to 1914 without great difficulty. The guarantee of **Belgian independence and neutrality** prevented trouble here.

When war did break out in 1914 Britain and France found themselves on the same side. They shared a hostility to Russian influence in the near east for instance, fearing Russian interference with their trading interests. The British also saw Russia as a major threat to their Indian interests.

**The Crimean War 1854–6.** The best example of Anglo-French co-operation as a result of their mutual suspicion of Russia was the Crimean War. Significantly it occurred at the one time that Palmerston was not influencing the Foreign Office.

This was the only time in the nineteenth century when the Eastern Question spilled over into a major conflict involving Britain. Britain and France fought against Russia's move into Turkish territory.

- The immediate cause of the Crimean War was the dispute over the guardianship of the Christian holy places in Turkish-held Jerusalem: should it consist of French Catholic monks or Russian Orthodox monks?
- But the more long-term cause was a misunderstanding that had occurred when Foreign Secretary Lord Aberdeen had met Tsar Nicholas I of Russia in 1844. Nicholas received the mistaken impression that Britain would accept a partition of the Turkish Empire at some point in the future. When Aberdeen became Prime Minister in December 1852 (and Palmerston was no longer Foreign Secretary but Home Secretary), the Tsar thought he saw his chance.
- When Russia made aggressive noises against Turkey in 1853, the Aberdeen government was seen as uncertain in

its opposition, but Nicholas miscalculated by thinking it would never declare war.

- Though it was not the main focus of Britain's strategic interests, most of the war was fought on the Crimean peninsula: this was at the southernmost tip of Russia where only the Black Sea separated it from Turkey. The winter conditions were appalling and the medical ' facilities for the injured crude in the extreme.
- The army generals' strategy was viewed as outdated and wasteful of lives.
- The Aberdeen government was removed by a vote in Parliament in the middle of the war in 1855 and there was a call for reform of the army and the British civil service (see Chapter 5).
- With Palmerston now Prime Minister a peace treaty was signed at the Congress held in Paris. The Treaty of Paris forbade Russia to put its warships or any kind of fortifications in the Black Sea area. Russia abided by this, the most important clause in the peace treaty, until 1870 (see page 118).
- Palmerston was satisfied with the treaty and that Russian expansion had been halted.

**Palmerston at the helm again 1855–8 and 1859–65.** The hesitant policy of Aberdeen had apparently led to war. It also led to Palmerston becoming Prime Minister and therefore exercising a great influence on foreign policy. His more aggressive style was once again popular. The championing of the cause of liberal and constitutional states continued with support of the moves towards Italian unity in 1859–60. These, however, proved not to be very great, amounting in the end to a friendly neutrality towards the crucial actions of nationalists such as Garibaldi in defeating the opponents of unity. Its main significance for British politics was that it united the Liberal Party: for once, Gladstone and Palmerston were on the same side.

Palmerston also upheld British trading interests abroad, as in China in 1856 and 1859–60. Following his defeat in the House of Commons over the *Arrow* incident in 1856 (see Chapter 3, page 42) Palmerston had called a general election in 1857 and had been triumphantly returned to power. Armed with this majority he was prepared to order the use of arms and in 1858 strategic Chinese forts were attacked. The Chinese agreed to a diplomatic mission and to the continuance of foreign trading interests. The opium trade was allowed to continue. The attack was undertaken purely to guarantee British trading interests in the area. Once Palmerston was friendly again with the Emperor after 1860 he was more than happy to back the Emperor's brutal suppression of a rebellion when surrendering rebels had been promised their lives.

On this issue Conservative policy was similar. When in office in 1858–9 the Conservatives dropped their previous criticisms of Palmerston's policy and Derby's government was the one that drew up the terms of the treaty legalising the opium trade. Significantly, Gladstone expressed his reservations about the policy in 1860 but agreed to go along with it.

**The Indian Mutiny 1857.** Further afield, Palmerston faced his greatest challenge in India where he had to deal with the crisis of the Indian Mutiny.

The general causes of tension in India were:

- Indian resentment at attempts to modify or abolish customs such as *suttee* – the burning of widows;
- the expansionist policies of the British governments and the use of Indian troops for this purpose;
- Indian Governor-General Lord Dalhousie's policy of annexing more Indian states when their rulers died, such as Oudh in 1856;
- the discontent of the Indian troops in the British army with their pay and conditions.

The immediate cause of the mutiny was the issue of cartridges for the new rifles used by the troops. The cartridges were smeared with animal fat and had to be bitten open before insertion into the firearm. Both Hindus, to whom cows are sacred, and Muslims, who will not eat pork, objected to having to do this.

The fighting was mainly in north India and there was great brutality on both sides. After English women and children were massacred at Cawnpore the British troops took vicious reprisals. The new Governor-General, Charles Canning, calmed the situation and though criticised for being too lenient with the rebels (English soldiers called him 'Clemency Canning') he was backed by Palmerston.

In 1858 the Conservatives under Derby reformed the government of India.

- The dual control with the East India Company was abolished: the government would undertake authority for the government of India.
- There would be a new ministerial post – the Secretary of State for India.

Control of India remained effective for another generation or more but a nationalist movement was soon to begin.

**Palmerston in difficulties.** In the early 1860s Palmerston's aggressive style of policy, which had been so effective in earlier years, began to run into trouble. Poor Anglo-French relations in the 1860s were mainly due to Palmerston's great suspicion of the Emperor Napoleon III whom he saw as dangerously aggressive in the Italian crisis in 1859, and when interfering in Syrian affairs in 1860 (in the area of the Turkish Empire). Palmerston obsessively and oddly came to believe that Napoleon III was intent on 'avenging Waterloo'. Having approved of the coup which brought Napoleon III to power in 1851, Palmerston appears to have felt that a French invasion of Britain was a real possibility in the early 1860s. Thus he organised a volunteer defence movement which recruited 150,000 men, and had new **Martello towers** erected on the south coast of England to watch for signs of French attack. Yet there was no evidence that the French seriously contemplated invasion. The Free Trade Treaty signed in 1860 between the two countries made conflict unlikely.

There was an uneasy relationship with the northern states of America in the Civil War. A clash with a northern warship (the *Trent*) on the high seas at the start of the war was only smoothed over by the intervention of a dying Prince Albert, and the fact that another ship, the *Alabama* (see page 119) was allowed to leave an English port in 1862 and attack northern states' shipping proved embarrassing.

KEY PLACE

**Schleswig-Holstein** Two provinces sandwiched between Denmark proper and German states. Schleswig was very largely Danish in composition and Holstein partly so. The two states had been connected to Denmark in political arrangements of staggering complexity. Palmerston claimed in 1864 that only three people had ever fully understood it: Prince Albert who was dead, a German professor who had become insane, and he himself, who had forgotten the details.

Protests from Palmerston and Russell to Russia about the harsh treatment of Poland in 1863, where there was a nationalist revolt, fell on deaf ears. Moreover, the growing power of Bismarck's Prussia in central Europe meant that Palmerston found his bluff was being called. In the Prussian dispute with Denmark over the ownership of **Schleswig** and **Holstein** in 1864, Palmerston's promise that if Denmark fought it would not fight alone was seen as a sham, as the Prussians easily overran the Danish forces.

## GLADSTONE AND DISRAELI: CHANGES IN FOREIGN POLICY

After Palmerston's death in October 1865, the excitement of the second Reform Act and the domestic activities of Gladstone's first ministry, it was apparent that a number of significant changes had occurred which would influence the possible new directions of British foreign policy. This led to a change in the attitude of Liberals and Conservatives to foreign policy. Just as the party system had emerged more clearly by 1868 so the different foreign policy approaches of the two parties were that much more apparent. Whereas Gladstone would inherit the tradition of Peel and Aberdeen, Disraeli would pursue more Palmerstonian-like policies.

Gladstone managed to unite the Liberals over foreign policy. He combined a belief in the Concert of Europe and the balance of power with a concern for morality in foreign policy and the desirability of an advance in international understanding. This could include a righteous campaign against injustice, most clearly shown in his protest against what he referred to as the 'Bulgarian horrors' in 1876 (see pages 120 and 180).

KEY CONCEPT

**A 'forward' foreign policy** One which attempted to assert British interests abroad in a vigorous manner, was prepared to intervene in disputes abroad, and sought to extend or at least maintain the colonial possessions of the country.

By contrast, Disraeli the Conservative took over the approach of the Whig, Palmerston. The previous Tory approach to foreign policy had usually been of the more cautious Peel/Aberdeen style, but after the death of Palmerston in 1865 – and Derby in 1869 – Disraeli saw an opportunity to take on what he saw as potentially popular foreign-policy principles. These principles would be combined in what was seen as a **'forward' foreign policy**, which, like Palmerston's, would be popular with many backbench MPs. In addition, however, it could well be popular with the wider electorate Disraeli had himself created with the second Reform Act in 1867. The emphasis, however, had changed from Palmerston's supposed sympathy with 'small nations struggling to be free' to a concern with the British colonies, or Empire as it was now becoming. This development was first apparent in the Manchester and Crystal Palace speeches of 1872 (see Chapter 6, page 93). However, Disraeli knew as well as Palmerston or any other diplomat the limitations on an ambitious foreign policy: while Britain's navy was one of the strongest in the world, the permanent army was not large, and was ill-equipped for a prolonged continental campaign.

The reasons for the changes in foreign policy were not confined to individuals. The political maps of Europe, Africa and the Near East were changing rapidly.

## GLADSTONE'S FOREIGN POLICY 1868–74

In what ways did Gladstone face a different European situation?

- The unification of Germany in 1871 after the Franco-Prussian War brought a powerful European country on to the diplomatic scene and also revealed French military weakness. The expansion of Prussia in 1864 and 1866 at the expense of Denmark and Austria led to a clash with France in 1870 and the final unification of Germany in 1871.
- The final stage in the unification of Italy in 1870 – when the Pope lost his remaining political power in Rome – meant there was another new major independent country in Europe and a potential ally for Britain.
- There was the more aggressive outlook of a stronger and reformed Russia. The Tsar took the opportunity afforded by the absorption of the major powers in the Franco-Prussian War of 1870–1 to denounce the Black Sea neutralisation clauses of the Treaty of Paris (see page 114), and Russia announced it now intended to construct a Black Sea fleet. A conference in London denounced the

Russian action in theory but accepted the reality of the change.

### KEY EVENTS

**The *Alabama*** The ship *Alabama* had been built in Liverpool in 1862 and, despite British neutrality in the American Civil War, had been allowed to leave port and sail to the United States where it inflicted major damage on northern shipping. It may be that Gladstone felt personally guilty about the affair because he was in the government that had carelessly allowed the ship to sail out of a British port in the first place.

**The construction of the Suez Canal** The canal was built between 1859 and 1869, largely with French engineers. Palmerston had been suspicious of it at first, but Disraeli saw it as a valuable route to India and purchased 4 per cent of the shares of the company in 1875 on behalf of the British government, thanks to help from his banking friends, the Rothschilds.

**The *Alabama* incident.** Nowhere is Gladstone's internationalist approach better shown than in his acceptance of the *Alabama* arbitration award which made possible a better future relationship with the United States. After the end of the war the Americans claimed compensation from the British government for the damage done by the *Alabama*. This was at first refused but Gladstone, when Prime Minister, agreed to an independent international tribunal to assess the claim. He then agreed to pay the figure decided upon: £3.25 million, a third of the figure claimed by the Americans. This arbitration, although it increased Gladstone's unpopularity, was a landmark in the development of international relations.

## FOREIGN POLICY 1874–86

Conservative foreign policy, dominated at first by Disraeli, was seen as the more forward-looking and active foreign policy with a strong emphasis on the traditional principles of maintaining British naval strength and trading interests. But time and circumstances had amended and added to these principles, and after 1880 Gladstone also found himself sucked into a more expansionist policy.

**The Suez Canal.** The **construction of the Suez Canal** (opened in 1869) was likely to make the control of the eastern end of the Mediterranean even more significant for Britain. The canal linked the Mediterranean to the Red Sea and thus the Indian Ocean.

**The Eastern Crisis 1875–8.** The most worrying feature of foreign policy for Disraeli was an expanding Russian Empire which Britain wished to hold in check while trying to prop up the increasingly sick Turkish Empire. In the 1860s and early 1870s Russia's main external interest was expansion into Asia after the Russian reverses in the Crimean War. The Russians steadily moved their borders south and east reaching the boundaries of Afghanistan, Persia (Iran) and China. To the new British imperial mind, this threatened India. By the 1870s Russia had emerged as a reformed state (not least having abolished serfdom) and once again looked hungrily towards Turkey. The growth of nationalism in late nineteenth-century Europe had affected the **Slav** areas of eastern Europe which were prepared to back increased Russian influence in the area.

The Eastern Crisis of 1875–8 brought foreign policy centre stage in a more profound way than Palmerston's antics in the 1850s and brought Gladstone out of what now proved to be a temporary retirement to condemn the Turkish atrocities in Bulgaria in 1876. With Disraeli intent on defending the Turks and playing down the news of the massacres of Bosnian Christians as 'coffee house babble', and Gladstone demanding the Turks leave with 'bag and baggage' the area they had 'desecrated and profaned', the scene was set for a confrontation over foreign policy where the parties were opposed to each other on principle.

KEY TERM

**Slavs** People spread over much of eastern Europe, including Russians, Bulgarians and Poles.

- Disraeli wanted to maintain the traditional support of Turkey as in the British interest in general and trade in particular. He was suspicious of Russian ambitions and power.
- Gladstone maintained a concern for moral behaviour in international affairs. Intervention should not be undertaken lightly but extreme behaviour of the kind the Turks had been guilty of in Bosnia and Bulgaria should be attacked.

Disraeli, who regretted the 'coffee house babble' remark when the full extent of the unspeakable atrocities became known, was momentarily wrong-footed. However, the Russian reaction to the atrocities – a military attack on Turkey – gave him a chance to recover.

Russia invaded Turkey in 1877 and by March 1878 they had concluded the Treaty of San Stefano. This created a large Bulgarian state which would be seen as under Russian influence if not control. With British hostility growing, the German Chancellor Bismarck called a Congress in Berlin in 1878 where the San Stefano Treaty was revised.

- 'Big Bulgaria' was carved up and Russian influence reduced.

- Britain, represented by Disraeli and Foreign Secretary Salisbury, obtained the island of Cyprus near the eastern end of the Mediterranean.
- Disraeli described this as 'peace with honour' and it emphasised the more imperial mood of the 1870s.

Although this temporarily settled the Eastern Question, other important new factors were coming into play at a time when Britain avoided formal alliances with any other countries.

- The expansion of the great powers into the interior of the African continent widened and complicated the activities of the British government's foreign policy and its diplomatic activity. It added to the possibility of clashes with other European powers.
- A closer interest was taken in the Far East with the result that by the end of the century formal British presence had been established with the ownership of the colony of **Hong Kong**.
- The discovery of valuable mineral deposits in areas such as South Africa committed the British presence to this area just at the time when it was becoming strategically less significant.
- The men on the spot could sometimes push for a more forward policy themselves, not necessarily with the

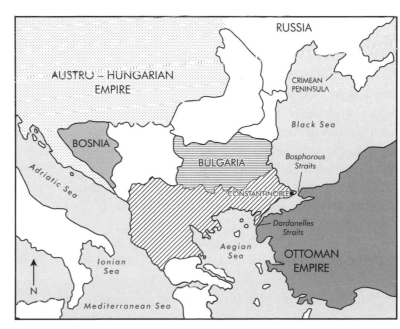

**The Eastern Question in the 1870s.**

approval of the government back home. There were occasions when colonial representatives determined policy detail more than the government at home, sometimes rather wildly. Disraeli particularly suffered from this in the late 1870s. In India the Viceroy of this period Edward Lytton pursued an aggressive policy towards the neighbouring state of Afghanistan in order to prevent it accepting Russian influence in the country. At almost the same time Sir Bartle Frere, High Commissioner of South Africa, committed Britain to a war against the Zulus by threatening war unless they accepted demands they were most unlikely to agree to.

- The 'white empire', for example Canada, Australia, New Zealand and South Africa, was seen to be moving towards self-government and independence: Canada became self-governing in 1867 and Australia and South Africa at the turn of the century.

**Gladstone and Egypt.** In fact, the forward march of British foreign policy and the degree of the government's commitment to a complex international policy became apparent in Gladstone's second ministry in the early 1880s. Britain was sucked more and more into Egyptian affairs, exercising an informal control over the country in order to maintain its interest in the now vital Suez Canal area. In 1882 this produced a crisis in the cabinet over principle. Gladstone authorised the bombardment of Alexandria and John Bright resigned from the cabinet. The alliance of the Radical Manchester School of Cobden (no longer alive) and Bright and the now more aggressive Gladstone was over. Perhaps the situation was influenced by Gladstone's investment in the Egyptian stock market. In any event, Britain and Egypt now undertook joint control of the area south of Egypt, the Sudan. Decisive action abroad was increasingly seen as essential to maintain British interests, and the kind of hesitation shown by Gladstone's government which resulted in the **death of General Gordon** in 1885 was much criticised.

## FOREIGN AND IMPERIAL POLICY 1886–1902

During this time British foreign policy, guided by Lord Salisbury, avoided formal alliances of any kind with

KEY TERM

**Franco-Russian Alliance 1894** This formal friendship (technically secret) between Republican France and Tsarist Russia meant that as the 1890s progressed the increasing formalisation of diplomatic relations between other countries in Europe made it harder and harder for Salisbury to avoid similar arrangements for Britain. Salisbury (unlike the Liberal Foreign Secretary Rosebery 1892–4) continued to lean towards Germany rather than France but Britain was by the mid-1890s relatively isolated in Europe. This was emphasised by the Kaiser's clear sympathy for the Boers in South Africa in their disputes with Britain.

KEY EVENT

**Results of the Berlin Conference** Nigeria was formally acquired by Britain in 1886. Britain also held a colonial conference over territory in West Africa with France in 1887. There was a colonial agreement over East Africa with Germany in 1890: Britain was granted the area of Uganda, Kenya and Zanzibar. Uganda was formally annexed by Britain in 1894. Britain, France and Portugal signed more agreements in 1891 to sort out boundary disputes. Nyasaland and Northern Rhodesia were formally obtained in 1892.

European powers. Salisbury maintained good relations with Italy and Austria with a Mediterranean Agreement of 1887 to maintain the status quo in that area. In giving the island of Heligoland to Germany in 1890 British control of potentially disputed areas in East Africa was accepted. However, the **Franco-Russian Alliance of 1894** was a significant influence on British policy as was the rapid growth of the German navy during the same decade. By the end of Salisbury's period of office there were pressures for Britain to ally formally with another country.

In this period dominated by Salisbury's Conservatives imperial issues became increasingly important in political affairs. The 'Scramble for Africa' was a dominant feature in this period, between the Berlin Conference of 1884 and the formal acquisition of Uganda in 1895. The great powers carved up the continent with only Liberia, Libya and Abyssinia remaining independent of colonial rule or domination.

Britain already had formal possessions in the far south of Africa from the first half of the century – Cape Colony and Natal – and informal influence in Egypt in the far north. In Gladstone's first ministry in 1873 the Ashanti tribes in West Africa had been attacked and influence in the Nigerian/Ghanaian area consolidated. In the north in 1882, Egypt effectively, if unofficially, became part of the British Empire as a 'protectorate'.

A series of agreements between the major European powers ensured that the carve-up of much of African territory was done relatively peacefully in the sense that no European war occurred. However, the experience was not without violence for the native African.

The **Berlin Conference** of 1884–5, attended by fifteen countries, decided on spheres of influence in Africa for the different European powers.

The Sudan, south of Egypt, was obtained by General Kitchener in a war against the natives in 1898, thus recapturing the area lost when Gordon had been killed in 1885. This led to the greatest moment of tension with a European power over the 'Scramble for Africa'. Fashoda

was a town on the west bank of the river Nile in eastern
Africa where French and British troops clashed in 1898
over possessions in this area of the Sudan. General
Marchand raised a French flag in the town but was
challenged by Kitchener. The tense atmosphere, however,
was relieved at the end of the year when the French,
uncertain of Russian support, agreed to withdraw.

The old principle of preferring influence to outright control
seems to have been abandoned. Significantly, the former
Liberal turned Conservative Unionist, Joseph Chamberlain,
chose the post of Colonial Secretary in Salisbury's
government in 1895 because he saw it as one of major
importance. Chamberlain's policies were those of a man
with as much drive and energy as in his earlier days as
Liberal Mayor of Birmingham in the 1870s. What did
Chamberlain achieve?

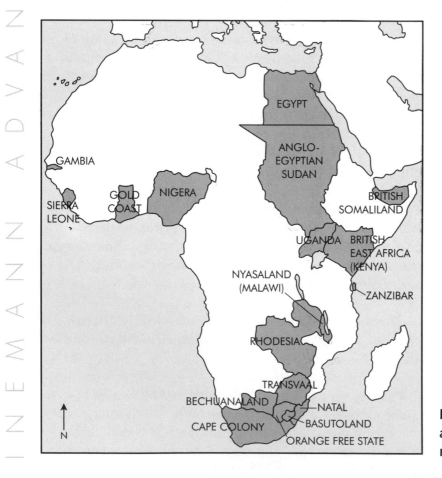

**Britain's African Empire
at the end of the
nineteenth century.**

- Organised a second colonial conference in 1897 attended by the Prime Ministers of the self-governing 'white' colonies.
- Financed public health improvements in the Empire and research into tropical diseases such as the founding of the London School of Tropical Medicine in 1899.
- Appointed a Royal Commission on the economic development of the West Indies in 1897.
- May well have been involved (though he denied it) in the unofficial British raid on Boer territory in South Africa by Leander Starr Jameson at the very end of 1895.

The imperial atmosphere was perhaps best captured by the **Golden and Diamond Jubilees** of Queen Victoria in 1887 and 1897.

Imperialist feelings were to reach a high with the Boer War of 1899–1902. Yet this clash proved to be the turning-point where disillusion with Empire began to set in.

- The war began with British forces attacked in Natal and Cape Colony.
- There was temporary relief when the sieges on the towns of Mafeking, Kimberley and Ladysmith were relieved between February and May 1900 and Salisbury won the 'Khaki' election of October 1900, called after the Boer town of Pretoria was captured.
- But there was an embarrassingly long ending to the war which lasted until May 1902, because Boer guerrilla forces put up very effective resistance.
- The British troops rounded up Boer women and children and 'concentrated' them into camps, the origin of what became a sinister term.
- It was revealed later that Chinese labour had been allowed into South Africa after the war but that the Chinese worked in scandalously squalid conditions that became known as 'Chinese slavery' for which the government, in being either unaware or unwilling to take action, was much criticised (see page 243).
- The fact that nearly half the young male recruits signing up to serve in the war were unfit through poor nutrition and lack of basic medical assistance was another scandal that caused many to feel that more emphasis on

KEY EVENTS

**Golden and Diamond Jubilees** Held to celebrate the Queen's occupancy of the throne for 50 and then 60 years, the lavish public celebrations had a military and imperialistic flavour, with all corners of the British Empire represented. Colonial conferences were held to coincide with the Jubilees. The celebrations reflected the contemporary enthusiasm for large empires and the political influence and economic power they were seen to bestow on the 'mother country'.

improving social conditions at home would now be welcome. The war had emphasised Britain's diplomatic isolation and before the end of it, in January 1902, the country had concluded its first formal alliance for many years: the **Anglo-Japanese Alliance**.

## CONCLUSION

- The Boer War had revealed that not all was well with the British Empire.
- Britain's isolation from formal diplomatic agreements with other European powers was causing some concern by the time Salisbury retired.
- Britain's economic power, spread throughout much of the world, was now being challenged by rapidly industrialising countries like the United States and Germany.
- The new century would bring much greater involvement in European tensions for Britain and the end of a long period both of peace and the avoidance of formal alliances.
- Nationalist objections to British control of overseas territory would loom increasingly large.

KEY TERM

**Anglo-Japanese Alliance 1902** The Japanese had first taken the initiative towards this with an approach in April 1901. Britain would recognise Japan's special interest in Korea. Either country would come to the other's aid if it were at war with more than one great power. It shows Britain needed an alliance but it did not end the country's diplomatic isolation in Europe.

## SUMMARY QUESTIONS

1 What were the main principles of British foreign policy in the period dominated by Lord Palmerston?

2 Why was the time between 1865 and 1873 so significant for the future direction of British foreign policy?

3 Why were relations with Russia so tense for much of this period?

4 How was there a change of emphasis from colonies to Empire in the late nineteenth century?

HEINEMANN ADVANCED HISTORY

# CHAPTER 8

## The era of Conservative dominance 1886–1905

### INTRODUCTION

Between August 1886 and December 1905 the Conservative Party was the most successful one in British politics, being in power for all but two and three-quarter years of the nineteen-year period. This was a time when the electorate had been widened to include male householders in both borough and county and when the Conservatives were still strongly associated with a landed interest that was clearly declining in power and prosperity. They kept out of office a potentially strong Liberal Party that had been united around Gladstone in the 1860s. With their Whig and Radical supporters, the Liberals had won more seats than the Conservatives in all but two of the thirteen elections between 1832 and 1885, the exceptions being 1841 and 1874.

During this period – 1886–1905 – the Conservatives were led by the Marquess of Salisbury until his retirement in 1902. The Marquess came from the heart of the English landowning aristocracy. He always used the word 'English' rather than British, and indeed it was in England that the Conservatives were the most successful electorally. Salisbury held traditional Conservative views, strongly opposing parliamentary reform in 1867, resigning from Disraeli's government rather than support the urban household suffrage that actually operated more widely when he was Prime Minister. Until the mid-1890s he faced Gladstone as leader of the Liberal Party but proved more successful at this time than the 'people's William'.

### WHY WERE THE CONSERVATIVES SO SUCCESSFUL IN THIS PERIOD?

Circumstances did not appear to favour a long period of Conservative rule. It surprised many, not least the pessimistic Salisbury, who constantly lamented the decline of aristocratic power. The signs of future problems for the Conservatives were all too apparent.

- After the Corrupt Practices Act of 1883 the landed interest and the wealthy industrial class would find it harder to exert their traditional 'influence' at elections and it was thought this would count against the Conservatives.
- Economically, this was a period when British industrial power and prosperity were seen to be less dominant than earlier in the century. It has been argued that, in Britain, the 1880s in particular were a time of industrial depression. Certainly there was a slowing of growth compared to previous decades. However, while wages were not rising, the general fall in prices, helped by cheap imports of food from abroad, ensured that living standards increased for all but the worse-off classes, whose poverty became greater relative to other social groups.
- There were increasingly widespread calls for a greater degree of social reform as more awareness of the extent of poverty among the lower working classes became apparent. The **surveys of Charles Booth** in London in the 1880s and **Seebohm Rowntree** in York at the turn of the century confirmed a growing feeling that the extent of poverty at the lower end of the working class was more severe than many had previously realised.
- There was a major challenge from nationalists in Ireland to Britain's refusal to grant Home Rule to Ireland.
- Demands for a further extension of the franchise in general and to women in particular, though expressed in moderate language, were quite apparent.
- Trade unionism spread rapidly to unskilled workers and grew in militancy with more strikes in the late 1880s and 1890s, such as the very successful dockers' strike of 1889 which received great public support.
- Socialist ideas, supported by only a few people before the mid-1880s, were gaining ground strongly by the turn of the century as arguments grew that 'labour' should be represented.

### KEY REPORTS

**Booth and Rowntree surveys** These surveys were undertaken by investigators going from house to house and asking questions of the inhabitants. Modern sampling methods were only developed in the early twentieth century.

It was gradually becoming accepted that those out of work may have been victims of the economic system rather than merely lazy individuals. Moreover, the surveys revealed that those in work could be extremely poor because wages were so low.

**Aristocratic Prime Minister, Lord Salisbury.**

Yet between 1886 and 1900 Salisbury and the Conservatives won three elections out of four quite comfortably and in Gladstone's one ministry he had to rely on Irish Nationalist support. So why were Salisbury and the Conservatives so successful in this period?

### Imperialism.

- Salisbury inherited from Disraeli the more forward looking foreign and imperial policy that became particularly associated with the Conservatives.
- The substantial gains made with the European carve-up of Africa were well received by the public at the end of the 1880s.
- After 1895, the dynamic colonial ideas of Joseph Chamberlain were available to the Conservatives as, having left the Liberals in 1886, he had by this time fully associated himself with the Conservatives and been accepted by them.
- In particular the election victory of October 1900 – called the 'Khaki election' because of the background of war and soldiers' voting – was dominated by the fighting in South Africa and was always likely to result in the electorate backing the government's war effort.

**Ireland.** The establishment of Conservative rule in 1886 was caused by the Irish Question. English public opinion was not in general pro-Roman Catholic or pro-Irish and the hostile reaction to Gladstone's proposal to bring in Irish Home Rule showed up this clearly. The substantial Conservative victory in 1886 was in effect the electorate's verdict on the desirability of Home Rule and the decision was clear: it was not wanted.

### Elections 1886–1905

| Date | Prime Minister | Party | Result |
|------|----------------|-------|--------|
| 1886 | Salisbury | Conservative | Con./Lib. Unionists 405, Liberals 190, Irish 85 |
| 1892 | Gladstone | Liberal | Con./Lib. Unionists 314, Liberals 272, Irish 81 |
| 1895 | Salisbury | Conservative | Con./Lib. Unionists 411, Liberals 177, Irish 82 |
| 1900 | Salisbury | Conservative | Con./Lib. Unionists 402, Liberals 184, Irish 82 |

(Plus two seats for Labour in 1900)

Salisbury's firm policy in putting down the Irish nationalist disturbances in the late 1880s also won electoral support. Salisbury's Irish Secretary from 1887 – his nephew **Arthur Balfour** – was nicknamed 'Bloody Balfour' for the ruthless way he suppressed uprisings by the Plan of Campaign of William O'Brien and John Dillon. Balfour was equal to the emergency and introduced the ruthless new Crimes Act. Not only did this make it easier to make arrests; it had been skilfully drafted by Balfour to make renewal by Parliament unnecessary, so removing opportunity for opposition from the Irish nationalist MPs. Moreover, Balfour exploited the fact that a number of the Catholic bishops were no friends of nationalist extremism. This resulted in the condemnation by Pope Leo XIII of the Plan of Campaign in 1888 (see page 214).

Balfour also had a more constructive side to his policy: the adoption of land purchase. He encouraged state-financed schemes to aid Irish tenants to purchase land from their landlords, quite a number of whom were happy to sell if the price was right. The first land purchase clauses had been included in Gladstone's first Irish Land Act of 1870 but this made little impact. Lord Ashbourne's Act in Salisbury's brief ministry of 1885–6 had shown the way forward, and Balfour sponsored two acts in 1888 and 1891. Most significant of all was Wyndham's Act of 1903, passed by another Chief Secretary for Ireland shortly after Balfour had become Prime Minister.

**Middle-class support.** Ever since the general election of 1868 there had been indications that the **growing urban middle class** was increasingly turning away from the Liberals and giving its support to the Conservatives (see Chapter 4). Wealthy commercial businessmen (sometimes known as plutocrats), city bankers, lawyers and a growing professional class of doctors, architects and university teachers, whose parents or grandparents may well have come from humble backgrounds, had now 'arrived' in society and had lost their radical edge and Liberal instincts. They tended to imitate the landed classes by sending their children to board at the **public schools** that had developed. They liked the relatively low-cost government with careful expenditure that Salisbury managed to retain until at least

**Arthur Balfour 1848–1930**
Nephew of Lord Salisbury, Balfour acted as his secretary at the Congress of Berlin. MP in 1880 when he worked with Lord Randolph Churchill and others such as John Gorst and Henry Drummond Wolff to criticise the Conservative leader in the Commons, Sir Stafford Northcote, and to put forward ideas that would make the Conservatives more of a reforming party. First entered the cabinet in 1886; Irish Secretary 1887–91; First Lord of the Treasury 1891–2; 1895–1902; Prime Minister 1902–5, continued as Conservative leader until 1911.

**KEY CONCEPT**

**The growing urban middle class** Two election results in 1868 had indicated the potential support for Conservatives in the new middle-class suburban areas: bookseller W.H. Smith (later an important cabinet minister in Salisbury's government from 1886 to his death in 1891) defeated the Radical Liberal John Stuart Mill. In Middlesex, another Radical, Henry Labouchere, was defeated by Lord George Hamilton. These results were against the national trend towards the Liberals.

## KEY TERMS

**Public schools** In reality private schools, though open to all who could pay the fees. Barely a dozen of them operated in the early part of the century but the number of schools rose sharply from the 1840s onwards as the railway system made boarding at them a practical proposition.

**Primrose League** Not officially a Conservative Party organisation until 1914, the Primrose League usually acted as if it was one. Founded in 1883 by Lord Randolph Churchill in memory of Disraeli and his supposedly favourite flower, it had, by the 1890s, about a million members, many of them middle-class women who were willing to do voluntary, unpaid work for the party of the envelope-licking variety. Its social activities linked the party with many ordinary voters and even non-voters.

the Boer War. Here, Salisbury owed a good deal to the financial skills of his Chancellor from 1887 onwards, George Goschen.

**Political circumstances.** The Redistribution Act of 1885, following on from the 1884 Parliamentary Reform Act, proved to be of considerable benefit to the Conservatives (see page 67). In addition, the Conservatives had an army of volunteer supporters, including many women. Organisations like the **Primrose League** as well as the National Union (see Chapter 5) would do a great deal to get the Conservative vote to turn out when the occasion arose.

## CONSERVATIVE REFORM

Despite the fact that Salisbury gave the impression of wishing to stem the tide of reform once he was Prime Minister, his two main ministries did introduce a few significant changes which would have commanded support from some of the electorate and which frequently aided the ordinary citizen.

### Reform 1886–92

The Local Government Act of 1888 was the most important piece of domestic legislation passed by Salisbury. The following changes were made:

- introduced county councils for all areas of England, elected by ratepayers (male and female) and modelled on the existing municipal boroughs;
- greatly reduced the administrative role of justices of the peace – magistrates;
- set up the London County Council. The reform of the government of London was long overdue. The government of the City of London had not been reformed in 1834 as were other corporations. London's growth in area way outside the city boundary and the vast increase in population had made for confused and complex administration;
- created a group of nominated senior council members called aldermen;

- introduced a more uniform and democratic system of local authorities, consistent with the national change to householder franchise in 1884.

The changes were extended in 1894 by the Liberals who created a further tier of local government with the creation of urban and rural district councils as well as the very local parish councils. The reforms lasted until 1965 in the case of London – with the creation of the Greater London Council – and until 1972 for other areas, when there were changes in the size and functions of the county councils, though most continued to exist.

Other reforms followed:

- The Housing of the Working Classes Act 1890 extended the Artisans Dwelling Act of 1875 by consolidating the powers of compulsory purchase and enforcing the requirement that local authorities replace the buildings demolished.
- Elementary state education, which had been rapidly growing since the Act of 1870, was now to be made free in all areas (as it was already in some) with legislation to this effect in 1891.
- The **Tithe** Act of 1891, by requiring (generally Anglican) landlords rather than (frequently nonconformist) tenant farmers to pay the tithe, pleased many different sectors of the community.

The 1895–1902 ministry was more concerned with imperial and foreign affairs but two further substantial acts were passed:

- Workmen's Compensation Act 1897. Industry had to compensate all workers for accidents occurring at work, cutting through exemption clauses about negligence. In subsequent years, seafarers, domestic servants and agricultural labourers, all exempt at first, were included.
- Small Dwellings Acquisition Act 1899. Assistance for workers to buy their own houses.

A Royal Commission set up by Joseph Chamberlain to investigate the possibility of a scheme for old age pensions

**Tithe** Literally 'a tenth'. Traditionally, the tenth of the produce of the land was to be given to the Church as a form of tax. It had long been changed to a money payment on land and, like Church rates, was especially resented by nonconformists. This was despite modifications to the arrangements in 1836.

reported in 1898, but the outbreak of the Boer War in 1899 delayed this and any other schemes of reform.

**Political skills of Salisbury.**  For all his throwaway style and prophetic gloom, Salisbury was in fact a shrewd operator who handled colleagues effectively on most occasions. In particular the way he handled the resignation of **Randolph Churchill**, and later enticed Joseph Chamberlain permanently into the Conservative ranks by 1895, illustrate his abilities. Churchill was made Chancellor of the Exchequer in Salisbury's second ministry in 1886. He resigned dramatically at the end of that year when he wished to make greater economies in the military budget than other ministers would allow. He had thought he was indispensable to Salisbury but the Prime Minister, who found Churchill a difficult colleague, accepted the resignation and appointed Goschen in Churchill's place. This was the first use of a Liberal Unionist in a Conservative government and Churchill admitted that he 'had forgotten Goschen'.

In 1895 Salisbury invited Joseph Chamberlain to be a prominent cabinet member. It was said that Chamberlain could have charge of any department he liked and to the surprise of many picked the Colonial Office, as the up-and-coming area of importance. Politically poles apart in the early 1880s, Salisbury and Chamberlain worked well together in the later 1890s.

## WHAT DIFFICULTIES DID THE LIBERALS ENCOUNTER IN THIS PERIOD?

The dominant issues of Ireland and imperialism were less favourable to the Liberals than the Conservatives.

**Ireland.**  Gladstone's proposal of Home Rule split the party badly.

- The Whig element in the party, led by Lord Hartington and including a number of Irish landowners, could not accept the idea of Home Rule. Hartington saw it, not as a chance for the Irish to govern themselves, but as a dereliction of duty by the English government.

- But, in addition, a Radical element led by Chamberlain and (for a time) **Trevelyan** also broke with the party over the issue. They felt Home Rule to be unnecessary: the Westminster government should itself attempt to bring about further reform and improvement in Ireland.
- These Liberal Unionists remained without a party rather like the Peelites after 1846. With a few exceptions (Trevelyan, for example) they were never to return and gradually connected themselves to the Conservatives over the next few years, as most famously did Chamberlain by 1895. In 1912 Liberal Unionists formally united with the Conservatives.
- The downfall of the Home Rule leader Parnell – cited in a **divorce case** in 1890 – meant the end of friendly relations between Liberals and many Nationalists.
- Gladstone remained as leader into his eighties because he believed he must try to obtain the Home Rule he failed to achieve in 1886. This became something of an obsession with him and the development of the party in other more constructive ways did not materialise. Even when he became Prime Minister for the fourth time in 1892, he had to rely on the votes of Irish Nationalists as well as Scottish and Welsh MPs.
- The House of Lords remained strongly opposed to Home Rule and, when the Bill did pass the Commons in 1893, the Lords threw it out by a massive vote of 419 to just 41.

**Imperialism.** Liberals were seen, not altogether accurately, as 'Little Englanders' whose vision was small, who played down the greatness of the English race and who had insufficient regard for the great British Empire. In fact a number of Liberals such as **Lord Rosebery** were keen imperialists, but therein lay the problem: the Liberals were divided on the issue. Nowhere was this more apparent than when it came to the Boer War, when a three-way split could be detected.

- Imperialists such as Rosebery broadly supported the position of the Conservative government.

## KEY PERSON

**George Otto Trevelyan 1838-1928** The son of Sir Charles Trevelyan, an author of the Northcote-Trevelyan Report into the civil service in 1853. Appointed Chief Secretary for Ireland 1882–4. Opposed Home Rule, like Joseph Chamberlain, despite his advanced Liberal opinions and resigned from the government in April 1886. However, unlike Chamberlain, he returned to the Liberal fold in 1887.

## KEY EVENT

**Parnell's divorce case**
Parnell was named as co-respondent in a divorce case brought by a close colleague, Captain O'Shea, against his wife Kitty. Whilst many had known of the affair for years, the publicity resulted in a general attack on Parnell by many English figures. Gladstone distanced himself from Parnell under pressure from English nonconformists, who denounced the Irishman as immoral and unfit for public office. Parnell's own party was split over the issue.

**Earl of Rosebery 1847–1929** Inherited title when child. Assisted Gladstone in Midlothian campaign 1879. Held cabinet positions; Prime Minister 1894–5, the choice of Queen Victoria. Handsome, rich and personable, he cut quite a dash in the Liberal Party but was essentially a Whig with imperialist views and little interest in social reform. Gave up Liberal leadership soon after the party's defeat in 1895.

**Sir Henry Campbell-Bannerman 1836–1908** Born in Glasgow, son of a very wealthy draper, he held minor office in Gladstone's governments. A middle-of-the-road Liberal who became party leader in 1898 and valiantly tried to hold the Liberals together during the Boer War. Helped them win a great election victory in January 1906 but suffered ill-health soon after. Nonetheless he was not the weak leader that some of his colleagues believed he would be.

**Herbert Asquith 1852–1928** Yorkshire-born lawyer and Liberal imperialist, but also quite radical on some social questions. Chancellor of the Exchequer 1905–8 where he devised the Old Age Pension scheme introduced in Parliament in 1908 by Lloyd George, after Asquith had succeeded the sickly Campbell-Bannerman as Prime Minister in that year. Remained Prime Minister until December 1916. Opposed votes for women during that time.

- A middle section led by **Campbell-Bannerman** did not oppose the war but criticised aspects of the strategy and tactics.
- The most radical group, of which Lloyd George was the most outspoken, criticised the war and were labelled pro-Boer by the generally pro-war press. Lloyd George's speech in Joseph Chamberlain's city of Birmingham in 1901, opposing the government's war policy, was not well received. His expressions of support for the Boers caused a riot and he had to be smuggled out of the Town Hall disguised as a policeman in order to avoid a lynching by the mob.

## LIBERAL PRINCIPLES: ACHIEVED OR OUTDATED?

1 **Political principles** Apart from Disraeli in 1867, it was Liberals who had been more associated with the extension of the franchise than had the Conservatives. But with the passing of the third Reform Act in 1884 and the Corrupt Practices Act the previous year, they had now run out of steam on the issue.

- There were divisions in the party on whether or not to extend the franchise to all men. There was a disagreement as to whether the vote was a privilege or a right.
- The question of votes for women put the Liberals in a quandary. More radical Liberals were sympathetic but were opposed to a limited franchise for wealthier women which they feared would benefit the Conservatives. Prominent Liberals such as **Asquith** remained firmly opposed to any form of female suffrage.

2 **Economic principles** Liberal belief in free trade remained as strong as ever. Unlike the issues of Ireland and imperialism it was also popular in the country as a whole. Throughout the second half of the ninetenth century Conservatives were as attached to it as their opponents and so the issue was hardly one on which the Liberals could gain votes. However, after a visit to South Africa in 1903, Joseph Chamberlain returned to Britain with the idea that Britain could reintroduce protective tariffs against foreign countries whilst

preferring imperial trade. Because of the unpopularity of the word 'protection', he did not use it in his campaign, opting instead for the less provocative-sounding tariff reform. Chamberlain acquired a good deal of support for his views but the suggestion split the Conservatives. Chamberlain thus managed to split both major parties in his political career. After this Conservative flirtation with ending free trade, the Liberals won a huge majority at the election of January 1906.

3 **Religious principles** Liberals had long stood for the removal of the religious discrimination still apparent in public life, and Gladstone's great 1868–74 ministry had clearly demonstrated this commitment. But here, Liberals were really victims of their own success. By the 1870s nonconformists for instance could feel that their chances of social, political or economic advance were not generally hampered by their religious background. Although **prejudice against Roman Catholics** remained strong in areas like **Liverpool** and **Glasgow**, it was becoming more of the informal than the institutional kind. Lord Salisbury complained when a civil servant was dismissed from his post for apparently no better reason than that he was a Roman Catholic. In 1886 Salisbury appointed Henry Matthews as Home Secretary, the first Roman Catholic to hold a cabinet post.

In the past Liberals could rely on the nonconformist vote because they were the party to look after their interests. It was nonconformists who pushed for the Licensing Act of 1872, unpopular with many other groups. But now the Liberals could no longer rely on a block nonconformist vote.

- As they rose socially, many nonconformists turned to Anglicanism, for social as much as religious reasons.
- The strength of the nonconformist churches had peaked mid-century and they were starting to decline by the last years of the century.
- Religious issues were less prominent in politics (though they could surface at times over issues such as education).

## KEY CONCEPT

**Anti-Catholic prejudice in Liverpool and Glasgow**

Prejudice against Roman Catholic immigrants from Ireland was common in these two cities. The tension between Protestant and Catholic communities led to the rival football teams of Everton (Catholic 1878) and Liverpool (Protestant 1892) and Celtic (founded by Catholic Irish immigrants 1888) and Rangers (Protestant 1872). Conservatives, with their anti-Home Rule policy, gained support from the strong Protestant population in these areas.

4 **Social questions.** The increasing demand for state action on social control was evident in the last years of the century. Moreover, the Liberals had an opportunity here to associate themselves with the need for further change, as Salisbury's range of social reform was limited. But here there was a problem. Social reform in areas such as housing, pensions, poor law reform or concern for children's welfare would involve state intervention on a scale many Liberals such as Gladstone's disciple John Morley found incompatible with their traditional view of the freedom of the individual. Gladstone's resistance to a great deal of activity in this area was obviously influential and the **Newcastle programme** of 1891 showed the struggle between traditional and more radical Liberals in the mixed agenda it proposed.

Writers such as T.H. Green and L.T. Hobhouse were moving towards the '**New Liberalism**' which would attempt to argue that a minimum standard of living for the ordinary people was necessary if the true fruits of freedom were to be enjoyed. A party divided on such an important question and arguing about a change in its fundamental philosophy was hardly one to be entrusted with the government of the country.

## WHY DID IMPERIALISM REPLACE IRELAND AT THE CENTRE OF BRITISH POLITICS IN THE 1890s?

From 1886 until at least 1890 Ireland continued to be at the centre of political activity as Parnell was still prominent and law and order in the country remained a central question. This did the Conservatives no harm as it kept the Liberal Unionists close to them. Leading Unionists such as Chamberlain and Hartington, though keeping their distance from the Conservatives on the Commons benches, gave broad support to their Irish policy. After about 1890 Ireland became less prominent as far as English politics was concerned. Balfour's policies as Chief Secretary for Ireland had proved successful. He had effectively halted the Plan of Campaign and seen his policy of land purchase in 1888 make available to tenants £10 million and a further £33 million in 1891.

The downfall of Parnell was sudden and complete and left the Irish nationalists bitterly divided.

**How far was the period 1885–1902 an age of imperialism?**

- The success of Disraeli and Salisbury in 1878 at the Congress of Berlin where 'peace with honour' was claimed with the acquisition of Cyprus, set a pattern for later years.
- In the 1880s the Liberal government became more and more committed in Egypt, and the Berlin Conference of 1884–5 ensured that Britain would take its share of the African possessions that were being portioned among Great Britain, France, Germany, Portugal and Belgium.
- Avoiding formal treaties with other European powers, Britain's army remained relatively small but the navy was seen as a world-wide protection force for British interests.
- The speed with which the Empire expanded in these fifteen years was greater than any previous period: the bulk of British African territory was acquired at this time.
- The two Jubilees of Queen Victoria in 1887 and 1897, as well as her eightieth birthday celebrations in 1899, associated the era ever more deeply in the public mind with the imperial idea.

The height of imperial grandeur: Queen Victoria's Diamond Jubilee. The celebration had to be held on the steps of St Paul's as the Queen was too frail to climb them.

- **Colonial conferences** were held at the same time as the Jubilee celebrations when political leaders from self-governing territories were in attendance. Britain was increasingly seen as the 'mother country'.
- There was a strong emphasis on the British Empire in the political discussions of the day, the deployment of the military, diplomatic discussion with other powers and in the education of children in schools.

During the Boer War, the public relief at the raising of the sieges of Mafeking, Kimberley and Ladysmith meant the Liberals could be attacked as unpatriotic and in some cases – such as **Lloyd George** who spoke out against the war – as pro-Boer. This was a name given to those Liberals, Radicals and Socialists who felt the Boer nation was being oppressed by the British who were not entitled to attack it. In the country as a whole it was not a popular position to take.

## THE END OF CONSERVATIVE DOMINANCE

The Conservative problems after Salisbury's retirement in 1902 led to Balfour's resignation in 1905 and a great Liberal victory at the general election of 1906. Revealingly, however, the principal issues at the election were ones that, for the last time, favoured traditional Liberalism.

- The Conservatives split badly over Joseph Chamberlain's suggestion that free trade be abandoned and replaced by 'imperial preference' (see pages 240–1). Free trade, clearly a Liberal policy, remained popular with the electorate.
- The image of Empire had been tarnished by the problems encountered in the Boer War and its immediate aftermath, including the embarrassment of Chinese slavery (see Chapter 7)
- The Education Act of 1902, by giving some ratepayers' money to Church schools, angered nonconformists who returned, if temporarily, to the Liberal fold.

- Similar Liberal support was gathered to oppose the Licensing Act of 1903 which was felt to favour the brewing interest too much in giving generous compensation to landlords whose pubs were forced to close.

In 1903 there were secret meetings between Liberal and Labour politicians to plan to work together at the next general election in order to defeat the Conservatives. This electoral co-operation between the Liberals and the Labour Party, the **Lib-Lab Pact**, made the Liberal victory in January 1906 seem even greater than it was: over 400 Liberals were returned to Parliament as against 157 Conservatives and 29 Labour. The Labour Party was keen to see the Liberals returned to power as they had promised to pass an act that would benefit the trade unions after the **Taff Vale judgement**.

## CONCLUSION

- Favourable political circumstances had enabled the Conservatives to retain office for much of the period 1885–1905.
- The effective leadership of Lord Salisbury undoubtedly helped.
- The popularity of imperialism until at least the turn of the century was also of great value to them. Irish affairs tended to benefit them electorally. Gladstone's ailing leadership and his concerns over Irish Home rule did not help the Liberal Party.
- The weaknesses and division of the Liberals over the major issues of the day were significant negative factors. This was especially true of the Conservative general election wins of 1895 and 1900.
- The Liberals, challenged by 'New Liberalism', underwent close self-examination in the 1890s.
- By appealing to the growing powerful middle-class interest, the traditional party of the landowning aristocracy, the Conservative Party, was able to survive with its power largely undiminished into the democratic twentieth century.

## SUMMARY QUESTIONS

1 Why might the Conservatives not have expected to do well in this period?

2 What political circumstances helped the Conservatives to stay in power?

3 What were the main problems facing the Liberal Party at this time?

# AS ASSESSMENT

## QUESTIONS IN THE STYLE OF EDEXCEL

In this unit you will normally have one extract of between 100 and 150 words. There will be three questions based on the extract. The first will relate directly to the extract; your answer, in your own words, will be based on its contents. The second and third questions will not be related directly to the extract but will be on a connected theme. In the second answer you are asked for an explanation of an event or theme. The third question will require a longer, essay-style answer, where causes or consequences of an event or theme could be addressed. Some sort of historical judgement will be required.

### Source A

As householders or as lodgers, the great bulk of the inhabitants of the boroughs will certainly be admitted to a right of which they have only too long been deprived . . . a principle which really opens Parliament to the people. . . . Great as were the effects of the Reform Bill of 1832, . . . we are perfectly satisfied that the Reform Bill of 1867 will produce still greater effects. Progress in all directions will presently be registered. Ignorance will give place to education, prejudice to justice . . . a glorious future is before us . . . Henceforth no class . . . will be excluded from the franchise except it may be for the impoverished peasants of our rural districts. The time will come when even the peasants will be entrusted with the suffrage. But sufficient for the present is the victory achieved.

Extract from the *Newcastle Weekly Chronicle*, 13 July 1867.

### Questions

1 Study Source A. Why is the *Newcastle Weekly Chronicle* so satisfied with the passing of the 1867 Reform Act?

(5 marks)

**Level of response required:**
A developed and fully supported statement making a number of different points. Note that the question straddles more than one bullet point: it concerns parliamentary reform, but also the rivalry of Gladstone and Disraeli.

**a** Start by thinking about the overall feeling of an extract: is there a word that could sum up its mood? In this particular case the writer is clearly very satisfied and it could be said that the piece is 'optimistic'. This could then be used as a theme for the answer with illustrations of the optimism shown. This kind of approach should help to avoid the trap of merely repeating or summarising the extract.

**b** Identify the main ideas: you can use key words from the extract to develop your answer.

- 'Justice' at last is done; many borough inhabitants will now gain the voting right 'long denied them'.
- With almost all classes now included in the suffrage, further 'progress' should be made in dealing with their needs.
- A sufficient degree of reform has been passed 'for the present', though even the 'peasants' may eventually gain the right to vote.

**2** What were Disraeli's motives in passing the 1867 Reform Bill?

(7 marks)

**Level of response required:**
A range of reasons which, at the highest level, judges the relative importance of the reasons given.

A question may be asked because, on the surface, something surprising has happened and an explanation is required. You can use this to your advantage. Why should Disraeli, a Conservative, pass such a substantial parliamentary reform bill that granted household suffrage, when his party had voted against a more moderate measure the year before? You then provide the answer to this puzzle. Make sure that with a limited number of marks available you stick closely to the question. Concentrate on Disraeli's 'motives', avoiding a blow-by-blow account of the complex events surrounding the passing of the Bill.

- Disraeli believed that the ordinary householder was essentially respectable and could be relied on to vote wisely.

- Moreover, the skilled working classes, proud of their independence, as Disraeli believed, might be reluctant to vote for the same party as their Liberal employers. Thus, party advantage will be seen to loom large.
- In addition, Disraeli could control the *terms* of the Bill if he was in power, to the benefit of his own party.
- His rejection of amendments suggested by Gladstone, in contrast to his acceptance of more Radical ones, suggests an intention to weaken his main rival in Parliament.
- Here, *link* the point about accepting Radical amendments (such as Hodgkinson's compound householder) to another Disraeli motive, i.e. the desire to quell public agitation for reform made apparent by the activities of the Reform League, the disturbances in Hyde Park and the large reform meetings in the north of England.
- Focus on a few clear reasons with appropriate illustration. Try to argue that one reason selected is the most significant in your opinion. Justify your choice from the evidence.

**3** What impact did the passing of the Reform Act of 1867 have on the direction and organisation of the Conservative and Liberal parties up to 1885?

(18 marks)

### Level of response required:
A developed and balanced explanation with a sustained argument.

The wording of the question needs careful examination to make sure you have understood its meaning and realise what material is required from you. Look for key words. Here, they are 'direction' and 'organisation'.

With a longer answer you also need to think carefully about the main factors that should be included in your script.

- Read the phrasing of the question carefully. Don't just rush in quickly thinking 'this is the question on the effects of the Second Reform Act' and reel off a list of things.
- Clearly you have to relate to the terms of the Act and also to the whole idea of a mass electorate, nearly doubled from approximately one to two million.
- But you need to consider the words 'direction' and 'organisation' and ensure you have material on each. Longer answers need balance in order to pick up marks in each section.

The points you need to consider include:

- The larger electorate, coupled with the secret ballot introduced in 1872, meant parties would have to appeal to voters' opinions rather than their pockets. Did policy move in new directions?
- For these policies to be noticed among the new voters, a new framework that would attract support and perhaps membership needs to be developed. What changes in organisation were made?

Make sure you also deal with both Liberalism and Conservatism in a balanced way with a reasonable amount of material on each. Specific material might include:

- Disraeli's speeches at the Crystal Palace and in Manchester in 1872 developed ideas designed to appeal to the new electorate. Did they move his party in a new direction?
- By 1874 the organisation of the Conservative Party had undergone radical improvement thanks to the efforts of John Gorst, and this played a part in the party's success in the general election of that year. What changes had been made?
- The two-party system was firmly established as a result of the 1867 Act.
- Both parties established organisations at local level. Local constituency associations would concern themselves with registration issues, selecting candidates and social activities.
- In Birmingham the Liberals led by Joseph Chamberlain developed an impressive organisation and the National Liberal Federation of 1877 was a sophisticated piece of political machinery.
- The Conservatives, forced to adapt by the much wider nature of the electorate, found a good deal of potential support in the new suburban middle classes.

These are all potential themes. Use these at the start of new paragraphs, relating clearly to the question and then bring in detail to back up your points.

For example, use the first sentences in the bullet points above to state your case and then decide on some specific detail to illustrate it.

*Disraeli's speeches at the Crystal Palace and Manchester in 1872 developed ideas designed to appeal to the new electorate.*

This relates to the new situation after 1867 and indicates the line of argument. Imagine you are told, 'show me how'. You would go on to bring in detail about Conservative policies with regard to a more outgoing foreign policy and an increased concern with social reform. Be careful in this particular question not to go off at a tangent and get involved in the minute detail of social reform.

## QUESTIONS IN THE STYLE OF OCR

Two answers of continuous prose will be required, the first worth 30 marks and the second 60.

The first will require you to show knowledge and understanding of significant events, and the second, historical assessments of particular developments, possibly with a comparative element.

### Questions

> 1 Identify and explain the main factors helping Palmerston stay in power for most of the period 1855–65
>
> (30 marks)

At this level you have to adopt a more *analytical approach* than for GCSE. So for this question you need to arrange your ideas paragraph by paragraph. For the top mark band A examiners will expect you to cover a wide range of reasons, all fully illustrated. How can you reach this level most effectively?

**Paragraphs.** Think in terms of each paragraph making a contribution to answering the question. If some people picked up your completed answer and selected one paragraph to read at random then, having done so, they should be somewhat the wiser as to the answer to the question. Moreover, they should have been able to work out what the question was, not because you have repeated the wording (though referring to key words or phrases at times is a good idea) but simply by the way you have angled your material to the question set. If all they read from the paragraph they selected was a *mere description of events* then a much lower band mark is coming your way however accurate your material. On the other hand, if you explain things clearly but fail to include enough detail to prove your point, you will always sell yourself short. You must include enough evidence to satisfy someone who doubts the truth of your assertions.

**Framework.** Once you have established a clear analytical shape for the whole answer, you have constructed the framework of the house. Now you can put in the soft furnishings – the detail that will justify the assertions made at the start of each paragraph. What you need to do is *prove* your points with *relevant* material. Stick to the simple but sound formula: point–proof. In planning the work you should recall some reasons why Palmerston was dominant in this period.

- The popularity of his vigorous foreign policy with Radicals.
- The support of the middle-class electorate at crucial times.
- The caution of his domestic policy appealing to the more conservatively minded.

- The relative weakness of the Conservatives, resulting in their acceptance of Palmerston's domination of the political scene fairly willingly.
- Palmerston's sound political judgement on most occasions.
- His successful handling of events such as the end of the Crimean War and the Indian Mutiny.

Devise a suitable first sentence for a paragraph for each of these ideas and then list the points of detail that would illustrate them. For example:

First sentence – *Derby's unwillingness to accept office in 1855 left the way open for Palmerston to assume power.*

### Detail.
- the circumstances surrounding Aberdeen's defeat and resignation in the middle of the Crimean War;
- the inability of Derby to form a ministry and the reluctant Queen Victoria finally resorting to Palmerston;
- the weakness and timidity of the Conservatives at this time.

> **2** What features of Gladstonian Liberalism were most apparent in Gladstone's first ministry 1868–74?
>
> (60 marks)

**Evaluation.** Your preparation will be more complex than compiling a list of reasons: more *judgement* and *selection* of material is called for, as 45 of the 60 marks are awarded for *evaluation*. You need to show *understanding* of Gladstonian Liberalism and *explain* rather then merely describe the links between its ideas and Gladstone's activities in his first ministry. You will need to show your ability to organise your material carefully and, as with all answers, communicate it clearly with accurate grammar, punctuation and spelling.

**Perspective.** Fifteen marks are reserved for *perspective*. That is, you show evidence of supporting historical knowledge and understanding around the question. For example, the highest-level answers in this case would show an awareness of the growing call for reform after the Crimean War, and how Liberal demands for change came to fruition in Gladstone's first ministry. An awareness of the *context* of the reforms would gain credit. You will be expected to make a *judgement* about which features of Gladstonian Liberalism were 'most' apparent

**Introduction.** An introduction could define the essential characteristics of Gladstonian Liberalism and these would be used as a framework for the rest of the answer. Each section of the answer should contain:

a reference to one aspect of Gladstonian Liberalism coupled with;

**b** supporting detail from events and legislation from the ministry in question.

So if, for instance, religious Liberalism is seen as significant, the nature of the need for true religious equality as opposed to toleration should be explained. This can be illustrated by the University Tests Act, Irish Church disestablishment and the general support for nonconformists from the Liberals led by Gladstone, an Anglican.

**Shape of the whole answer.** The answer needs to be a coherent whole. Think carefully about the order of the points that you will make. It may be a good idea to jot these down roughly and quickly in pencil at the start of an examination to see how they look. Factors that will influence your order could include:

- chronology;
- theme;
- degree of importance;
- maintaining the flow of the answer from one point to another.

This last point means having regard for ideas that will connect to your previous paragraph. Thus, having written about religious Liberalism you could start a paragraph on the removal of unjustified privilege, by writing:

*Not only did Gladstone show concern for equality of opportunity for non-Anglicans: it was also reflected in his concern for the introduction of competitive examination in the civil service.*

It should now be possible to work out what is required in the next few sentences, in order to *back up* your assertion with *evidence*.

**Conclusion.** At the end there should be a conclusion that brings the piece to a coherent end without stopping too abruptly. It need not be long: it brings together the main factors you should have made clear in your analysis already. In a well-written answer, the conclusion will not come as a surprise.

When you have completed the answer try reading:

- the introduction;
- the first sentence in each paragraph;
- the conclusion.

If you have constructed your answer well then what you have read should make sense and provide the framework for your assignment. If so, then your analysis is in place. Now look at those first sentences again and the assertions you have made. Does the material in the rest of the paragraph prove your point? If it does you should now have a higher band answer providing your material is relevant, comprehensive and balanced.

# A2 SECTION: INTRODUCTION

This part of the book focuses on the maturing of Gladstone's and Disraeli's political opinions after 1846 to help explain their characteristics and policies when they later both occupied the position of Prime Minister. Their contrasting attitudes to foreign, economic and Irish policy are closely examined. The individual rivalry of the two men is well known and was both political and personal. However, other important figures of the time are examined and the general economic, social and international forces that helped to determine the direction of political developments are not neglected. For example, the dominance of the idea of free trade and the importance of social class in this period are both given due weight. The impact of the changing international situation around 1870 is also considered. Attention is also paid to the impact of parliamentary reform on both the Liberal and Conservative parties.

With the death of Disraeli in 1881 and the crisis in the Liberal Party ushered in by the Home Rule controversy of the mid-1880s, the later sections of the book look at the increasing dominance of the Conservative Party under the underrated figure of Conservative Prime Minister Lord Salisbury in the last years of the nineteenth century. In the final section the political wheel turns full circle and the reasons for Liberal success in the general election of 1906 are surveyed. The impact of the Irish Question on the politics of the time is also explored in some depth.

After a short general introduction to each section, the views of historians on the relevant theme are examined. The historians themselves have been quoted to allow them to speak for themselves and to enable students to develop their own views and debate the principal issues amongst themselves.

# How far did Gladstone and Disraeli alter their political opinions 1846–68?

## INTRODUCTION

- Gladstone's moves towards Liberalism proceeded at an uneven pace.
- His commitment to free trade had become fixed by 1846 and never deserted him for the rest of his life. In some ways he always remained a Peelite.
- His moves towards religious liberalism were apparent, but uncertain and faltering, right through to 1868.
- Not until the 1860s was his support for political reform apparent.
- Disraeli was consistently committed to the Conservative Party throughout the period.
- It is debatable, however, how far he was committed to anything else.

### Historical interpretations

**Gladstone and historians.** How consistent were Gladstone's views in this period? Heavily influenced by Peel he seems to have embraced religious liberty and belief in free trade by 1846. However, Colin Matthew, *Gladstone 1809–1874* (1986), whose biographical writings owe much to a thorough study of Gladstone's voluminous diaries, argues that this did not exclude a strong belief in the role of the state. Politicians must give a lead, Gladstone believed. The economic Liberalism he displayed was, Matthew believed, born out of the conviction that it would produce the greatest possible prosperity and ensure a continuation of the status quo.

In his biography, *Gladstone* (1995), Roy Jenkins, an Oxford man himself, sees considerable significance in Gladstone's choice of Oxford University for a parliamentary seat in 1847. 'It exaggerated his natural tendency to mix politics and religion' since Oxford was the centre of current theological dispute (see page 153). But it also brought a strain between the Conservative Oxford and the increasingly Liberal train of thought in Gladstone's mind. It thus took him a long time to cross the 'swirling waters of both political and religious uncertainties'.

An earlier biographer, E.J. Feuchtwanger, in *Gladstone* (1975, 1989), argues that in addition to his growing economic and religious Liberalism, Gladstone's Neapolitan experience in 1850 ended his sympathy with the traditional continental governments and encouraged his belief in liberal nationalism. This belief, together with his loyalty to free trade and coupled with his doubts (rather less liberal) about extending the franchise, made it possible for him to accept office under Palmerston in 1859.

Feuchtwanger also argues that his change to a greater sympathy with franchise extension in the 1860s (which so concerned Palmerston) was linked to his belief in free trade and the importance of government economy. He had decided that the majority of new voters would be keen to keep taxes down and maintain a close scrutiny of government expenditure.

**Disraeli and historians.** There is a difference of opinion amongst historians who analyse Disraeli's political opinions. The Conservative Party, of which Disraeli became undisputed leader in 1868, hardly conformed to his Young England ideal (see page 154). It is on this point in particular that historians have differed. The standard life is the superbly written biography of Disraeli by Robert Blake, published in 1966. Blake answers his own question 'how seriously then should we take Disraeli's "philosophy"?' with the words 'not very' and argues that 'when he became a leading political figure he never attempted at all seriously to carry out the sort of programme that he and his friends (in Young England) seem to have envisaged'.

Writers of briefer lives in the 1990s, John Vincent, *Disraeli* (1990), and Paul Smith, *Disraeli: A Brief Life* (1996), have taken a different stance. Vincent argues that Disraeli's ideas and analysis of the state of society were acute and ahead of his time, but that he lacked the political ability to put them into practice. Smith sees Disraeli not as a consistent thinker but as someone who tried to fashion the nature of the Conservative Party into a body to fit a Jewish outsider, 'reconciling the diverse aspects of his inheritance and personality with each other and with the society in which he had to operate'. John Walton, in *Disraeli* (1990), argues that that there is consistency in Disraeli's opinions. He never really defended protection; it was more that he attacked Peel for going back on his word. As Chancellor in 1852, 1858–9 and 1866–8, Disraeli introduced budgets that supported the economic free trade orthodoxies that he had persuaded the Conservatives to accept. Disraeli himself claimed consistency, and stated in 1867 that he had educated his party to accept that a widening of the franchise would be beneficial to the Conservatives (or Tories as Disraeli preferred to call them), as working people would support aristocracy, Church and monarch. None of this invalidates his central belief, which was, argues Blake, in the fitness for rule of the English landed classes as a whole, rather than a narrow Whig clique.

## DISRAELI AND GLADSTONE: POLITICAL BEGINNINGS

When Gladstone and Disraeli began their political careers in 1832, it was Gladstone who was the Conservative, elected for the seat of Newark which was effectively controlled by the anti-reform Duke of Newcastle.

Disraeli, in his less successful attempt to be elected at Wycombe, described himself as a Radical.

Thirty-five years later, Gladstone and Disraeli, already political opponents for some time, were to alternate as Prime Minister for some 13 years, a rivalry ended only by Disraeli's death in 1881. Yet it was Gladstone, as leader of the Liberal Party, who was seen as the more Radical character. How had this situation come about?

When Disraeli was finally elected to Parliament in 1837, his fifth attempt in five years, he was standing in the Conservative interest, though his motives for doing so were certainly not similar to Gladstone's. One consistent theme in Disraeli's beliefs that *can* be detected is that he was anti-Whig. But when he realised that the Conservatives – rather than the Tories – were not '**worn out**' he was happy enough to attach himself to them. In 1837 he was elected for Maidstone but this time *defeating* a Radical candidate. His Radical allegiance had always been lukewarm. In his second attempt to get elected for Wycombe he had been flattered and surprised to receive Tory support. They had no candidate and were anxious to exclude the Whigs by any means. In 1836 he became Private Secretary to the Tory peer and ex-Lord Chancellor Lord Lyndhurst and the die was cast.

## WHAT WERE THE DIFFERENCES IN GLADSTONE AND DISRAELI'S ATTITUDES TOWARDS SIR ROBERT PEEL AND CONSERVATISM IN THE 1840s?

The 1840s were to prove a crucial period of development. Though Gladstone and Disraeli were both seen as Conservatives in Peel's government from 1841 to 1846 there were major differences of outlook in their overall philosophy and they ended up in 1846 going their separate ways.

**The issue of the Church.** Gladstone's Conservatism put a lot more emphasis on maintaining the privileges of the Church of England than did that of Disraeli. Although Gladstone never totally shed all aspects of his Evangelical Liverpool background, particularly in regard to personal piety and religious expression, he was much influenced in the 1830s by the **Oxford Movement** which emphasised the importance of the Church of England as an institution. It stressed the corporate and sacramental side of faith more than individual conversions and Bible-based preaching. It meant maintaining the traditional aspects of the Catholic – though not the *Roman* Catholic – faith. To Gladstone, the Whigs were threatening the position of the Church with proposals such as the one in 1834 to transfer some of the revenues of the Anglican Church in Ireland to non-religious purposes. In 1838 he attempted to express his views in a book

KEY TERM

'Worn-out' Tories After the passing of the 1832 Reform Act against Tory wishes and their heavy election defeat later in the year Disraeli saw Toryism as 'worn out'. It seemed doomed to extinction in the new industrial age. However, Peel's Tamworth Manifesto accepted the spirit as well as the letter of the Reform Act in 1834. The subsequent recovery of the party as Conservative gave Disraeli fresh faith in its future, albeit not in the same way as Peel saw it.

**Oxford Movement** The movement to try to recapture the independence and catholic practices of the Church of England. Its beginning is traditionally ascribed to a sermon given in Oxford in 1833 by John Keble protesting at proposals to divert Church revenues into secular channels. Several of the movement's notable supporters, such as John Henry Newman, later converted to the Roman Catholic Church, though Keble himself did not.

*The State in its Relations with the Church* which had a vision of a government and a society entirely in harmony with the beliefs and principles of the Established Church. This meant, for instance, that all office holders should be members of that Church. The book did not make easy reading with a very flowery style (Gladstone never used one word when two would do), and was not well received. Peel, Gladstone's party leader, and certainly not an irreligious man, is recalled – by his biographer Norman Gash – as commenting: 'That young man will ruin a fine career if he writes such books as these'. It was at this time that Gladstone was described by the Whig Thomas Macaulay as being 'the rising hope of the stern unbending Tories'.

Disraeli never showed Gladstone's religious intensity, though he did have a regard for the Church, albeit in a much broader context. He saw it as a central plank in the maintenance of the English way of life upheld by a disinterested and paternalistic aristocracy, rather than by what he saw as the narrow-minded, money-grubbing middle classes to whom the Whig party paid far too much attention. To Disraeli, the Church was part of the glue that held society together and, as such, should be supported. This was a more pragmatic view of the institution than the beliefs maintained by the religious certainties of a youthful Gladstone.

**For and against the Maynooth Grant.** In any case Gladstone, moving away from the earlier rigidity of his religious views, was coming to accept that his thoughts concerning the all-embracing role for the Church of England were unrealistic. This is shown in his complex approach to Peel's decision to increase the annual grant to the Roman Catholic College at Maynooth in 1844–5 (see pages 33 to 35). Gladstone now accepted the validity of this move but still resigned from the government because of his previously stated public views in his State and Church book, which effectively opposed the grant. His complex letter explaining his actions left Peel as bewildered as he was when he had first read Gladstone's book.

Disraeli's opposition to the grant increase was quite unqualified. It emphasised that Roman Catholicism, though he found its mystical aspects intriguing, meant little to him and it divided Young England since his Young England friends (see below) supported the change. Disraeli's speech opposing it criticised the government for going back on stated principles. Blake puts Disraeli's opposition down to his desire to attack Peel, but it was nonetheless an effective speech. For once he had made a better impression in Parliament than Gladstone.

### Political office 1841–6

Gladstone's greater political success continued under Peel: he had been given office in the Conservative government whereas Disraeli was not. Gladstone occupied a junior post in the Treasury at the very end of 1834 and then early in the new year was promoted to the position of Under-Secretary for War and the Colonies. But it is their contrasting fortunes in 1841 that are most significant; Gladstone was appointed Vice-President of the Board of Trade – and raised to President with cabinet rank in 1843 – but Disraeli was completely passed over, an imagined slight he chose not to forgive. Yet, as his generally sympathetic biographer Robert Blake argues, Disraeli was not well connected and had little to recommend him. Peel was never likely to have offered him office.

**Free trade and Young England.** The dominant interests of the two men in the early 1840s show how they were moving in different directions. Gladstone's interest and ability in financial matters (never Disraeli's strong point) were apparent. He became convinced, as did Peel, that the encouragement of free trade by a lowering of tariffs, was the key to economic success. Gladstone became a strong supporter of the budgets brought in by Chancellor of the Exchequer Henry Goulburn (see Chapter 3) but essentially inspired by Peel, such as the ones in 1842 and 1845 which removed tariffs on many duties. Gladstone was not without achievement himself, piloting the complex Railway Bill of 1843–4 through the Commons.

In contrast, Disraeli, without office and more of a free agent, attached himself in 1843 to a group known as Young England led by two younger ex-Cambridge graduates, George Smythe and Lord John Manners. Partly protesting against the party discipline imposed by Peel, they stood for a romantic view of England where aristocratic tradition and influence could combine with the true working classes to outflank what they saw as the narrow-minded and heartless Whig-led middle classes, who were imposing a cruel Poor Law on the country and had little concern for the social welfare of the ordinary people.

**Repeal of the Corn Laws.** The differences between the two men became more apparent over the issue of the Corn Laws. When, in December 1845, Peel proposed to repeal the Corn Laws, Lord Stanley (from 1851 the Earl of Derby) resigned and Gladstone returned to the government as Secretary for War and the Colonies. He was going to support Peel in his hour of need, whereas Disraeli's opposition to him grew to its climax. If Disraeli's speech over Maynooth had mildly impressed Parliament, his speech on repeal created a sensation. Saying little about the merits of the issue itself, he attacked Peel for going back on his pledges regarding the retention of the Corn Laws when he took office in 1841.

Gladstone had become a Peelite and Disraeli a Protectionist Conservative. With the fall of Peel's government soon after repeal they were both out of office. Gladstone was the member of a small band of Peelites whose merit

> ## Disraeli's speech against repeal of the Corn Laws
>
> Disraeli's speech involved personal attacks on Peel, who was:
>
> *No more a great statesman than the man who gets up behind a carriage is a great whip. Certainly both are disciples of progress. Perhaps both may get a good pace. But how far the original momentum is indebted to their powers, and how far their guiding prudence applies the lash or regulates the reins, it is not necessary for me to notice.*
>
> Peel had gone back on his principles – he should resign:
>
> *Let men stand by the principle by which they rise, right or wrong. I make no exception. If they be wrong, they must retire to that shade of private life with which our present rulers have so often threatened us.*
>
> Peel had done great damage by splitting the Conservative Party:
>
> *Above all maintain the line of demarcation between parties, for it is only by maintaining the independence of party that you can maintain the integrity of public men, and the power and influence of Parliament itself.*
>
> (Extracts quoted from Robert Blake, *Disraeli* (1969 edition, page 227.)

was in the quality rather than quantity of their loyal support for their leader. By contrast, Disraeli found himself in a much larger group – the protectionists – but one where his parliamentary skills and especially his speaking ability would be much in need. The prejudices that had been evident against him ever since Members of Parliament laughed at his maiden speech did not disappear, but he was too valuable an asset to be ignored. He was passed over for the party leadership in the Commons at first but in effect occupied the position of the leading Conservative speaker in that House.

## HOW DID THE DEVELOPING IDEAS OF GLADSTONE AND DISRAELI CONTRAST IN THE PERIOD 1847–51?

**Protection?** Between 1846 and 1852 Gladstone and Disraeli both found themselves in opposition to the Whig/Liberal government of Lord John Russell. It was a time when the views of the two men developed: Gladstone's Liberalism became more apparent and Disraeli struggled with the possibility that, despite his efforts in 1846, protection might have to be abandoned as a policy. This issue first became apparent in 1848 with the resignation and subsequent death of the protectionist leader in the Commons, Lord George Bentinck. Although Derby was not prepared to make Disraeli the official party leader in the Commons, this is what he effectively became. In 1849, when Derby made a strong protectionist speech in the Lords, Disraeli was less enthusiastic in the Commons. Also, he was reproved by Derby for a speech at Aylesbury (Buckinghamshire) when he suggested that repeal could remain if farmers were to be compensated in other ways. After the sudden death of Peel in 1850, Disraeli was keener than ever for the Conservative Party to accept free trade, but the time had not yet come.

Gladstone had no such hesitations about embracing free trade. In March 1848 his speech defending the general direction of Peel's policy in this area since the budget of 1842 was impressive and marked him out as a possible Chancellor of the Exchequer in a future government, though whether this would be a Conservative or Liberal one, it was hard to tell. In 1849 he supported the Russell government's repeal of the Navigation Laws, another important free trade measure. Perhaps Gladstone would return to the Conservative Party if its members could swallow the free trade pill. Lacking financial talent of their own they certainly needed him, and as early as 1848 tentative enquiries were made to see if he would rejoin his other colleagues. The resignation of Russell's government in February 1851 was followed by a week of frantic negotiations between Peelites and protectionists but this merely confirmed Disraeli in his feeling that protection must go. It was clear that talented financial men like Gladstone who were badly needed would not accept the offer of a post from Derby while the Conservatives were still officially protectionist. Derby, with very little ability to draw on in the protectionist ranks alone, gave up his attempt to form a government, and Russell resumed his ministry for a few more months.

**Other issues.** Although free trade was the area where Gladstone's emerging commitment to Liberalism was most clearly seen, there were others. In 1847 Gladstone and Disraeli found themselves in the same parliamentary division lobby: they both supported the removal of Jewish disabilities – the fact that a Jew by religion could not enter Parliament because he had to take a Christian oath. This had been occasioned by the success in the general election of that year of the Jew, Baron Lionel de Rothschild, for the City of London. It was not surprising that Disraeli supported the motion since it was only his father's quarrel with his synagogue when Disraeli was young that had resulted in a Christian baptism of his children. For Gladstone, however, the move was more significant. It seemed to contradict his earlier views on the desirability of a purely Christian, if not Anglican, state. Gladstone's speech explaining the modification of his views was another of his more complex and obscure efforts. Roy Jenkins remarks that 'subordinate clauses hung like candelabra throughout his oration, with few of his sentences containing less than 70 words and some twice as many'. It seems that he had come to realise that his religious ideal was unattainable and there would have to be a less restrictive approach. The change did not endear him to his new constituents, the **graduates of Oxford University**, whose MP he had just become.

On foreign policy it appeared that Gladstone and Disraeli both had reservations about the style of Palmerston's conduct in this area. This was particularly reflected in the Don Pacifico debate (see Chapter 7, page 112) in 1850 when Palmerston defended himself against Peel, Gladstone and Disraeli in the Commons and was also criticised by Aberdeen and Derby in the Lords. As a sign of things to come, it was Disraeli's speech which was the least critical, objecting to Palmerston's actions not on moral grounds, like Gladstone, but because of the possibility of Palmerston's actions offending other major powers.

A central event in the more general development of Gladstone's liberal thought was his visit to the **Kingdom of Naples** in the winter of 1850–1. The corrupt legal system and lack of free speech or any prospect of a parliamentary system appalled him; he called it 'the negation of God erected into a system of government'. The overcrowded prisons and the dreadful treatment of their inmates made a deep impression on him and confirmed the increasingly liberal direction of his thinking.

## KEY PEOPLE

**Graduates of Oxford University** Those who possessed a degree from Oxford or Cambridge universities were entitled to vote for two MPs from each place. The views of Oxford graduates in the nineteenth century were staunchly Conservative and strongly supported the traditional institutions of the country such as the Church of England.

## KEY PLACE

**The Kingdom of Naples** Country occupying the southern half of the Italian peninsula before most of Italy was unified in 1860. A very illiberal and repressive state.

## HOW SIGNIFICANT WERE THE PARLIAMENTARY CLASHES OF 1852–3?

**Disraeli's budget speech 1852.** During this year Gladstone and Disraeli both held the office of Chancellor of the Exchequer. It was Gladstone's speech attacking Disraeli's budget of December 1852 which really marks the start of the intense rivalry between the two figures. In February 1852 the first Derby ministry took office, lacking in ministerial experience. Disraeli protested his unfitness for the post of Chancellor but received it all the same. Although unclear before the election, it was certain afterwards that the Conservatives would not attempt to reimpose the Corn Laws. Disraeli's budget at the end of the year was an attempt to compensate farmers for this by such measures as the reduction of the malt tax, but Gladstone did an effective demolition job on Disraeli's figures. In addition, however, he launched what Disraeli regarded as something of a personal attack: Gladstone asserted of Disraeli 'he has not yet learned the limits of discretion, of moderation and forbearance that ought to restrain the conduct and language of every member of this House'. As a result the budget was rejected by 21 votes. This triumph did much for Gladstone's reputation in liberal quarters, but it ensured the coolest of relations between the two men. The Derby ministry resigned and, in the new Whig-Peelite coalition under the leadership of Aberdeen, Gladstone replaced Disraeli as Chancellor.

**The dispute of 1853.** At the start of 1853 there was a financial dispute between the two men, as childish as it was complex. New Chancellors traditionally paid outgoing Chancellors compensation for the furniture in the public rooms at 11 (then numbered 12) Downing Street and also for passing on the Chancellor's gown. However, as in future under new regulations the furniture was to be dealt with by the Board of Works, Gladstone argued that the Board rather than he himself should compensate Disraeli. Disraeli argued, probably technically correctly, that the new arrangement would only apply from the new Chancellor onwards. The nineteenth-century formality in letter writing added to the tension as the exchanges became more and more stiff and unfriendly. There were Gladstone's rigidity of manner and extreme desire for economy and Disraeli's indefensible desire to use the quarrel to avoid relinquishing the Chancellor's gown. In the end Gladstone conceded the financial point on the furniture, but never received the gown, which remains in Disraeli's country house at Hughendon Manor in Buckinghamshire to this day. Formality was now to mark their relationship for some time. Moreover, they were clearly political opponents. Disraeli now had the mortification of watching Gladstone produce a budget to replace his own. It was an outstanding success and the first of the supremely confident free trade budgets that Gladstone was to produce intermittently over the next fourteen years.

## HOW DID GLADSTONE'S POLITICAL CAREER DEVELOP 1853–60?

**Success in implementing free trade.** Gladstone's first period as Chancellor of the Exchequer (1852–5) coincided with a growing economic confidence, only brought to a halt by the British involvement in the Crimean War. He had the opportunity to plan a progressive reduction in income tax and he made impressive use of it in the budget of 1853. His mastery of detail and intimate understanding of tax schedules and intricate financial detail were unmatched. After this impressive first budget, forcefully delivered, he found he had raised the status of the office of Chancellor to a position matched only, after the Prime Minister's, by the Foreign Secretary's.

Interrupted by the Crimean War and the political complexities that kept him out of office, Gladstone was able, in 1859, to resume his work on lowering tariffs and planning for a phased reduction and eventual abolition of the income tax. In his speeches he continued eloquently to explain (although he was often long-winded) how the increasing prosperity of the country could allow for both tariff and tax reductions and still produce a surplus. For instance, in 1860 the Commons sat in rapt attention as Gladstone, with total mastery of the subject, tantalised his audience by outlining hypothetical budgets more or less generous than the one he actually went on to propose. His achievement was great. He had, to use his own words in the great free trade budget of 1860, 'set free the general course of trade'.

**Back to the Conservatives?** Now that it was clear that the Conservatives had abandoned protection there was always the possibility that Gladstone, still regarded as the most Conservative of the leading Peelites, might rejoin them. When Aberdeen resigned early in 1855 the Queen sent for Lord Derby and there was briefly a possibility that Gladstone and Disraeli might be members of the same government. But Derby decided he had insufficient support to form a new government and Gladstone was reluctant to serve under anybody except Aberdeen. However, Aberdeen could not, at this moment, become Prime Minister after the Commons vote of no confidence in his ministry. So eventually Victoria, with reluctance, asked Lord Palmerston to form a government. He was the Whig-Liberal whom Gladstone least wished to serve under. Gladstone disliked what he saw as Palmerston's rude and aggressive foreign policy. Initially the Peelites accepted Palmerston's offer for Gladstone to continue as Chancellor. However, they resigned days later when they realised that Palmerston was proposing to set up a Committee of Inquiry into the previous ministry's handling of the Crimean War.

For four more years Gladstone hovered uneasily between party groupings, uncertain of his final political home. He continued to be critical of Palmerston's aggressive foreign policy, as did other prominent political figures. Gladstone (and Disraeli) voted against Palmerston in 1857 over his handling of the *Arrow* incident (see Chapter 3, page 42). He also opposed Palmerston in 1858 when, for once, the Prime Minister was thought to be standing up insufficiently strongly to a foreign power with his Conspiracy to Murder Bill (see Chapter 3, page 44). Revealingly, however, Gladstone attacked the measure for being repressive rather than for being unpatriotic.

Gladstone's dislike of what he regarded as Palmerston's 'lax moral tone' was evident when in 1858 Palmerston appointed Lord Clanricard to a senior post in government. This scandalised the more upright section of Victorian society, for Clanricard had not only been a notorious adulterer, he was also said to have induced his late mistress to leave her estate to their bastard son rather than to her legitimate children. It is possible that only the likely presence of Disraeli in a prominent position in Derby's government prevented Gladstone from joining the Earl when he replaced Palmerston in 1858. However, Gladstone's most recent biographer, Roy Jenkins, feels it was more the influence of the collective reaction of the erstwhile Peelites, including **Graham** and **Herbert**, who all seemed reluctant to take office. Gladstone had nonetheless seriously considered it and even voted on Derby's side in the motion that brought them down after the 1859 election. Nor did he attend the important meeting at Willis's Rooms traditionally taken to be the foundation of the modern Liberal Party. It was only after this in June 1859 that Gladstone threw in his lot with the new Palmerston administration as Chancellor of the Exchequer and thus became a fully fledged Liberal.

## WHAT ROLE DID GLADSTONE AND DISRAELI PLAY IN BRINGING ABOUT PARLIAMENTARY REFORM?

However, party definitions and labels meant less then than now and Gladstone did not become less 'conservative' or more 'liberal' for not rejoining the Conservatives. Indeed, in 1859 the Conservative Disraeli introduced a Reform Bill into the House of Commons where it was opposed by Gladstone. The 'fancy franchises' Bill (see Chapter 4), as it became popularly known, was no radical measure and it reflected Disraeli's attitude to reform; essentially pragmatic and looking for possible party advantage. Gladstone's long speech opposing the proposals struck a more generally anti-reform stance in that he defended the small, corrupt boroughs where voters had frequently been bribed or where there was just one candidate elected unopposed. Extraordinarily, it sounded more like an old-fashioned Tory speech defending the pre-1832 system of election. Given these views it can be seen how Gladstone could accept office as Chancellor of the Exchequer under Palmerston in 1859. The two men were both sceptical on the question of reform and, for once, in agreement over foreign policy, as the major question of the day was Italian unity. Gladstone, given his previous attitude towards the Kingdom of Naples, could not be anything but pleased to see its position undermined and eventually destroyed.

In the early 1860s Gladstone's views on parliamentary reform seem to have undergone a remarkable transformation. By 1864 he was in the position to make his noteworthy 'pale of the constitution' speech (see Chapter 4) that, however misinterpreted as democratic, clearly represented an advance on earlier views. The American Civil War had been a difficult issue for Gladstone with his memories of the family's involvement in the slave trade and his **early defence of the slave-owning**

**Sir James Graham 1792–1861** From an aristocratic background, resigned from the post of First Lord of the Admiralty in Whig government of 1830–4 over proposed use of Irish Church revenues for secular purposes. Became a Peelite Conservative. Home Secretary 1841–6 when he supported Peel over the Corn Law dispute. First Lord of the Admiralty again in Aberdeen's Whig-Peelite coalition of 1852–5.

**Sidney Herbert 1810–61** Aristocrat who was at school with Gladstone who much admired him. Peelite: brought into cabinet as War Secretary 1845–6 during Corn Law crisis, held the same post in Aberdeen's government 1852–5 and in Palmerston's 1859–61 until his early death. Responsible for Florence Nightingale being sent out to the Crimea.

planters in Parliament, and he had at first favoured the South believing they had 'made a nation'. But he was full of admiration for the stoical way the average Lancashire cotton worker had endured the hardships caused by the cotton shortage. They had shown a 'willingness to suffer patiently', he told the working men of Chester at the end of 1862, which should be 'instructive to us all'. However, one Gladstone biographer, Richard Shannon, argues that Gladstone naively exaggerated their virtues and the extent to which they supported the northern states on principle and in direct opposition to their self-interest. He argues that Gladstone, in saying that 'cotton is but the instrument in the hand of God', was developing 'a stage setting for a morality drama of his own devising'.

Gladstone was now coming to believe that thanks partly to his own efforts as Chancellor of the Exchequer the working classes' growing prosperity, independence and loyalty to established authority were making them fit for the privilege of the franchise. There is no doubt that Gladstone was popular amongst the working people and his speaking tours of Tyneside and Lancashire in the early 1860s were well received. The phrase 'the people's William' was born. As Chancellor, his **abolition of the paper duty in 1861** was popular not only because it opened up the way for a cheaper press for the increasingly literate, skilled working class; it also demonstrated the fact that Gladstone could take on and defeat the opposition of the House of Lords.

So, with Palmerston dead and Prime Minister Russell in the Lords, it was Gladstone who was the logical choice to introduce the 1866 Reform Bill which would by its £6 limit grant a modest extension of the franchise to just that class of person he now deemed fit for the honour. But he found himself outmanoeuvred by Disraeli. As Blake says, Disraeli's views on parliamentary reform were 'purely opportunistic' throughout this period. There was no reason why the Conservatives could not support this moderate Reform Bill and so prevent the likelihood of anything more radical coming along for some time. Neither Derby nor Disraeli were totally opposed to reform on principle – Derby had been a strong supporter of it in 1832 – but Disraeli, seeing the possibility of a split in the Liberal ranks, urged Derby to oppose the Bill which, with the aid of the Adullamite opposition, brought down the government and put Derby and Disraeli into office with the chance of settling the reform question on their own terms (see Chapter 4).

Disraeli's handling of the situation was initially impressive. He persuaded the majority of his party of the need for reform, overriding the opposition and surviving the resignations of Cranborne and Carnarvon from the cabinet without the fracturing within the party that had occurred with the Liberals. But his touch deserted him somewhat when a combination of public agitation, uncertainty over the fine detail of the terms and a desire to get one over Gladstone at almost any cost resulted in acceptance of amendments so radical that some contemporaries could hardly believe what was happening. Perhaps Disraeli took some satisfaction from the fact that working men were now enfranchised in such numbers as to outvote the middle classes in some areas. For Disraeli had traditionally seen an alliance between the landed classes and the working people of England as being a more satisfactory arrangement for government than the 'rule' of a middle class of limited vision and hard-nosed, laissez-faire individualism. But had Disraeli's earlier opinions on these questions changed by 1867?

## WHAT WERE DISRAELI'S POLITICAL AND SOCIAL IDEAS?

**Disraeli's novels.** Disraeli's views in the 1840s can be ascertained by looking at his novels of the period. In the first of a trilogy, *Coningsby* (1844), a survey of political attitudes of the day, he makes clear his distaste for the Whigs. He describes them as a narrow-minded clique wishing to exclude all other groups from power, including the monarchy and the ordinary people of England (for it is *England* that most interests Disraeli). His political heroes were **Lord Bolingbroke** and **William Pitt** (whose Chancellor's gown he so wished to retain), who, he argued, had provided truly national leadership based on sound principles. Disraeli was also critical of Tories who opposed all change and reform, but this did not mean that he approved of Peel's attempt to reform the Conservatives in the 1830s. The Tamworth Manifesto (see Chapter 1) was 'an attempt to construct a party without principles'. What Disraeli seemed to want was a third way: to combine the powers and influence of the traditional institutions of the country – the Church, Parliament including the House of Lords, the monarchy and the landed interest – with the ordinary people in order to improve their conditions. In *Sybil* (1845), Disraeli's most famous passage bewails the 'two nations' of rich and poor 'between whom there is no intercourse and no sympathy' and suggests the solution to be a revival of the monarchy and the traditional landed interest who will care for the social welfare of the ordinary people. The Church will have a role in raising the aspirations of the people as Disraeli also indicates in his writings, particularly in the third of the trilogy, *Tancred* (1847).

Disraeli's views could be seen as romantic, pining for the happy days of good old rural England before 'dark satanic mills', grasping industrialists and greedy Whig lawyers. Unfortunately, circumstances did not favour the implementation of his views. **Chartist pressures** made it impossible to put forward a further extension of the franchise so that the alliance with the people could be cemented. Worse still, in 1846, political circumstances forced Disraeli into alliance with the **more reactionary sort**

### KEY PEOPLE

**Henry St John, Viscount Bolingbroke 1678–1751** and **William Pitt 1759–1806** Both regarded as leading political thinkers at either end of the eighteenth century. Bolingbroke held office only briefly, whereas Pitt was Prime Minister for almost 20 years.

### KEY CONCEPT

**Chartist pressures** Passing major reform in the face of Chartist demands would be seen as giving in to pressure and showing signs of weak government.

## KEY CONCEPTS

**More reactionary sort of Tory**
'Reactionary' was a word used after the French Revolution to describe those of conservative opinions who were reacting against recent changes and wished to put the clock back. The more reactionary sort of Tory would be one who disliked the growth of middle-class political influence and wished to maintain and re-strengthen the landed aristocratic hold on political power.

**The days of Pitt and Fox** The debates between William Pitt and Charles James Fox were a feature of parliamentary life between 1783 and the death of the two men in 1806. Pitt opposed the more liberal Fox's championing of causes such as the freedom of the press and his greater willingness to accept the essential principles of the French Revolution.

**of Tory** in opposing Peel's repeal of the Corn Laws; Young England broke up for good and for over 20 years the Tories remained largely out of office. Disraeli's interest in parliamentary reform is seen in his Bill of 1859 and the Act of 1867, in his concern for the welfare of the people in his social legislation of the mid-1870s, and in his strong nationalistic feeling in his development of imperial ideas from about 1872.

## CONCLUSION

By 1868 the views of both Gladstone and Disraeli had changed.

- They now both embraced free trade, Disraeli having come to this later than Gladstone.
- They both accepted the need for parliamentary reform, although it was 'the people's William' (as Gladstone had been called) who had been slower to come to this conclusion. Overall, however, Gladstone's Liberal instincts were the stronger, not least over religion, a surprising development when one compares the views of the two men in this area 25 years before.

By the late 1860s Gladstone and Disraeli had both become acknowledged party leaders and, though not young themselves, had taken over from older men of more aristocratic background. Both seemed confident of winning support from the newly enfranchised working man, yet able nonetheless to maintain an essentially aristocratic rule. Firmly entrenched in opposing parties and opposing both personally and in policy, they prepared to face each other in the new political world with which the second Reform Act had presented them. This new world entailed more head-to-head conflict of the party leaders than there had been seen since the **days of Pitt and Fox** at the end of the previous century.

# How did Gladstone and Disraeli perform in the role of Prime Minister?

## INTRODUCTION

- Gladstone exerted a strong leadership over a potentially disunited Liberal Party in his first and second ministries, though undertaking some courses of action reluctantly.
- Disraeli enjoyed early domestic success in his 1874–80 ministry but had a mixed record in foreign policy and found the struggle against bad health increasingly difficult.

### Historians' views: the nature of Liberalism

Traditionally historians have argued that the forces of Liberalism were somewhat disunited. Beyond a general acceptance of free trade and 'retrenchment' in public spending, they argued, was there anything to hold the Liberals together? The divisions over the passage of the 1867 Reform Act seemed all too obvious. Historians have been divided on exactly what Liberals believed in at this time. John Vincent, *The Formation of the British Liberal Party* (1966), and D.A. Hamer, *Liberal Politics in the Age of Gladstone and Rosebery* (1972), argued that they stood for little that was concrete. Vincent asserted that it was really only 'sentiment' that bound the party together and that coherent thought among Liberal leaders was rare. Hamer argued there was 'no single accountable and general system of thought' in Liberalism and they were 'not held together by any strong sense of common purpose'. It was politicians outside Westminster that often made the running in terms of policies; but they were mainly **faddists** who only cared about their own particular concern.

However, more recent writing has claimed that the Liberals did stand for something coherent and that specific ideas *were* important to the party. J.P. Parry, *Democracy and Religion* (1986), sees religion as a central factor. It provided a 'moral purpose' for the party and a number of issues in Gladstone's first ministry were related to it: Irish Church disestablishment in 1869 for instance. The extension of religious liberty, directly or indirectly, can be seen in the Education Act of 1870 and in measures such as the University Tests Act of the same year. Eugenio Biagini, in *Liberty, Retrenchment and Reform* (1992), sees a long line of liberal thought going back to Tom Paine and the supporters of the French Revolution who were suspicious of state or church control and enthusiastically supported free trade. It has been argued that the link was not only in ideas but in language. This reflects a recent – and

### KEY TERM

**Faddists** People concerned with only one issue such as restriction on alcohol sales (the United Kingdom Alliance) or disestablishment of the Church of England (Liberation Society).

## KEY TERM

**High politics**
Political discussion
and decision-
making at the
highest level such
as with cabinet
ministers.
Historians disagree
about the relative
importance of high
politics compared
with other factors
when looking at
significant political
developments such
as the 1867
Reform Act.

controversial – trend amongst some writers of history known as the 'linguistic turn'. It sees more significance in the language and discourse of the time than in **high politics** and economic and social structures. So, potential support for the Liberal Party was present in the ideas and ideals of the skilled working man. This latter phrase, too, was significant. It emphasised the *male* working world of the time but also seemed to suggest more independence than the term 'worker'.

The writings of Terry Jenkins, *Gladstone, Whiggery and the Liberal Party 1874–86* (1988) and *The Liberal Ascendancy* (1994), have shown that the development of the Liberal Party was more complex than just increasingly powerful Radical demands being resisted by an increasingly weak Whig fragment. The Whigs, argued Jenkins, should be defined more broadly than the small aristocratic clique identified by Vincent (1966). He argues that they continued to play a major role in the party in this period.

### Historians' views: what qualities did Gladstone bring to Liberalism?

As to Gladstone's performance as Prime Minister, could he weld the different Liberal groups together? Traditionally Gladstone's achievement here has been seen as great. As Parry (1986) points out, he had qualities that appealed to the wide-ranging nature of Liberal support. However, recent historians such as Colin Matthew, in *Gladstone 1809-1874* (1986), have argued that the Prime Minister was less than happy about a good deal of the legislation that his government passed through Parliament. 'Several proposals were repugnant to him' he asserts. This view stresses the traditional side of Gladstone's views. In his book *Rise and Fall of Liberal Government in Victorian Britain* (1994) J.P. Parry argues that Gladstone was frequently out of sympathy with much Liberal thinking, whereas Biagini (1992) regards his charismatic leadership as significant in Liberal success. His degree of control partly depends on the issue. Roy Jenkins (1995) views him as 'in full and direct command' over the drawing up of the Bill to disestablish the Irish Church in 1869. But he too sees Gladstone disliking a trio of measures, University Tests, Education and the Ballot.

### WHAT DID GLADSTONE'S FIRST MINISTRY ACHIEVE?

Gladstone's first ministry was seen as one of the great reforming ministries of the nineteenth century. A wholesale assault on the Irish Question, a passion for economy and efficiency in government, the extension of religious liberty, economic prosperity based on free trade principles, the removal of unjustified privileges in different areas of society, political reform with the introduction of a secret ballot and even a very modest dose of social reform, combined to give the impression of frenetic activity and considerable achievement in little more than four years from December 1868 to the early months of 1873. How much credit could Gladstone as Prime Minister take for all this? Did he suggest or even approve of all the measures taken? Could the ministry be said to have been a success for the Liberal Party? At first glance the achievements appear considerable in view of the political background against which they were undertaken.

### Why was Gladstone's first ministry always likely to be a time of change?

It is true that the election of a new Liberal government in 1868 was always likely to bring change: for instance, recent Royal Commission reports on subjects such as the civil service, schools and army and navy recruitment might well prompt government action. Palmerston, seen as an opponent of more widespread reform, was dead and gone. Now, there was a large number of new MPs, especially Liberal ones, from a much wider social background than previously. Rubinstein (1998) calculates that the proportion of legal and professional Liberal MPs rose from 27.7 per cent in 1859 to 37.6 per cent in 1868, the landed interest declining from 30.2 to 24.7 per cent. Economic liberalism in the form of free trade and a limited role for the state was generally accepted, but further political changes were expected in the wake of the Reform Act of 1867.

After the extension of the franchise in 1867, Liberals attracted a wide social range of support from traditional Whig landowners through the manufacturing and commercial middle classes, the legal and other professions to the skilled artisan and rural worker. Could Gladstone weld the different Liberal groups together? Ex-Peelites could admire his concern with efficiency and economy that stemmed from his mercantile background; his popular appeal had grown in the 1860s through his oratory, his concern for popular causes and his willingness to meet the people **on the stump**. 'God knows I have not courted them' he alleged: but he had. Yet those of a more conservative cast of mind would be re-assured by his traditional High Church principles, landed connections (with his estate at Harwarden) and his admiration of the qualities of aristocratic rule. No other living figure could claim all these potential advantages. Gladstone, before he became Prime Minister, had shrewdly chosen the abolition of Church rates and the Irish Church resolutions on disestablishment as a focus to bring Liberals together. He would aim to maintain this unity.

### How central a figure was Gladstone in the reforms of the first ministry?

Gladstone was a man of enormous energy and drive and spent a good deal of time and effort on certain aspects of his government's activities. Keeping a wary eye on his Chancellor, Robert Lowe, he became Chancellor himself in 1873 when Lowe resigned over misappropriation of

**KEY TERM**

**On the stump**
Stumping – or walking – around the country: in fact by this time probably travelling by train. The idea was to meet ordinary electors and address them with political speeches hoping for their support.

funds by subordinates. The Prime Minister took a personal interest in the Irish Question and the disestablishment of the Irish Church reflected the direction of his thinking on the religious question in Ireland. He also spent some time studying the intricacies of Irish land tenure in preparation for the Land Act of 1870. After the death of Lord Clarendon in 1870 Gladstone appointed his confidant, Lord Granville, as Foreign Secretary. His personal interest in this area is apparent in the studied neutrality of Great Britain in the Franco-Prussian War and in the insistence on the *Alabama* arbitration payment in 1872 (see Section 3). Other measures of the ministry appealed to his sense of administrative order and fairness such as the civil service reforms.

However, Gladstone had an instinctive dislike of pulling down institutions in order to achieve reform and of major constitutional change. Not for him a reform of the House of Lords or an extension of Church disestablishment to England. Only if an institution had badly fallen short should it be reformed. He reluctantly accepted that this was partly so with the army and in fact wished to see greater administrative changes than the ones Cardwell introduced.

Despite his apparent conversion to religious liberalism, Gladstone was reluctant to accept the terms of the University Tests Act and allow complete equality of nonconformists at Oxford and Cambridge. Even the Civil Service Act, of which he approved, and which threw open all posts to competitive examination, exempted the Foreign Office, traditionally staffed by those from an aristocratic background.

Gladstone had serious reservations about the 1870 Education Act. It was not a subject that he studied with the meticulous preparation that he gave to some others and he still believed in the virtues of a traditional classical education. What most concerned him was the provision for religious teaching in the new system. He was anxious that **religious formularies** were included and had a dread of simple undenominational teaching. However, this is what he got with the Cowper-Temple clause (see Chapter 5, page 75).

He appears to have been lukewarm over the Ballot Act, taking the long-standing argument against change that an Englishman – and for Gladstone it could never be anybody other than a *man* – should not be ashamed of the way he voted. The amendment to the Municipal Voting Act in 1869 that gave female householders the franchise at local level was put forward by a backbench Liberal MP, Jacob Bright, brother of John, and was not government policy.

### What was Gladstone's relationship with the nonconformists?
Nonconformists were a vital element of the Liberal Party in the late

nineteenth century, though before 1868 only a few such as Edward Baines were actually in Parliament. High Church Anglican as he was, Gladstone may appear an odd hero for dissenters, but that is how he appeared to many of them. Circumstances in the 1860s brought them closer together. For their part, nonconformist leaders such as Samuel Morley concluded that voluntaryism in education would no longer cope with the demand and that state assistance was essential. The result was the uneasy compromise of the Education Act of 1870. Gladstone in his turn admired nonconformist religious zeal in promoting an actively Christian society, upright behaviour, thrifty outlook and an increasingly wider vision in international affairs. And they were pleased when, as Chancellor, he established post office savings accounts in 1861, insisted on abolishing the paper duty in the same year and introduced reductions in income tax. More directly, his conversion to the abolition of the payment of compulsory Church rates and his policy of the disestablishment of the Irish Church found unanimous approval from this group.

Ironically Gladstone could count on their support more in his early days as Prime Minister than he could on the Anglican property owners who viewed what they saw as his Radicalism with some suspicion. With their increasing prosperity and greater acceptance within society, nonconformists could see themselves taking advantage – for themselves or for their children – of the opportunities provided by the civil service, army and university reforms. But here the faddist element in the Liberal Party showed up most clearly. The National Education League was not happy with the compromises of the Education Act and the continued prominence of Anglican schools. The Liberation Society, approving of Irish Church disestablishment, now wished to push for English and Welsh disestablishment. The United Kingdom Alliance wanted temperance measures: the Licensing Act of 1872 was in part a reaction to its pressure and alienated many other Liberal supporters with its illiberal and restrictive air. Historians in the early twentieth century such as Sir Robert Ensor made much of Gladstone's comment at the end of his ministry that he had been 'borne down in a torrent of gin and beer'. While more recent researchers have proved this incorrect, the Bill was a sign of the fact that the ministry was starting to run out of steam as well as alcohol.

### Conclusion: how successful was Gladstone as Prime Minister in his first ministry?

How well did Gladstone hold the party together? After the death of Palmerston the Liberal coalition had fallen away, yet Gladstone had quickly managed to rebuild it with a different complexion. There was a complex mixture of forces at work within the party and it is too simple to see it as torn with division between Radicals wanting more and more reform and Whigs wanting none.

The ministry was certainly an efficient one. The appointment of Henry Thring as first parliamentary counsel to the Treasury helped to bring clarity to the organisation of government. Gladstone brought charisma to the leadership without courting the electorate as directly as in the days before he was Prime Minister. Evidence from his diaries suggests his cabinets were run efficiently with all ministers having a chance to express their opinions. Gladstone could handle some ministers well as is shown in the sympathetic handling of John Bright at the Board of Trade when he was far from well.

However, Gladstone did find the Lords difficult on occasion, as over the amendment to the Irish Land Act (see Chapter 5) and their resistance to the abolition of purchase of commissions in the army. Moreover, it was clear by 1873 that the ministry was collapsing when it was defeated in the Commons on the Irish Universities Bill. Gladstone had devoted great attention to the drafting of it and displayed his usual impressive, statistically backed knowledge of a subject on which he felt strongly. But he failed to pass on his commitment to most other Liberals. From then on the ministry's days were numbered. Though Disraeli refused to take office after Gladstone resigned and the ministry staggered on, it was clear it would not last, as by-election defeats showed. If Gladstone thought that his promise to abolish the income tax if re-elected would win him the election of February 1874, he was to be sadly disappointed. The Liberals suffered their heaviest defeat since 1841. Perhaps they had been too successful and upset too many interests.

## DISRAELI AS PRIME MINISTER 1874–80

### Historians' views

Disraeli's performance as Prime Minister has provoked less controversy than Gladstone's. There is general agreement that Disraeli was an opportunist; as John Vincent (1990) has remarked, the main dispute is whether this was wholly or just partly so. Paul Smith, *Disraelian Conservatism and Social Reform* (1967), has shown that Disraeli took little part in the detail of the drive for social reform and Richard Millman's study of the Eastern Crisis of the late 1870s suggests that beyond wanting to assert British presence abroad – in a way that (he complained) Gladstone had not done – Disraeli had a flexible policy.

There has been more recent emphasis by John Vincent and Paul Smith, *Disraeli* (1996), on Disraeli as a coherent thinker than as a consistent politician and Smith sees his Jewishness as more significant than did Blake (1966). In 1878 there were some such as Lord Carnarvon – who, with the Foreign Secretary Derby (son of the former Prime Minister), resigned in protest against Disraeli's anti-Russian policy – who saw his preference for the Muslim Turk over the Christian Russian as a product of his non-Christian origins. It helps to explain the suspicion with which Disraeli was regarded, even when Prime Minister, by many High Church Conservatives who had a considerable regard for the Russian Orthodox Church. Blake (1966) argues that 'he instinctively lacked sympathy with small nations struggling to be free'. He also feels that Disraeli's early thinking was not related to his performance as Prime Minister and that the one consistent principle he carried over into the days of his premiership was the maintenance of the aristocratic settlement. It could be argued, however, that while accepting the earlier researches of Paul Smith, showing clearly that Disraeli was not involved in the detail of social reform, the general social concern expressed in his novel *Sybil* in the 1840s does surface in his ministry's reforms especially in the year of greatest legislative activity, 1875.

### Background

Disraeli did not take office in the same circumstances that Gladstone did in 1868. In that year a Liberal government had been expected for some time and its policy direction was clear. Gladstone had emerged as a recent strong leader at the peak of his powers in his late fifties. By contrast, Disraeli, in his seventieth year, bemoaned that real power had come too late. There was no clear sense of direction for the ministry, many of whom were surprised that the Conservatives had won the election so comfortably.

### How far was Disraeli in control of affairs as Prime Minister?

The result of this uncertainty was that much of 1874 was taken up with the Public Worship Bill pushed for by Queen Victoria and the Archbishop of Canterbury rather than the Prime Minister. Disraeli had his interests, particularly in foreign policy, but his indifferent health and his temperamental aversion to detail (hardly a characteristic of Gladstone) meant he was not likely to take a day-to-day interest in the running of affairs. Economic affairs were viewed with the eye of the ex-Chancellor that he was, but the detail was left to the current holder of the office, Sir Stafford Northcote.

His appointments to the cabinet showed some originality. Richard Cross as Home Secretary proved an outstanding appointment and it was partly a gesture of thanks to Lancashire for its support in the election. Disraeli used the power of his office to back Cross's social legislation proposals through the cabinet, particularly the Trade Union Act, which few other cabinet ministers were keen on. Disraeli, however, was listening to his backbenchers, who argued that such a measure was necessary to win the goodwill of the newly enfranchised working people. However, whether it could be concluded that the desire for working-class support was a dominant feature of Disraeli's policy can be questioned. He was already becoming conscious of the fact that the growing area of support for the party was the suburban middle class.

Moreover, Disraeli's support for Cross did not extend to influencing the detail of reform. Disraeli apparently fell asleep in cabinet when its more intricate clauses were being discussed. The conclusions of Paul Smith and Robert Blake have not been challenged: Disraeli let others make the running in social reform. His association with it stems from his earlier writings and references to it in his speeches of 1872 (see Chapter 6). Still, in retrospect, the years 1875 especially and also 1876 could be seen as his most successful and active. Then the ministry ran out of ideas in domestic affairs and ran into trouble in foreign policy.

Vincent argues that Disraeli was 'boxed in' when he became Prime Minister. Free trade and the general course of economic policy had been established for years and confirmed by Gladstone. Abroad, Britain's power was naval and commercial, not military; a 'forward policy' could court disaster. He could not match the campaigning style of Gladstone shown to greatest effect over the foreign policy in both 1876 and again in 1879 (see Section 3). In the end, however, by waiting until Russia had threatened the very heart of Turkey he recaptured the initiative for the government. Moreover, his opportunism had been used to good effect in 1875 when he saw the chance to buy Suez Canal shares for Britain: decisive action was immediately taken. He also handled the relationship with the Queen far more effectively than Gladstone, and the Royal Titles Act was a useful piece of imperial window-dressing. But Disraeli's health was always problematic in these years. He was ill soon after becoming Prime Minister and in 1876 he accepted the offer of an earldom – to become Lord Beaconsfield.

### 1879: Why was this a difficult year for Disraeli and his government?

As with Gladstone in 1873–4, the last year of Disraeli's ministry, 1879–80, was fraught with difficulties. An economic downturn resulted in pressure on Disraeli to return to protection – which he knew was impossible; the Conservatives lost a number of by-elections, which were becoming an increasingly important political barometer in the post-1867 political age, and the ministry faced problems abroad in both Afghanistan and southern Africa. Economic distress in Ireland had particularly serious consequences. After four quiet years under the firm control of Irish Secretary Hicks Beach, Land League activists were making a serious challenge to the authority of the government. Other than setting his face clearly against Home Rule – for Disraeli disliked aggressive nationalism – the Prime Minister had little to offer in the way of policy. His health deteriorated further and he dreaded the onset of winter. The unexpected victory for the Conservatives in a by-election in February 1880 at Southwark persuaded Disraeli to go to the polls at the end of March. But another Conservative victory was not to be. Gladstone was returned with a majority of 115 over the Conservatives.

## WHY WAS GLADSTONE LESS SUCCESSFUL AS PRIME MINISTER IN HIS SECOND MINISTRY 1880–5?

**Ireland and imperialism.** Gladstone and the Liberals inherited a daunting political situation in 1880. Both Ireland (see Section 5) and foreign entanglements (see Section 3) were to prove draining and difficult. His 'mission to pacify Ireland' had clearly not been achieved and now loomed increasingly large in his priorities. Matters imperial were to prove an equal strain, culminating in the embarrassing disaster of the death of General Gordon. In particular, Gladstone found himself under attack on *moral* grounds for the deal done with Parnell in the Kilmainham Treaty in 1882, the bombardment of Alexandria in Egypt in the same year and the scandalous delay in sending out the relief party for Gordon in 1885.

**Relations with Joseph Chamberlain.** At home Gladstone's problems came as much from his own side as from the opposition where Lord Randolph Churchill and his 'fourth party' (maverick Conservatives) were attacking the Conservative leadership as much as the Liberal administration. As to his own side, Gladstone's relationship with Radical leader Joseph Chamberlain was an uneasy one on both sides. Chamberlain complained there were insufficient Radicals in the government and it is true that Gladstone was inclined to appoint aristocratic Whigs if he could. Chamberlain also felt Gladstone was dragging his heels over social reform in areas such as housing. In 1883 he produced the Unauthorised Programme (see page 86). Among his suggestions were proposals for an increase in taxation generally and land tax in particular, free elementary education, and more provision to enable local authorities to introduce a wider range of social reform. For his part Gladstone disliked the aggressive speeches of Chamberlain outside Parliament, such as the one attacking Lord Salisbury as a member of an aristocratic class 'who toil not neither do they spin'. Chamberlain equally resented being told off by Gladstone for the self-same speech. Gladstone failed to handle Chamberlain well with disastrous consequences to come in the split over Home Rule in 1886.

**The Bradlaugh case.** The republicanism and atheism of some of Chamberlain's more radical colleagues must have been hard for Gladstone to accept. Yet he managed to extend his religious liberalism beyond the nonconformists, with aspects of whose beliefs he could readily identify. Another nonconformist grievance was largely removed with the Burials Act of 1880 allowing nonconformists to be buried in Anglican churchyards. But a greater challenge to Gladstone was the Bradlaugh case.

Charles Bradlaugh, an avowed atheist, had been elected MP for Northampton in 1880. After initially refusing to take the parliamentary oath (swearing by Almighty God) he then agreed to do so, but the House of Commons voted against him being allowed to take it. Despite his obvious distaste for Bradlaugh, Gladstone did his best to get the House of Commons to agree to allow Bradlaugh to take his seat and even introduced a bill to allow affirmation rather than swearing of the oath; but it was narrowly defeated. In a speech that still reads well today Gladstone argued that the persecution of Bradlaugh was in fact bringing him unmerited sympathy and that 'tepid deism' was a much greater threat than outright unbelief. It was a classic statement of Liberal values. A bill similar to the one Gladstone proposed was eventually passed in 1888.

**Political reform.** On the question of political reform, Gladstone accepted the necessity of the Corrupt Practices Act of 1883 to make the aims of the Ballot Act of 1872 a reality (see Chapter 4). But his commitment was not personal and, somewhat rarely where one of his major bills was concerned, he left the drafting of it entirely to others. He did, however, negotiate personally with Salisbury a good deal over the Lords' reluctance to pass the third Reform Bill in the following year. The 'compromise' – which was for the Lords to pass the bill as long as there was a separate re-distribution bill the following year – was seen, after the event, as politically damaging to the Liberals, because the single-member seats created tended to favour the Conservatives more.

Nonetheless, Gladstone's achievement in getting the two measures through Parliament with far less difficulty than the first and second Reform Bills was considerable. Gladstone was personally opposed to votes for women but some of his legislation would indirectly create the climate where this would become politically possible. These measures included the cleaning-up of elections as a result of the Corrupt Practices Act and the passing of legislation giving women greater property rights, such as the Married Women's Property Act of 1882.

**The old gentleman and the old lady.** Old age was also beginning to catch up with Gladstone in certain ways. Though he remained for many more years a person of formidable energy and determination, his eyesight had weakened and his social unease with those who did not share his background and values was even more noticeable. He found it harder and harder to get on with Queen Victoria, and the feeling was mutual. On one occasion he used his poor eyesight as an excuse: he had not read some of his colleagues' speeches that the Queen had complained about on the question of the third Reform Bill. She also professed to be 'utterly disgusted with his "stump" oratory'. His other excuse for not reading the speeches had been lack of time. Busy enough as he was in 1884 he had been even more so before. Unwisely he insisted on being his own Chancellor of the Exchequer again for the first two years of the new ministry until giving it up to H.C.E. Childers who could well have had the position in 1880 if Gladstone had not been so certain that none of his colleagues could do the job as well as he could. But it was not his over-work that persuaded Victoria to consult Foreign Secretary Granville rather than Gladstone when she could: it was a mutual incompatibility.

## CONCLUSION

- Gladstone, in his first ministry of 1868–74, managed to hold together a very wide Liberal coalition, though not without tensions nor without his disapproval of some of the measures passed.
- His ministry weakened dramatically in 1873.
- His second ministry of 1880–5 was not without its achievements but ran into greater problems both political and personal.
- Disraeli did not play an active role in the domestic legislation of his second ministry but he did handle the monarchy well and achieved some personal success in foreign policy.
- As with Gladstone's first ministry, the last twelve months of office proved a great strain for Disraeli and were followed by a sound defeat.

# SECTION 3

## Gladstone and Disraeli. What were the main differences in their approach to foreign policy?

### INTRODUCTION: GENERAL APPROACHES TO FOREIGN POLICY

- As with their political careers overall, there were times in their younger days when Gladstone and Disraeli could be seen on the same side in foreign-policy debates in the House of Commons.
- Later, however, with altered conditions abroad and Palmerston dead, foreign-policy occasioned frequent divisions of opinion between the two men.
- Disraeli acquired a reputation for a more interventionist foreign policy than Gladstone and one that emphasised the imperial dimension.
- Gladstone, however, was not an isolationist and firmly believed in the principle of the Concert of Europe for settling diplomatic disputes peaceably.

### Historians' views

Early biographers of the two men such as Moneypenny and Buckle, *Disraeli* (1910–20, six volumes), and John Morley, *Gladstone* (1903, three volumes), tended to defend the approaches of their subject while unearthing sufficient material (on all issues not just foreign policy) for later historians to come to more impartial judgements. In the *Oxford History* volume written in 1936 the Liberal historian Ensor argued that Gladstone understood better than Disraeli the powerful force of nationalism that was shaping events in so many places, but especially in the Balkan region of the declining Turkish Empire. Kenneth Bourne, *The Foreign Policy of Victorian England* (1970), however, regarded Gladstone's Concert of Europe idea as merely 'pious hopes' and believed it was Disraeli who recognised better the nature of the new post-Palmerston, Bismarck-dominated Europe. 'Gladstone's Concert was quite incompatible with Bismarck's policy of ensuring German security by maintaining controlled tension among all the powers.' What was needed, Bourne argued, was a more assertive policy based on the imperial idea. Blake, in *Disraeli* (1966), argues, however, that when Disraeli took office in 1874 'it is doubtful whether he had any clear ideas on foreign policy other than doing something ... to reassert Britain's power in Europe'.

More recent work has played down the differences between the two men on foreign policy. Colin Matthew's *Gladstone 1809–1874* (1986) sees Gladstone as some way removed from the isolationist Cobden school of foreign policy. Whereas Radicals saw diplomacy as 'corrupt dealing between landed castes', Gladstone felt only good could come from close connections between different nations. Matthew quotes Gladstone himself that England's 'hand will not be unready to be lifted up, on every fit and hopeful occasion, in sustaining the general sense of Europe against a disturber of the public peace'.

Smith, in *Disraeli: A Brief Life* (1996), argues that Disraeli was fundamentally cautious when it came to dealing with major powers, appreciating the fact that Britain's power was essentially commercial rather than military. He defends Disraeli from Shannon's criticism in *The Age of Disraeli 1868–81* (1992) that he only waited on events because he did not know what to do. Smith argues that Disraeli's major difficulty was in keeping his cabinet on the same road, as when Derby and Carnarvon resigned over the Eastern Crisis in 1878. Roy Jenkins (1995) points out that there was also a split in the Liberals, with Hartington and Granville less than enthusiastic about Gladstone's dramatic campaigns of the 1870s. Many of the Liberal and Conservative leaders were 'clustered on some fairly moderate ground in the middle'.

## WHAT WAS THEIR ATTITUDE TO FOREIGN POLICY IN THE 1850s?

**The Don Pacifico debate.** The contrast between the two men in foreign policy was not particularly apparent at first. In 1850 Gladstone and Disraeli spoke in the Don Pacifico debate (see Chapter 7, page 113). Gladstone's speech was regarded as by far the stronger and more critical of the two. Analysing why highlights a difficulty frequently encountered when examining Disraeli's policies. Was his reluctance to criticise Palmerston based on a sneaking regard for his aggressive assertion of British interests, or was it motivated more by political calculation? In 1850 Disraeli did not regard the time as ripe to vote down the Russell government since the Conservatives were still not clear on whether to try to restore protectionist policies. By contrast, in 1858, Disraeli was at first inclined to support Palmerston's Conspiracy to Murder Bill but soon changed his mind when he realised it was unpopular in the House of Commons and the government *could* be brought down. This time, the Conservatives were seen as ready for office and duly took it when Palmerston was defeated.

**Crimean War.** During the Crimean War Disraeli said little. He defended the principle of the war but not some of the tactics and he and Gladstone – as a member of the government – were, unsurprisingly, on opposite sides when it came to a vote on whether Roebuck's demand for a committee of inquiry into the conduct of the war should be held. Disraeli voted with the majority and the Aberdeen government resigned. Ironically this might have brought Gladstone and Disraeli into the same government had Derby managed to form one at that stage. By the time he did three years later, Gladstone was on the verge of committing himself to the Liberals, partly because he saw eye to eye with them on the main foreign-policy question of the moment: Italy.

**Italy.** Gladstone's extreme distaste for the government of Naples (see Section 1, page 157) made him a supporter of a liberal unification of Italy and helped to clear the way to join Palmerston's government in 1859. On this occasion Disraeli was torn between principle and **expediency**. He shared Conservative suspicions about French intentions but not Liberal regard for liberal nationalist movements in Europe. Nonetheless, when he saw how public opinion was moving in the Italian direction – the start of that feeling which made Garibaldi a fêted hero a few years later when he visited Britain – he urged Derby at least to refrain from positively supporting Austria. In the event Derby's government fell and a pro-Italian Liberal Party returned to power with Gladstone as Chancellor.

**KEY TERM**

**Expediency** To act expediently is to act on the basis of convenience or necessity rather than belief or principle.

## WHAT WAS THEIR ATTITUDE TO INTERVENTION IN FOREIGN AFFAIRS?

**The American Civil War.** Disraeli's inclination towards non-intervention – a trait more popularly, though not always accurately, associated with Gladstone – was also apparent on other issues such as the American Civil War. He may have shared Gladstone's views privately about the desirability of a separate southern nation, but he said nothing. Gladstone, by contrast, was indiscreet. As early as October 1862 in a speech in Newcastle he argued that, although there might be a debate about the rights and wrongs of slavery, the South had 'made a nation'. This not only got the military situation wrong: it gave a misleading impression of the British government's attitude to the question. Might it intervene to help the South? Palmerston was forced to disown the remarks of his Chancellor.

**Schleswig-Holstein question.** There were only a limited number of opportunities to criticise the government on foreign-policy questions, since the early 1860s represented a time of broad Conservative support for the Liberal Palmerston and – as he neared 80 years old – a sense of waiting for his political end. The main attack was on Palmerston and Russell's meddling in the Schleswig-Holstein question (see Chapter 7, page 117) where the government's threat to intervene was seen as unrealistic. Disraeli, conscious of royal sympathy for Denmark, complained that Palmerston had betrayed the Danes by promising they would not fight alone and then doing nothing to help them.

**Changed European circumstances.** Within a few years of Palmerston's death came the new order of affairs in Europe with German and Italian unification, leading to a powerful Germany and a weakened France. There was also a renewed interest in European affairs by a reformed and strengthened Russia. The growth of nationalism (pan-Slavism) in the Balkan area of south-east Europe came to a head in the 1870s and raised the issue of a possible Russian-supported pan-Slav bid for independence from the Turkish Empire. This meant that Gladstone faced a very different European climate from his predecessors. Later he was to find himself sucked into the mentality that required the protection of British imperial interests abroad, but for the present at least his principles remained unchanged.

**Neutrality in the Franco-Prussian War.** Neutrality was the only realistic policy in the Franco-Prussian War of 1870, given the geographical circumstances, the divided state of British public opinion, Gladstone's distrust of both the Prussian Prime Minister Bismarck and the French Emperor Napoleon III, and the agreement by the Prussians to respect the neutrality of Belgium in the conflict.

Yet Gladstone was not as completely non-interventionist as some of his colleagues. His belief in the Concert of Europe became apparent when he tried to persuade his cabinet to oppose Prussia's forcible taking of the French provinces of Alsace and Lorraine at the end of the short war. Gladstone proposed a stand of neutral countries in Europe against annexation. He failed to persuade his fellow ministers to agree. He did manage to convene a conference in London on a related issue in 1871. The Russian denunciation of the Black Sea neutralisation clauses of the 1856 Treaty of Paris was the kind of unilateral announcement (one of independent action) that Gladstone so disliked. The conference did not reverse the Russian move but the principle that in future such actions should be subject to international ratification was accepted. Gladstone also applied this principle to the long-running debate on whether the USA should receive any compensation for the damage done by the British-built ship the *Alabama* in the Civil War in the early 1860s. Gladstone accepted both the principle of arbitration and the amount – 15 million dollars – despite public hostility at home.

**How did the changed circumstances affect Disraeli's approach to foreign policy?** With all the changes in both the European and international scene since the time of Palmerston, Disraeli's opportunism was again given a chance to come to the fore. He sensed the change of atmosphere early in 1872. Victories for the Conservatives in by-elections in middle-class urban seats amidst criticisms of Gladstone's 'concessions' to the Americans over the *Alabama* arbitration, combined with a renewal in the popularity of the monarchy after the Prince of Wales' recovery from illness, encouraged Disraeli to make his dramatic set piece **speeches** at

## KEY SPEECH

**Disraeli at Manchester 1872**
Related economic strength to new opportunities abroad: 'I express here my confident conviction that there never was a moment in our history when the power of England was so great and her resources so inexhaustible. And yet, gentlemen, it is not merely our fleets and armies, our powerful artillery, our accumulated capital and our unlimited credit on which I so much depend as upon that unbroken spirit of her people, which I believe was never prouder of the imperial country to which they belong.'

Manchester and the Crystal Palace which foretold the new direction in foreign policy – an *imperial* one. Disraeli sensed that it was not merely British economic strength but also public opinion that meant the time was right for a more active foreign policy.

**Suez Canal shares.** The dramatic purchase of the Suez Canal shares three years later and its popular public reception seemed to bear him out. This was very much a personal triumph for Disraeli since Palmerston had previously been wary of involvement in the canal's construction, seeing it as a French plot to disturb British trade and threaten India, and both Foreign Secretary Derby and Chancellor Northcote had their doubts about the policy. Disraeli acted quickly and decisively, arranging at speed the £4 million needed to buy the shares from the bankrupt Khedive (ruler) of Egypt. He used his connections to get the money advanced by his old friend Lionel de Rothschild: clearly, the idea of the British government effectively being the security for the loan satisfied Rothschild.

The incident brings out particularly clearly the difference between Gladstone and Disraeli at this stage. Gladstone criticised the deal as getting Britain potentially too involved in overseas affairs which might give rise to complications later. In contrast, Disraeli boasted to the Queen of a great triumph. Both had a point.

## WHY DID THE EASTERN CRISIS PROVE SUCH A DIVISIVE ISSUE?

But by far the greatest foreign-policy dispute between them was yet to come. The feared complications over Russian ambitions and Balkan nationalism had begun in 1875 with a nationalist revolt by the Bosnian Serbs against Turkish rule. The Russians were anxious to support Slav nationalism, and, along with Austria and Prussia, tried to persuade the Turks to agree to reforms and more self-government for the Serbs. However, the revolt spread to Bulgaria in 1876 with more devastating consequences. Short of troops and money with which to put down the revolt the Turks allowed the irregular troops of the Bashi-Bazouks to suppress the uprising. This they did with great brutality.

**Gladstone's pamphlet.** The reaction to these Bulgarian atrocities, when some 12,000 Bulgarian Christians were massacred, engulfed not just Gladstone and Disraeli but much of the nation. To Gladstone this was not a question of becoming involved with affairs that were none of Britain's business. Ever since the Crimean War Gladstone felt Britain was responsible for the fate of Christians in this area, even if the powers of Europe had failed to guarantee their protection in the way that the Treaty of Paris that had concluded the war had intended. His outrage and desire to intervene could, he asserted, be justified. Yet here, it was Gladstone who was not without his opportunism. He did little for two months. It was only when protest meetings occurred in August that Gladstone felt something of a crusade could be launched. He then produced his pamphlet *The Bulgarian Horrors and the Question of the East* early in September 1876. It sold 40,000 copies in the first few days and 400,000 by the end of the month. It touched a chord in the British public, shocked at the revelations of massacres on a scale which the nineteenth century was not used to. It embarrassed Disraeli, since his dismissal of the early reports of the massacre was seen as ill-founded. But, in addition, what Gladstone had done was to divide public opinion on the question down the middle. This made the launch of any active policy very difficult for Disraeli.

**A country divided.** The division of opinion was profound. Much, though not all, of the press backed Disraeli, who also had support from the powerful forces of the monarchy and the majority of high society and city finance. But both Anglican – especially High Anglican sympathisers with the orthodox Bulgarians – and nonconformist clergymen were prominent in their support for Gladstone. He also had on his side much of the academic world, especially the new breed of university historians.

There is no doubt that the dislike that Gladstone and Disraeli had felt for one another for some time was now turning to loathing. Disraeli accused Gladstone of using the agitation to further his own political ends and suggested privately he was 'an unprincipled maniac', and publicly 'of all Bulgarian horrors the greatest'. This tasteless remark must have upset Gladstone, although his reaction to insults from Disraeli was publicly muted. His respect for Disraeli at this time was so low that he correspondingly despised any criticisms his opponent might make of him. There was nothing, said Gladstone, 'serious or sincere in any of his utterances, however vehement'. His greatest anger was reserved for the suspicion that Disraeli was manipulating the views of Queen Victoria. Gladstone also disliked the fact that the £6 million Treasury surplus that his government had left to Disraeli's was being turned into an even larger deficit – £8 million by 1880.

Although Gladstone's campaign had great support the country was divided over the affair. Anti-Russian feeling from the days of the Crimean War back in the 1850s had died hard, and Gladstone was even accused of being a Russian agent. Russia declared war on Turkey in April 1877 and excitement in England reached fever pitch. In May, Gladstone, against all advice, moved five resolutions in the House of Commons arguing that Turkey had forfeited all right to support from the British government. After pleading from Hartington, Gladstone only actually moved the first two resolutions, but still found them comfortably defeated. The tide of excitement had turned.

**Jingoism.** When the Russians attacked Turkey and eventually overpowered stiff Turkish resistance at the fortress of Plevna, the whole existence of the Turkish Empire seemed threatened. Even Gladstone had only suggested that the Turks leave the area of Bosnia. Public opinion now began to swing back to the idea that Britain should attempt to stop the Russians. Many supported Disraeli's decision to move a British fleet into the eastern Mediterranean in January 1878, although Derby, his Foreign Secretary, was not among them and subsequently resigned. The music hall song went:

> *We don't want to fight but by Jingo if we do,*
> *We've got the men, we've got the ships, we've got the money too.*

This first example of jingoism – or aggressive nationalism – seemed to confirm Disraeli's feelings about the way public opinion among both middle- and working-class Englishmen (and it was mainly English and mainly men) was going. In February and March 1878 jingoism reached its peak. The windows of Gladstone's house in London were broken by stones thrown by a mob, and on another occasion he and his wife had to be protected by four mounted policemen from assault. His second pamphlet, *Lessons in Massacre*, published in March 1878, sold only 7000 copies, 393,000 fewer than his previous one.

**The Congress of Berlin 1878.** Fortunately for Disraeli, the Russians had overreached themselves in the Treaty of San Stefano, early in March 1878, by creating a large puppet state of Bulgaria. This offended Austria – who had wrongly assumed that the Russians, if given a free hand, would let the Austrians fulfil their desire to annex Bosnia. This enabled the Prussian leader Bismarck to call a Congress of European powers in Berlin in the summer of 1878, giving Disraeli and his new Foreign Secretary Salisbury a chance to play a major role on the European stage. 'Big' Bulgaria was dismantled and Britain obtained the island of Cyprus; 'peace with honour' in Disraeli's description. Gladstone, though relieved at the outcome of events which apparently seemed to demonstrate the Concert of Europe in action, publicly criticised the treaty and referred to the acquisition of Cyprus as 'an act of duplicity not surpassed and rarely equalled in the history of nations'.

## WHY DID DISRAELI'S FOREIGN POLICY RUN INTO DIFFICULTIES IN 1879–80?

Yet just as the pendulum of public opinion had swung against Gladstone in 1877–8 so it was to return in his favour in 1879. During the Midlothian campaign (see Chapter 4, page 65) Gladstone regained the political initiative from Disraeli and foreign-policy issues loomed large in his assault. Disraeli's wasteful policy pursuing what Gladstone called 'false phantoms of glory' brought an attack on the Conservative administration's policies in Egypt, Cyprus, the Transvaal, Zululand and Afghanistan. The acquisition of the Suez Canal shares and the desperate financial plight of the Khedive had led to a virtual control of Egypt by Britain and France through their domination of international boards which effectively ran the country. Disraeli would have seen his policies in both Egypt and Cyprus as successful. Where Gladstone really struck home, however, was in attacking the troubles that befell Disraeli towards the end of his ministry on the borders of Britain's Indian and southern African possessions.

**Afghanistan.** Was it true that Disraeli's problems in these two areas stemmed from the men on the spot being too 'forward' in their policy, thereby bringing the British government into a difficult position? Afghanistan was regarded as a **buffer state** against Russian designs upon India. Lord Lytton, the Viceroy of India, complained to the Amir (ruler) of Afghanistan that a Russian mission (diplomatic group) had been accepted in his country and a British one refused. Ignoring orders of caution from London he ordered British troops from India to march on Kabul, the Afghan capital. The move was successful at first as the Amir fled, Britain effectively controlled his son and the Russians remained inactive. However, in September 1879, civil war broke out, British officials were murdered and there was a major crisis which became known in Britain just before Gladstone tramped the Scottish roads on the Midlothian campaign. He made full use of it, pointing out that 'the sanctity of life in the hill villages of Afghanistan … is as inviolable [untouchable] in the eyes of Almighty God as can be your own'.

While Lytton had certainly exceeded instructions, Disraeli's own 'forward' policy must take its share of the responsibility for what occurred. Disraeli had appointed Lytton in the first place in 1875 and told him to persuade the Amir to accept a British mission in return for money and assistance against aggression. It is hardly surprising that he refused this obvious attempt to control him, becoming wary when Lytton pressed the terms on him a second and third time.

In Gladstone's second ministry that followed in 1880 Afghanistan reverted to being a buffer state, but tensions were never far from the surface and one of Disraeli's involvements that Gladstone inherited caused a scare at the end of March 1885. A Russian force attacked and defeated an Afghan one in the disputed border town of Penjdeh. Gladstone and Foreign Secretary Granville threatened retaliation, but negotiated a settlement whereby the Russians acquired Penjdeh but not the important Zufilkar pass which would take them into the heart of the country.

**KEY TERM**

**Buffer state** A country – usually modest in size, power or population – whose existence physically separates two major powers or their possessions.

KEY TERM

## KEY TERM

**Beaconsfieldism**
Became a critical term used by Gladstone's supporters to describe what they saw as the meddling, expensive and unsuccessful foreign policy pursued by the Conservative government from about the time Disraeli was ennobled as the Earl of Beaconsfield in 1876.

**The Zulus and the Boers.** There was a similar problem with another 'man on the spot'. Sir Bartle Frere, again appointed by Disraeli, as Governor-General of Cape Colony in South Africa in 1877, behaved in a manner reminiscent of Lytton's, when he sent an ultimatum to a ruler he had no right to treat in such a way. This was the Zulu chief Cetawayo, who was commanded to disband his army in December 1878. Although Frere was backed by the new Colonial Secretary Hicks Beach, Disraeli and Salisbury (who disapproved of Frere) failed to act decisively and by the beginning of 1879 the British had a Zulu war on their hands. The first news was not good. Before the end of January a British force of over 1000 men had been wiped out at Isandhlwana. Although there was a British victory in July at Ulundi there had by that time been much criticism of the government and what Gladstone termed **Beaconsfieldism**. Gladstone again expressed his anger at the treatment of the Zulus: thousands had been slaughtered for no reason other than, as Gladstone's biographer Philip Magnus quotes him as saying, 'their attempt to defend against your artillery with their naked bodies, their hearths and homes their wives and

**The crucial position of Afghanistan around 1880.**

families …. to call this policy Conservative is in my opinion pure mockery, and abuse of terms. Whatever it may be in its motive … it is in its essence, thoroughly subversive'.

## WHAT WERE THE INFLUENCES ON GLADSTONE'S FOREIGN POLICY AFTER 1880?

**South Africa.** These events created another problem for the Gladstonian inheritance in 1880. Gladstone's first government had not been inactive in South Africa: it had annexed the diamond region of the Orange Free State back in 1871. In opposition he had severely criticised Disraeli's policies in the area but Frere was not recalled immediately as many expected when the Liberals came to power in 1880 and Gladstone's regard for national self-determination did not apparently extend to the Boers in the Transvaal.

A year after Ulundi with the Zulu threat to them removed, the Boers declared the creation of a republic in the Transvaal, breaking away from British control. Gladstone sent a force to resist this move but the force was defeated by the Boers at Majuba Hill in February 1881. Now, Gladstone accepted the independence of the Transvaal in reality although still retaining the right to British 'suzerainty', a vague word that suggested ultimate control was still in British hands. He had in Ensor's words 'conceded to force what he had refused to reason'. Gladstone had not handled the situation well. A Convention in London in 1884 modified the terms but failed to repeat the word 'suzerainty', leading to difficulties later on that ultimately culminated in the Boer War of 1899–1902.

**Egypt.** The difficulties Gladstone inherited from Disraeli were not confined to the problems in South Africa and Afghanistan. In fact Gladstone's greatest problems could be said to have come from one of Disraeli's apparent successes: the acquisition of the Suez Canal shares. For from this a gradual British–French control over the area of Egypt became apparent. When a nationalist revolt under Arabi Pasha broke out in late 1881, Gladstone was in difficulty. His instinct was to support Egyptian independence from the ever-weakening Turkish Empire. But the anti-European element in the revolt and the French unwillingness to undertake a joint mission led to a British expedition to preserve the 'securities of Empire'. In practice he had adopted a policy at least as interventionist as Disraeli, if not more so. The bombardment of the Egyptian port of Alexandria followed, and met with general approval back in Britain: only John Bright's resignation from the cabinet was a reminder of the non-interventionist policies of the Manchester School. A further military victory inland at Tel-el Kebir by Sir Garnett Wolseley was also celebrated back in the mother country but it was a reminder of the magnitude of the controlling task now facing whoever was in command

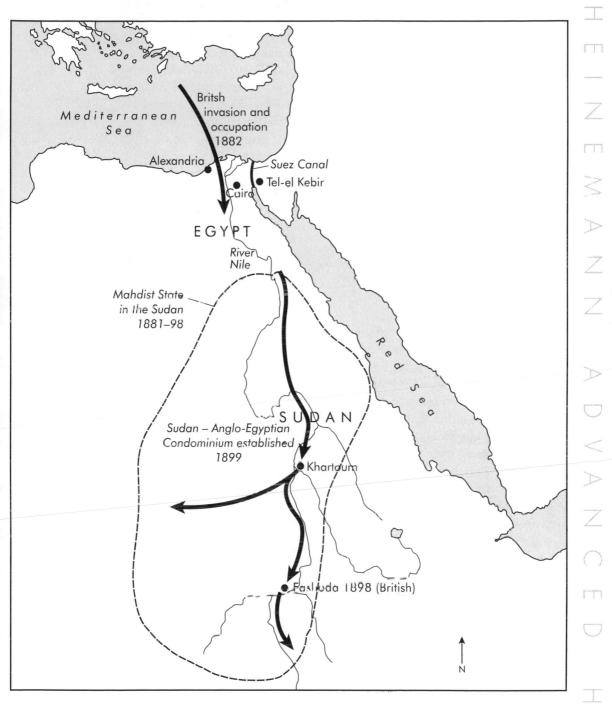

Labels within image:

_Mediterranean Sea_

Britsh invasion and occupation 1882

Alexandria

_Suez Canal_

Cairo

Tel-el Kebir

E G Y P T

_River Nile_

Mahdist State in the Sudan 1881–98

_Red Sea_

S U D A N

Sudan – Anglo-Egyptian Condominium established 1899

Khartoum

Fashoda 1898 (British)

N

**Egypt and the Sudan in the last quarter of the nineteenth century.**

of Her Majesty's Government.

Gladstone's concern for the Concert of Europe, however, had not disappeared. Britain attended a Conference in Berlin at the end of 1884 to establish the ground rules for what effectively became the partition of Africa among the major powers, even though Gladstone himself felt that involvement with Egypt and the Boers was quite enough. As far as Egypt was concerned, Britain was not to annex it in a straightforward manner into the British Empire. After long negotiations, a Board of Control was established in March 1885. Although all the major European powers were represented, the presence of the British army and the shrewd command exercised by the British Consul-General Sir Evelyn Baring meant that Britain was effectively in control. This also meant responsibility in time of crisis as with the nationalist revolt in the Sudan, south of Egypt, in 1885. It was the attempt to deal with this issue that led to the tragic isolation and death of General Gordon in Khartoum in January 1885. Gladstone's policy in Egypt had only been cheered while it was successful. Now the GOM – Grand Old Man – had become the MOG – murderer of Gordon.

## CONCLUSION

- Disraeli took opportunities to give Britain a decisive position in Europe through an active foreign policy, but was careful in his dealings with the major powers.
- Gladstone also believed Britain had a role to play in European affairs, but saw the role as one which would work in concert with the other major powers rather than looking solely to British interests.
- Gladstone's spectacular intervention in foreign affairs in 1876 over Bulgaria raised the political temperature between the two men.
- Disraeli pursued the imperial foreign policy he began to outline in his speeches in 1872, though not always with success, especially at the end of his second ministry.
- Gladstone inherited Disraeli's 'forward' policy and found himself going still further down the same road.
- Disraeli realised the electoral appeal of a patriotic and imperial foreign policy.

The circumstances in which the two men and their Foreign Secretaries conducted foreign policy had changed enormously from the days of Palmerston. Disraeli's policy had an element of opportunism as it always did, but Gladstone's belief in a Concert of Europe was a consistent one. Whether this was still appropriate by the 1880s was questionable. As Colin Matthew in *Gladstone 1874–1898* (1995) points out, this idea was based on the theory that international free trade would spread and render conflict futile. But in the late 1870s countries like Germany were turning to protection. The great Gladstonian vision was in decline.

# SECTION 4

## Economic development. How important was free trade to Gladstone? How did Disraeli and the Conservatives adapt to free trade?

### INTRODUCTION

- Mid-Victorian political rivalries were played out against a backdrop of economic prosperity.
- Britain's economic development in the 1850s and 1860s was second to none and was seen to owe much to the financial efforts of Gladstone.
- The Conservatives came round to accepting free trade in the early 1850s and, with varying degrees of enthusiasm, largely held to this view for the rest of the century.
- After 1873 economic expansion slowed down a good deal but the Liberals maintained an almost religious belief in the sanctity of laissez-faire in general and free trade in particular.
- Disraeli held to the principle of free trade from around 1850 until his death over 30 years later.

### Views of historians

There is general agreement about the importance of British economic prosperity in the middle part of the century in providing the foundation for the optimistic political mood. The main disagreement has been over the degree of appropriateness for the phrase 'Great Depression' to describe the relative economic decline after 1873. Writers at the time were aware of a slow-down in growth and the term 'Great Depression' became an established phrase early in the twentieth century. However, the severity of the depression of the 1930s called the use of the term for the 1873–96 period into question. In an article written in 1934, H.L. Beales cast doubt on the validity of the term. But it is a title that has obstinately persisted.

As late as 1969 a standard text like R.K. Webb's *Modern England* (Unwin) would still have a chapter headed 'The Great Depression', though in the same year Derek Beales in *From Castlereagh to Gladstone* used the phrase but described it as 'thoroughly misleading'. S. Saul's title *The Myth of the Great Depression* of the same year, made clear his views about the phrase. Though there had certainly been a slowing-down in growth with a general fall in profits, Saul did not feel the word depression was suitable for an economy that still showed many signs of growth. It should, he argued, be consigned to the historical scrap heap. However, the significant point for the political historian is that contemporaries *perceived*

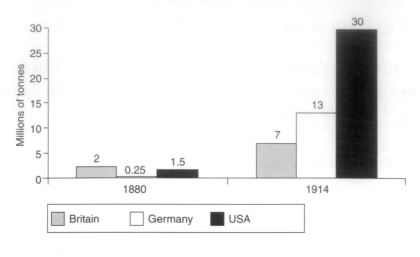

Fast but not fast enough: British steel production is overhauled by Germany and the USA between 1880 and 1914. (Source: Eric Hobsbaum *Industry and Empire* (Penguin revised edn, 1999), diagram 22.)

there was something of an economic crisis and responded accordingly. The psychological shock of strong foreign competition and a consequent slowing of growth made a considerable impression at the time.

Saul's call for abandonment of the term in historical circles has not altogether succeeded. Though writers such as Hobsbawm in *Industry and Empire* (1999) refer to it as 'misleading', Hobsbawm argues that if it suggests a 'state of mind of uneasiness and gloom about the prospects of the British economy, the word is accurate'.

## WHAT WAS MID-VICTORIAN PROSPERITY?

The 20 years from 1853 to 1873 were a time of great and rapid economic growth and also the period when Gladstone had considerable influence over the Exchequer. He was either Chancellor or Prime Minister for fifteen of those years, when favourable economic conditions inspired the coal, textile and iron and steel industries to achieve impressive rates of growth. The railway network spread all over the country, doubling its mileage between 1850 and 1868, British engineering led the world and there was an impressive expansion of overseas trade. Farming came out of the uncertain period immediately after the repeal of the Corn Laws to enjoy a 'golden age'. Britain was regarded as the 'workshop of the world', developing the most advanced industrial economy that existed.

Industrialists went through a particularly successful phase in this period. The earlier teething troubles of many manufacturers were over and increases in production were steady. The concentration – unlike in France – on the everyday rather than the luxury market paid off and exports

**KEY CONCEPT**

**Free trade favours the strong** Free trade favoured Britain as an advanced industrial country because it had many potential markets for its manufactured goods if there were no tariff barriers. In return, the country could import valuable materials and cheap foodstuffs from abroad. Countries with a less developed industrial base tended to prefer tariffs to 'protect' their infant industries.

blossomed. Coal, industrial machinery, ships and railway iron were all exported in increasing amounts encouraged by the free trade philosophy. **Free trade favoured the strong** and Britain *was* the strongest. In this period there was no fear of serious foreign competition in these fields where the country reigned supreme. The achievement in textiles was particularly impressive. It was said that in Manchester enough cotton goods were produced for the home market before breakfast time and the rest of the day was spent producing for export. Expansion of woollen production was also notable with exports doubling in the 1850s and 1860s. The speaking tours of politicians in the 1860s reflected areas of growth, such as Gladstone's visit and address to the ship workers at Newcastle upon Tyne in 1862 or Palmerston's in woollen-dominated Bradford in 1864.

**Was prosperity uninterrupted? The ups and downs of commercial life.**
Britain was not only the workshop of the world but also the world's banker and financier, moneylender and commerce dealer and trader. The growth of ports and shipping reflected this development. Tonnage of sailing ships increased dramatically until the mid-1860s and ran parallel with steamship production towards the late 1850s and early 1860s. In fact the policy of free trade may be said not only to have put agriculture behind industry, but industry itself second to overseas trade and commerce. The invisible exports of merchant shipping and investment services were important to the economy. In the 1860s the flow of capital, labour and goods was at its most unrestricted, yet the fluctuations in the economy were less noticeable than either before or since. The Crimean War caused a temporary setback in 1855 and there were brief recessions (as we would call them now) in 1857 – when English banking houses with American commitments suffered from a slow-down in trade – and in the winter of 1866–7 with the collapse of the finance house Overend and Gurney, which may have contributed to the degree of parliamentary reform in 1867 (see Chapter 4). None of these, however, proved serious or long-lasting. Local areas may have suffered from external factors, such as the Lancashire cotton workers during the Civil War in America 1861–5, or the silk weavers in Coventry. These workers were, untypically, hit by free trade itself. The free trade treaty with France in 1860 allowed French silks to come into the country without restriction immediately the treaty was ratified.

**What was the effect of mid-Victorian prosperity on agriculture?**
Agriculture shared in the prosperity. Improvements at home, combined with the lack of any initial effective competition from abroad, helped what many saw as the 'golden age' of British agriculture. The railways greatly aided the distribution of goods, and threshing machines and steam power also helped to increase production. The repeal of the Corn Laws forced

the producers to become more efficient or go under. Soil drainage and increasing knowledge of fertilisers also helped to prevent them from doing so, especially those in arable farming. The availability of loans to undertake drainage schemes also helped. Mixed husbandry assisted in adapting to the demands of the moment. Prosperity fed off prosperity as the greater wealth of the population as a whole led to increased demands for a wider range of foodstuffs.

**How did mid-Victorian prosperity benefit the Liberals?** Although the period 1846–68 was a time of relative *political* instability it was also a period of *national* stability. Two enduring popular fears were fading and a third was somewhat reduced: famine (except tragically in Ireland) and violent revolution no longer seemed likely, and the terrible diseases of the early nineteenth century, smallpox and typhoid fever for instance, were still killers, but on a declining scale.

Britain was being transformed from an agricultural and rural society into an industrialised and urban one. The prosperity of the period contributed to the Liberal political domination at this time. The values of this new society fitted in well with the Liberal approach to political issues – that of laissez-faire and an emphasis on state retrenchment. This was recognised in Parliament by the early 1850s by Peel's policies in the budgets of 1842 and 1845 as well as the Corn Law repeal of 1846 – but because of the Tory break-up in 1846 it fell to the Whig-Liberal grouping to put these views into practice. Significantly, however, they needed a Peelite in Gladstone to see the policy fulfilled.

## HOW DID GLADSTONE'S FREE TRADE POLICY CONTRIBUTE TO MID-VICTORIAN PROSPERITY?

**Gladstone's initial hostility to free trade.** When Gladstone fought the 1841 election at Newark he was not a free trader and regarded the free trade organisation, the Anti-Corn Law League, with disdain. Later, he admitted that his support of protection had not been based on his own analysis but on accepting the views of those he respected in other matters. In his move from Conservatism to Liberalism, his support of protectionism was the first of his views to change. This was because the government post in which he was placed by Peel – Vice-President of the Board of Trade – required him to make his own analysis of the issues. Moreover, the job required the practical application of principles and theories and up to this point in his life his ideas had been largely theoretical.

**Gladstone's change of mind.** When Peel's government undertook a major revision of the tariff, Gladstone, working incredibly hard, did much of the labour. He also spoke on the subject in the Commons, since the President of the Board of Trade, Viscount Ripon, was naturally in the Upper House – and not as energetic or as diligent as Gladstone. Given the Prime Minister's interest in the subject, Gladstone and Peel were brought closer together when discussing the relevant issues and Gladstone's whole Peelite philosophy developed at this time, much of which never left him. This philosophy did not embrace only economic policy, but also a concern for efficient and honest administration, a regard for the Concert of Europe principle in foreign policy and a statesmanlike attitude to the current questions of the day, rather than a narrow party political approach.

Gladstone gained the respect of Peel for his obvious control of the administrative detail of his job and his conscientious approach to the task in hand. Few other people could have gained such a mastery of the complexity of over 700 different tariff regulations; it would stand Gladstone in good stead when, as Chancellor of the Exchequer in the 1850s and 1860s, he came to reduce many of them. To Peel, these abilities overrode a certain personal awkwardness in Gladstone and some doubts as to whether he would be a sound 'team player'; the qualities Gladstone displayed outweighed these reservations. In 1843, with Ripon's retirement, Gladstone was promoted to the presidency of the Board of Trade and a seat in the cabinet. Tariff reductions on imports were already under way. Some 769 duties were cut down or abandoned in 1842, and in 1845 over half the remaining duties were abolished

The dispute over the Corn Laws in 1845–6 clearly highlighted Gladstone's commitment to free trade and in a very particular way. Having not long before resigned from the government over the Maynooth Grant question in January 1845, Gladstone was asked by Peel to return in the following December to take the place of the Colonial Secretary who had resigned. Thus, when many Conservatives were arguing that Peel had betrayed them with his decision to repeal the Corn Laws, Gladstone returned in Peel's hour of need.

**Free trade remains important.** Between 1846 and 1852 Gladstone remained out of office; it was a time when his views were uncertain and changeable on a number of questions. His religious opinions moved further towards abandoning the close links between Church and State that he had held with such passion in his youth. There was also his realisation of the powerful force of nationalism as demonstrated in the European revolutions of 1848, and the general development of his Liberal instincts with his visit to Naples in 1850. All this caused a good deal of soul searching in his diaries. But he remained faithful to the economic ideas on free trade which he had acquired before 1845.

His political reputation for financial competence was such that the Conservatives were anxious to see him back. However, when Lord John Russell's government temporarily resigned in 1851 and Lord Derby attempted briefly to form a ministry, Gladstone made it clear that he could not accept office if Derby reimposed even the smallest duty on corn. Since Gladstone had been offered any post he pleased except the post of Foreign Secretary and since he was anxious to hold office again after five years out of government, this was a principled refusal emphasising the importance of the free trade/protection issue.

## How important was Gladstone's first period as Chancellor?

Virtue was rewarded; before the end of the following year Gladstone had been appointed Chancellor in Aberdeen's Whig-Peelite coalition and proceeded to make a great impression. Gladstone felt that Peel's economic experiment in the early 1840s had worked. The argument had been that the increase in trade which resulted from tariff reduction would lead to greater prosperity, more than compensating for any loss of income from the tariffs. In the short run, however, governments needed to compensate for the immediate loss of revenue that tariff reduction entailed.

Gladstone did have the long-term aim of **abolishing income tax**, an aim which he still cherished as late as the mid-1870s, but he did not intend to do it immediately, for two reasons. Firstly, now that he was in his new post, he wished to pursue further tariff reductions – a development somewhat neglected by his immediate predecessors since 1846. Logically, therefore, the income tax should stay a little longer while free trade policies were extended. And, secondly, the tax had become extremely valuable in a very short space of time. As early as 1846 income tax was producing nearly 10 per cent of government revenue and tapping into the new-found industrial and commercial wealth more effectively than the more traditional forms of taxation. As more and more cracks appeared in the veneer of the laissez-faire doctrine and government expenditure rose, the tax gradually became indispensable.

Gladstone's budget of 1853 proved to be a masterly demonstration of the free trade principle. Abolishing duties on 123 partially manufactured goods and foodstuffs, he also halved duties on 133 more manufactured goods. But the Crimean War undid his carefully explained plan to make do without the income tax by about 1860 unless there was an emergency. In fact, in the summer of 1854 it was doubled from **7d to 1s 2d** in the pound because of the Crimean War. For Gladstone, the war

**KEY EVENT**

**The Cobden Treaty** In 1860 the Palmerston government asked Richard Cobden to travel to Paris – as a private citizen – and inquire into the possibility of a free trade treaty between Britain and France. He met the French Minister Chevalier and together they negotiated an agreement later incorporated by Gladstone into his budget of 1860. British duties were lowered on French silks and on wines and spirits. French duties were lowered on coal and many manufactured goods to a maximum of 30 per cent and later 24 per cent.

**KEY TERM**

**National debt** Money owed by the government to other countries or private investors. A substantial but not overwhelming debt was unofficially seen as a sign of strength at this time though Chancellors were generally anxious to reduce it.

was bad news politically as well as financially, since it led to the downfall of the Aberdeen government and a further period in the political wilderness for him. However, this was to change when he was able to swallow his reservations about joining a government led by Lord Palmerston in 1859.

## How important was Gladstone's second period as Chancellor?

Gladstone was able to spend seven continuous years as Chancellor between 1859 and 1866 and effectively complete the transformation of Britain into a free trade country. In his budget of 1860 he incorporated the free trade changes brought about by Richard **Cobden's Treaty** negotiated with France in that year.

**Gladstone and the paper duty.** The financial strength and stability produced by Gladstone's policies were used to his advantage in the dispute over the paper duties in 1861 (see page 161). Palmerston expressed his preference for an income tax cut rather than the abolition of the paper duty but Gladstone produced a budget that abolished the paper duty *and* cut income tax. It was the strength of the economy produced by his free trade policies that had enabled Gladstone to achieve this triumph, fulfilling both his financial aims and his growing Liberal instinct that the ordinary person, if well informed, had a real contribution to make to the political debates of the day.

**Retrenchment.** What some saw as Gladstone's great financial achievements were not universally appreciated. He was regarded as being very strict over government expenditure and certainly did not anticipate a major role for the state in questions of social reform. Nonetheless, retrenchment – the drawing-in of government expenditure – was seen as one of his qualities; a popular Liberal and Radical rallying cry was 'peace, retrenchment and reform'. The creation of the Public Accounts Committee in 1861 to oversee public expenditure was a good example of this. A balanced budget was seen as very important, with some attempt to pay off the **national debt** if at all possible. Gladstone had turned the post of Chancellor of the Exchequer into one of the most important in government, which it has remained ever since.

## How did Disraeli and the Conservatives adapt to free trade?

Free trade was clearly accepted by the Conservatives after the election of 1852, and so ceased to be a controversial issue for at least the next 40 years. But even before this, Disraeli's first budget as Chancellor in 1852 had not attempted to reimpose protection. The caution of Treasury officials and the alarm in the armed services caused by the recent proclamation of Louis Napoleon as Emperor rather than President of France gave Disraeli little room for manoeuvre. His only other measures

– some relief for the sugar and shipping interests – were minor changes. His budget was criticised by a combination of Whigs and Peelites and Disraeli tried to ridicule this alliance with his parting quip in the debate, 'England does not love coalitions.' But his technical changes to the income tax were exposed as unworkable by Gladstone in a brilliant speech given extra sparkle by his growing personal dislike of Disraeli. He showed up the technical inconsistencies in Disraeli's rescheduling of the income tax, but it was probably the description of the budget as 'subversive' and the unflattering comparisons of the Chancellor with Peel, that most upset Disraeli and began to make the bad feeling between the two men mutual.

**Disraeli: Chancellor again.** After his first unfortunate experience as Chancellor Disraeli became cautious on subsequent occasions. He delivered three more budgets – in 1858, 1859, and 1867 – but they were all very cautious and balanced the finances carefully. Perhaps he was determined to rival Gladstone's reputation for economy. He was not keen, for example, to allow the navy extra money at a time when it wished to transform the fleet by introducing ironclad steamships. Disraeli was conscious of the need for the Conservatives to take measures to widen the appeal of the party beyond the landed gentry, but lacked the opportunity, the expertise and the courage to take any bold steps: once again, as Chancellor, he was upstaged by Gladstone.

## How did Gladstone's free trade policies fare in his first ministry?
In his own first ministry from 1868 to 1874 Gladstone at first entrusted the chancellorship to Robert Lowe, a generous offer to a man who had split the Liberals over reform in 1866. But Gladstone had clearly established the framework of free trade and balanced budgets by 1866 and could rely on Lowe to follow a strict path of laissez-faire. In 1869 Lowe adopted a Gladstonian pose repealing the tea and other duties and yet still managing to cut income tax by a penny. Thereafter he ran into difficulties. The Franco-Prussian War in 1870–1 and the army reforms already planned by Cardwell, but now seen as urgent, spoilt plans for further reductions and the match tax of 1871 was unpopular. The tax hit ordinary working people far more than a rise in income tax from which many of them were exempt. The working classes had appreciated Gladstone's parsimony (extreme care with money) with the country's finances since it had been they who often suffered the most when indirect taxes on goods were imposed. When Lowe left the chancellorship in 1873, Gladstone could not resist taking on the role himself.

## What was the 'Great Depression'?
The relative decline in prosperity after 1873, known somewhat misleadingly as the Great Depression, and lasting until about 1896, did not bring about an immediate demand for the end of the free trade predominance. However, production methods no longer seemed so

innovative and the United States and the newly united Germany in particular were beginning to compete in the industrial areas Britain had always regarded as dominating throughout the world.

Agriculture particularly suffered: the extension of the benefits of free trade and industrialisation to other countries now began to take its toll on Great Britain. By the later 1870s, for instance, the American railways, once the country had recovered from its debilitating Civil War, made it possible to export cheap grain. As late as 1873 it still cost well over £3 to move a ton of grain from Chicago to Liverpool but by 1884 the cost had plummeted to little over £1. Fatal diseases may have claimed fewer premature deaths among humans but disease was no less virulent in animals; cattle plague in 1867 was followed by rinderpest in 1877, liver rot in 1879 and foot and mouth in 1883. This combination of foreign competition, animal disease and bad weather brought things to a head at the end of the 1870s.

## How did Disraeli react to calls for protection?

The indication of just how entrenched free trade had become in the mind of all political figures can be seen in 1879. The wet summers of the previous three years had produced disastrous harvests and a sharp decline in the price of corn. This declined from just under £3 a quarter (12.7 kg) in 1868 to little over £1 just ten years later. But Disraeli turned down the request of a farming deputation to reintroduce protection. He was aware of the problems in the rural community not least because his own tenants were threatening not to renew their contracts. Yet there was no realistic possibility at that stage of a return to protection. Ironically, 1879 was the year that Bismarck in Germany introduced protective tariffs and the general European support of free trade began to come to an end. It was a long time, however, before Britain considered retaliation and abandoned the precious policy of free trade.

Meanwhile Disraeli and his Chancellor Northcote had to deal with a budget deficit of well over £3 million for the financial year 1879–80. With an election impending there was nervousness about putting up taxation, especially as duties had been raised the year before. The attack by Gladstone on Beaconsfieldism included the charge of financial extravagance. Disraeli felt he had been unlucky that economic stability and colonial disasters had occurred at the same time. 'I have had to struggle against four bad harvests and four wars', he complained. Still, he remained a strong believer in low taxation and had, after all, made most of his social reforms 'permissive'. He believed that they should not result in much higher local taxes unless that was what the local electorate wanted.

### How did Gladstone react to changed economic circumstances?

But was the 'Great Depression' something that a Chancellor as distinguished as Gladstone could do anything about? His argument for holding this post as well as the premiership in his seventies was that it signalled a return to normal retrenchment after the excesses of Beaconsfieldism. The 'Great Depression'– though not a concept just of historians – went largely undiscussed in government. Matthew (1995) argues that this was because 'the mid-century view of government as parallel to and completely distinct from economic activity was, from a Liberal cabinet, now thoroughly entrenched and instinctive'. No action would be either appropriate or beneficial. In Gladstone's mind voluntary giving through charity and the operation of the Poor Law was the way to deal with cases of individual hardship.

The 1880s saw no improvement in the rate of growth in rural areas. The new technology of refrigeration on ships made possible importation of meat from as far afield as Australia and South America (Argentina). The main effect, however, of government inaction was on arable farming as prices remained low in response to competition. Arable farmers in the south and east were hardest hit as prices fell, leading to falls in wages as well as profits. By the time of Gladstone's final government in 1892 another slump was about to set in. Gladstone appointed a Royal Commission on Agriculture in 1893. By 1897 its report concluded that foreign competition was to blame for the problems but it did not think to suggest tariffs as a solution.

### What were the social and political effects of the slow-down in growth?

Industry was also affected, especially the iron and steel industry, as German and American competition became apparent, overtaking British production by 1895. But the greatest economic danger to the British seemed to be the fact that they were resting on their laurels won in the 1850s and 1860s. The satisfied middle classes lived off their investment income in suburbia and showed less interest than their forebears in the newly developing chemical industries, electricity supply and the development of the internal combustion engine. Their ambitions were filled by seeing their children go to prestigious public schools – where technical subjects were hardly in vogue – and their social climbing rejected the old strident nonconformity for a comfortable Anglicanism and a smart new property well away from the working-class areas around their workplaces. Increasingly they looked to a Conservative rather than a Liberal government to secure their interests with the greater safety. Salisbury's gain politically was the country's loss economically.

Yet it was the Conservatives who were more likely to challenge the status quo on free trade. A Royal Commission on the Depression of Trade and

Industry was set up in Salisbury's first ministry in 1885, but the chairmanship of Northcote guaranteed a free trade outcome to the deliberations. The word 'protection' would not darken the doors of an English discussion on how to deal with a depression, but the phrase 'fair trade' *had* begun to appear.

## How serious was the demand for 'fair trade'?

After the election of 1885 when the poorer rural householder possessed the vote for the first time, Salisbury had to scotch rumours that protection would make a come-back in the form of the reintroduction of the Corn Laws. From the time of his own entry into Parliament at a by-election in 1853 over 30 years before, this question had not been an issue. It was significant that he had to issue the denial. Moreover, though he did so clearly, Salisbury did not look upon free trade with the divine favour of Gladstone. He argued that 'retaliation' in the form of tariffs imposed in turn on those putting them on British exports might be appropriate in certain circumstances. But he opposed any general attack on free trade. Quite a number of parliamentary seats, such as North Devon, were thought to have been lost because voters feared a return to a 'dear loaf'.

The National Fair Trade League was founded in 1881 and in 1887 a National Union of Conservative Associations Conference at Oxford almost unanimously voted for a fair trade resolution. Salisbury thought the case for a retaliatory tariff on sugar was now justified, though he always played down the issue conscious of the need for party unity. The pressures for protection were so strong in 1891–2, after a heavy American tariff was imposed, that Salisbury promised retaliation in the 1892 election campaign. This definitely did not help him. As in every election between 1847 and 1931, parties advocating the undiluted continuation of free trade were successful. In vain in 1892 did Salisbury argue that he only favoured a very limited retaliatory tariff on luxury goods.

Never a dogmatist on the question, Salisbury just managed to hold to the Victorian consensus on free trade. With the electorate's opinion plain, and his dependence on an alliance with Unionists largely still strongly committed to free trade, there was little else he could do without courting disaster. But just after Salisbury's death in 1902 the Conservative Party split over whether to abandon free trade. The Victorian **consensus** on free trade was just that: Victorian. Within a couple of years of the Queen's death it had ended.

**KEY TERM**

**Consensus** Broad agreement on a line of policy.

- Free trade issues did not produce major differences between the parties in this period.
- Gladstone played a dominant role in the maintenance and expansion of free trade in the second half of the nineteenth century.
- Britain was no longer a confident economic world leader after about 1873.
- There was some demand for fair trade after 1880 but Salisbury handled the demands for this in the Conservative Party with sufficient skill to postpone a heated debate on the issue.

# Why did Ireland take up so much of Gladstone's time?

## INTRODUCTION

- Although Gladstone was aware of Ireland as a potential flashpoint as early as the 1840s he did not pay full attention to the issues raised there until he was about to become Prime Minister in 1868.
- He then saw it as his 'mission' to deal with 'the Irish question' in his first ministry of 1868–74.
- After some real achievements early in that ministry, Gladstone found it an increasingly difficult and demanding problem to deal with and one which helped to weaken his government.
- In his second ministry he was forced to a greater degree into a more coercive policy towards the country while still attempting a considerable degree of reform.
- When Gladstone was converted to the idea of Home Rule, the issue broke the Liberal Party. Yet Home Rule remained Gladstone's abiding but elusive aim until the end of his political career.

### Historians' views

Historians' views about Gladstone's Irish policy have undergone many changes. Morley's *Life of Gladstone* (1903) saw Gladstone's Irish policy as an heroic attempt to deal with the question. But Morley was closely involved himself, being Gladstone's Chief Secretary for Ireland in 1886 and 1892–4. Gladstone's efforts were also appreciated by other Liberal/Radical inter-war historians such as J.L. Hammond in *Gladstone and the Irish Nation* (1938) and Sir Robert Ensor in *England 1870–1914* (1936). The latter argued that Gladstone's coercion policy in the early 1880s was 'inevitable' given the circumstances but that it was 'not in his statecraft to pursue it alone': he always coupled it with a more constructive measure. By the 1950s, Magnus (1954) was a little more critical, pointing out that although Gladstone claimed to have known well before 1868 that action was needed on Ireland 'he had done little to prepare public opinion for it', a problem which remained. Nonetheless, he regarded Gladstone as having done as much as he could in the first Irish Land Act 'given the prevailing climate of current opinion'.

The most critical comments often came from Irish historians who doubted that Gladstone, for all his study of the subject, really understood either the intricacies of Irish land tenure or the psyche of the Irish people. F.S.L. Lyons' *Ireland Since the Famine* (1973 edition) argued that the 1881 Land Act was inadequate to deal with the challenge of the agricultural depression in Ireland at the time and quotes Barbara Solow, *The Land Question and the Irish Economy* (1971), as arguing that the Act was 'less ... an economic policy than ... a political stroke'. Gladstone was merely trying to deal with the *political* threat of the Irish nationalist party. Nonetheless, Lyons praises Gladstone for his 'fresh way of looking at Irish problems'. More recently there are the contrasting interpretations of Shannon, *Gladstone: Heroic Minister* (1998) and Matthew, *Gladstone 1874–1898* (1995). The former argues that the Land Act of 1881 made 'little difference', while Matthew, who regards the Act as a 'legislative triumph', sees the relative quietness of Ireland in 1883 and 1884 as in part a tribute to the law's effectiveness.

The most significant debate has been over the Home Rule crisis of 1885–6. Here Gladstone's motives and sincerity have been substantially challenged. Despite Richard Shannon's earlier work in 1963, *Gladstone and the Bulgarian Atrocities* (not only on the Bulgarian atrocities but ranging much more widely), Gladstone became the victim of the tendency among historians writing in the 1970s and early 1980s to see 'high politics' as being the principal driving force behind political motivation and action. Cooke and Vincent's *The Governing Passion* (1974), in a very detailed blow-by-blow account of the crisis, concluded that Gladstone's motivations had everything to do with English politics in general and Liberal unity in particular. This view was supported to some extent by historians such as Hamer, who, in *Liberal Politics in the Age of Gladstone and Rosebery* (1972), stressed the tendency of the Liberals to break up and argues that Gladstone needed a great issue like Home Rule to try to keep the party together. But there has been a revival of a less cynical analysis with books like Parry's *Democracy and Religion* (1986), arguing that the importance of religion has been underplayed by secular-minded twentieth-century historians. Gladstone by this analysis had a sincere desire to achieve justice for the Irish. Where he went wrong on Home Rule was in lack of consultation with his colleagues, believing that the Liberal Party would just follow on behind him.

In more recent times the arguments have continued. Jenkins (1995) dismisses the attack on Gladstone's motives: 'Whatever else characterises his handling of the Home Rule issue it was not the tactics of party manoeuvre'. Matthew (1995) argues from a study of Gladstone's diaries and other writings that Gladstone moved gradually to a position in favour of Home Rule and there was no 180-degree turn such as he made over Irish Church disestablishment. He points out that a serious throat condition made it difficult for Gladstone to do much speaking in the summer of 1885 when he might have revealed his hand. However, Shannon (1998), while not going as far as Cooke and Vincent and not discounting Gladstone's religious motivation, does see some element of high politics and struggle for the leadership mixed up with the crisis.

## WHAT WERE GLADSTONE'S VIEWS ON IRELAND BEFORE THE 1860s?

As with other issues in his political life, it was difficult to foresee Gladstone's later views and actions from his early voting record on Ireland in the Parliament of 1832–5, when opposition to any change in the financial position of the established Church was strongly supported by the earnest young Tory. In April 1835 Gladstone, in a junior post in the Colonial Ministry, vainly attempted to prevent the opposition's successful motion which brought down Peel's brief government. It was to use Irish Church revenues for non-religious purposes such as education. However, his views were soon to change.

One of Gladstone's rare references to Ireland in his years in Peel's government was in a letter to his wife in 1845, just before the Great Famine: 'Ireland, Ireland, that cloud in the west, that coming storm … Ireland forces upon us … great social and … religious questions. God grant that we may have the courage to look them in the face' (quoted in Magnus, *Gladstone,* 1954, page 75).

Although a fascinating forecast of future problems, it was not acted upon for over 20 years. Yet the seeds of change were clearly in Gladstone's mind: he was in the process of abandoning his former rigidly held views about the relationship of Church and State as was shown in his tortuous acceptance of the justice of the Maynooth Grant in the same year (1845) (see Chapter 3). From here, the logical pathway to supporting disestablishment of the Irish Church beckoned.

But for the moment economic matters dominated Gladstone's mind. When he was Chancellor in the Aberdeen coalition ministry in 1852–5 he extended the income tax to Ireland in his first budget of 1853, a measure regarded as insensitive in a country only just recovering from its catastrophic famine. It is a good example of Gladstone's theoretical analysis running ahead of his common sense – a not infrequent occurrence.

## WHY DID IRELAND BECOME A MORE DOMINANT ISSUE FOR GLADSTONE IN THE LATER 1860s?

In the late 1860s the Irish Question emerged as a more intrusive factor in British politics than at any time since the famine of 1845–6. This coincided with Gladstone's own developing views. His Liberalism in economic matters had extended more clearly to other fields; despite the fact that he was Chancellor of the Exchequer in Palmerston's government he was becoming bolder about making comments that related to his own opinions rather than the government's as a whole. One example had been the 'pale of the Constitution' speech in 1864 (see Chapter 4), and another was his support for a private member's bill advocating the disestablishment of the Irish Church in 1865. When defeated for the **Oxford University seat** in the 1865 general election, he **transferred his allegiance to South Lancashire.** This, coupled with Palmerston's death soon after the election, seemed to set the stage for a disestablishment measure. Gladstone announced significantly to his new constituents: 'At last, my friends, I have come amongst you. And I am come … **unmuzzled**'. However, parliamentary reform was to take priority.

Once the dust had settled on the 1867 Reform Act, there were good political reasons as well as ones of principle to bring disestablishment to the fore. It would reunite the Liberal Party, wrenched apart by the reform issue, and in a notoriously fractious party only six Liberals were to vote against it (see Chapter 5). It would also address the increasing challenge from the Fenians (see Chapter 5). The extension of their activities to the English mainland was succeeding in drawing their grievances to the attention of a wider English public. In particular there was the bold plan of Fenian John McCafferty to attack Chester Castle in February 1867, release Fenian prisoners and seize 2000 rifles which would immediately have been sent to Ireland. Although it failed, an action of this kind so close to the **Gladstone home at Hawarden** just over the Welsh border could hardly have failed to make an impression on him. The story goes that Gladstone was chopping down a tree on the Hawarden estate (a favourite pastime) when news came of the Queen's invitation to form a government. After commenting on the significance of this event he continued chopping until the tree was down. Then he stated: 'My mission is to pacify Ireland.' The tree felling was not totally incidental. Dealing with the Irish Question, Gladstone believed, was like chopping down a **upas tree.** Three branches needed to be cut: Church establishment, the land and education.

### Why was Irish Church disestablisment such a successful measure in 1869?

Gladstone took a good deal of personal interest in the legislation. He insisted on complete disendowment, a point which delayed the appointment of the best Liberal lawyer for the position of Lord Chancellor, Roundell Palmer. He obtained this government post later in October 1872 as Lord Selborne, but at the time he could not accept the disendowment principle. Gladstone drafted the Bill himself over Christmas and New Year 1868–9. He then introduced it with a three and a quarter hour speech which a wide variety of people, from Disraeli through to Gladstone's biographer and friend John Morley, thought was one of his finest and – despite the length – least long-winded. Gladstone also did a good deal of personal negotiating with awkward Whig peers

**KEY TERMS**

**Oxford University seat** Between 1847 and 1865 Gladstone sat for the parliamentary seat of Oxford University elected by the graduates of that institution. They had become increasingly concerned with Gladstone's growing Liberalism and rejected him as a candidate in 1865.

**Unmuzzled** Able to speak without fear or favour: Gladstone, no longer representing the Conservative graduates of Oxford, now felt freer to speak his mind.

**KEY CONCEPT**

**Transfer of allegiance to South Lancashire** Because elections were held over several weeks a prominent candidate, if defeated for one seat in the early stages of the contest, could probably find another seat where he was more likely to be elected.

and doubtful bishops in order to ensure the passage of the measure through the Lords. Archibald Tait, the Archbishop of Canterbury, for instance, did not vote against it. To get a bill of this nature past an Anglican-dominated Parliament with the near unanimous support of Roman Catholic and nonconformist alike was no mean achievement. The measure broke the traditional United Kingdom Church–State link for the first time and ushered in a period when the whole nature of the Anglo-Irish relationship would be re-examined.

The Act was undoubtedly a success, yet none of Gladstone's subsequent pieces of Irish legislation was quite as well received in Ireland or quite as effective in its application. Gladstone faced three major difficulties when trying to introduce subsequent Irish legislation. There was the danger of splitting the Liberal Party, the likely resistance of the House of Lords and the fact that public opinion was not very well disposed to further Irish reforms.

## How successful was the Irish Land Act?

The Irish Land Act of 1870 demonstrated these points, though it also demonstrated Gladstone's continuing commitment to the Irish issue and his mastery of intricate detail. He set himself the task of studying the complications of Irish land tenure; the qualities he had previously brought to the mastery of financial complexities were now equally well applied to this extremely tricky issue. His knowledge was entirely theoretical. He had never visited Ireland and was to do so only once, in 1877. However, his success in getting any sort of bill through at all was notable. Between 1835 and 1851 Tenant Right Bills had been regularly introduced by the Irish MP Sharman Crawford but without success and the small tenant right party had continued the task in the 1850s, but again with no success. The sticking point had always been that any bill in this area would be seen to be interfering with property rights: the poverty of the Irish tenants did not justify stealing from the landlord, as Lord Salisbury put it.

Gladstone, however, made it clear that he would not shirk from any measure that would 'liberate the principles of freedom and justice'. He clearly appreciated the depth of feeling that the Irish had on the land question, arguing that feelings sustained for so long must have some validity. But here the difficulties began to become apparent. The Liberal Party was less united on this issue than it had been over Church disestablishment. Gladstone's Chancellor Robert Lowe, regarded as a **doctrinaire Liberal,** eventually accepted the Bill, though not before the prominent newspaper, the *Daily News,* had predicted that he was as capable of splitting the party over land as he had been over the Reform Act in 1867. His eventual agreement stresses the nature of Gladstone's achievement. John Bright inserted clauses in the Act which would enable tenants to purchase land, though at this stage not many were able to take advantage of this possibility. The House of Lords found the sections of the Bill that concerned modifications of property rights less than acceptable and insisted on amendments such as the change from 'excessive' to 'exorbitant' (rent) that rendered the Bill less effective. Here Gladstone could not win the battle outright.

### Why did the Irish Universities Bill fail?

When it came to the Irish Universities Bill in 1873, it was the House of Commons, including some Liberals, that Gladstone failed to convince. It indicated both the difficulty of dealing with the very sensitive area of education and also that the Liberal Party's unity was breaking up. Radicals such as Henry Fawcett disliked the restrictive clauses in the Bill; other Liberals were disappointed that Gladstone had not moved on from Ireland to deal with *English* disestablishment. Nonconformists were disinclined to support another controversial educational measure, having been disappointed with the compromises of the England and Wales Education Act of 1870 (see Chapter 5). Educational concessions to the Catholic Irish did not appeal. But neither were the Catholic bishops satisfied with the restrictive clauses in the Bill.

## HOW DID HOME RULE IDEAS DEVELOP?

Gladstone's Irish reforms in his first ministry, though considerable, did not go far enough for many Irish Liberal MPs to support him to the full. The Home Government Association, set up in 1870, was a group led by protestant lawyer Isaac Butt (a man of Tory background who had defended accused Fenians) and this organisation was moving towards the idea of self-government with 'full control over our domestic affairs'– or Home Rule for Ireland. In November 1873 Butt replaced it with the Home Rule League and in the 1874 election the Liberal vote in Ireland collapsed, so that the party's strength declined from 65 seats (out of a total of 105 Irish seats) to twelve, with the new Home Rule group winning 59. Although many of these 59 were still prepared to support Gladstone and the Liberals it was a significant development for the future. In passing the Secret Ballot Act of 1872 and reducing Irish landlord electoral influence, Gladstone had made the creation of an Irish Nationalist Party more likely.

The most significant factor, however, in the growth of the Home Rule idea was the change in the economic position in Ireland at the close of the 1870s. Under **Hicks Beach**, Disraeli's Irish Secretary until 1878, the land question had remained relatively quiet and **agrarian outrages** had remained at a fairly low level. However, the agricultural depression that coincidentally came just after Hicks Beach's departure in February 1878 was a serious one and showed up the inadequacies of the Land Act legislation. For at this point there was a return to wholesale poverty among the Irish tenantry; many of them failed to pay their rents and the number of evictions rose rapidly. Between 1879 and 1883 more tenants were evicted than in the previous 30 years. This was met with a nationalist response. The Land League of Michael Davitt and the militant leadership of the Home Rule Party under Charles Stewart Parnell created a serious situation by the time Gladstone was Prime Minister again. In the 1880 election Parnell's Irish nationalists had 65 seats and soon made an impact in the House of Commons. Gladstone had been more concerned with the Eastern Question and the supposed iniquities of Beaconsfieldism. He had not anticipated Ireland being at the forefront of events; but so it proved.

## HOW DID GLADSTONE TRY TO DEAL WITH THE NEW IRISH CHALLENGES 1880–1?

**Compensation for Disturbance Bill 1880.** In his very first piece of Irish legislation on his return to office, Gladstone immediately fell foul of the House of Lords again. His attempt to introduce a measure of compensation for Irish tenants evicted for non-payment of rent in the troubled times of the previous two years was rejected in the Upper House by 282 votes to 51. The measure offended their Lordships' notions of the rights of property, was felt to be encouraging future non-payment and aiding those who had supported the agrarian outrages and violence of the Land League in the **New Departure** of Davitt (one of the leaders of the Land League). Lord Salisbury, who led the opposition in the Lords, commented to his nephew Arthur Balfour on Gladstone: 'there are marks of hurry which in so old a man are inexplicable'. Another phrase had been born which described Gladstone, this one used by his opponents rather than his supporters: 'an old man in a hurry'. Seventy Liberals in the Commons had failed to vote in the Bill's favour and Lord Lansdowne had resigned from the government in protest, all of which made it easier for the Lords to reject the Bill than the Irish disestablishment measure of 1869. It was not automatically regarded as something that the electorate would support.

**Coercion and reform: the second Irish Land Act 1881.** Gladstone's policy was a carrot and stick one. But on the first occasion the stick broke: his attempt at the end of 1880 to prosecute Parnell and other leaders of the nationalist agitation for *inciting* non-payment of rent ended in a jury disagreement. With outrages continuing on a large scale, Gladstone's Irish Chief Secretary Forster introduced a Coercion Act in January 1881. This met such fierce resistance from Parnell's nationalist MPs that the debate on it lasted over 40 continuous hours until the Speaker, **unprecedently,**

KEY TERM

**New Departure**
Irish tenant protests against English landlord control in Ireland at the end of the 1870s. Regarded as a 'new' departure because, unlike previous movements, their leaders were essentially ordinary tenants.

KEY TERM

**Unprecedented
suspension of
the sitting**
Unprecedented:
something that
had not happened
before. The
Speaker of the
House of
Commons ended a
session of
Parliament while
MPs still wished
to speak.

**suspended the sitting.** Gladstone had had to be persuaded of the
necessity for this coercion and wished, as before, to couple it with a more
constructive measure. He now felt that a more radical land act was
required if Ireland was to be pacified. This would provide for the 'three
Fs'– fixity of tenure, fair rents, and free sale.

The first of these meant that tenants could apply to a special commission
for judicial arbitration of their rent, the amount being fixed for the next
fifteen years. The second, making it hard to evict except for non-payment
of rent, would now be more effective than in the 1870 Act, because the
landlord could no longer simply raise the rent and then evict. The third
ensured a fair price for the improvements made not just in Ulster as in
the 1870 Act but all over Ireland. As in 1870 there was a very modest
section of the Bill to encourage the purchase of land by Irish tenants.
Resistance from the Lords was again possible but the senior Irish
Conservative Sir Edward Gibson advised against rejection. As one recent
historian, Andrew Roberts, has put it, 'the Irish landlords preferred to
receive reduced rents than none at all'. If the Bill passed, the Land League
would probably call off the mass refusal to pay rent.

**Gladstone and Parnell: 1881.** Parnell's language was still confrontational
and aggressive, perhaps to prevent his more extreme supporters from
taking the law into their own hands. He planned to test the new Act in
the courts and, if it proved unsatisfactory, he threatened further
disturbances. Yet Gladstone's concession had been a substantial one and
given a little more time might well have taken the sting out of the land
campaign. But in October 1881 Parnell's language was so extreme and
full of incitement to violence that the government decided to arrest him

under the Coercion Laws and imprison him in Kilmainham Jail where he could hardly either control, or be blamed for, subsequent outrages. This was clearly a tactical error on Gladstone's part. Not only was he making a martyr of Parnell, the agrarian violence became worse as the mythical figure of 'Captain Moonlight' stalked the Irish countryside wreaking havoc. It was soon regarded as necessary to release Parnell via the unofficial 'Kilmainham Treaty' negotiated by Joseph Chamberlain. In return for Parnell attempting to control the violence of the agitators, an Arrears Act would be passed to wipe out previous tenant rent debts. This had the effect of antagonising more Liberals and Chief Secretary Forster, feeling his policy had been undermined, resigned on 2 May 1882, the day Parnell's release was agreed.

## 1882: ANOTHER DIFFICULT YEAR FOR GLADSTONE'S IRISH POLICY

Gladstone's policies do seem to have persuaded Parnell and the Irish nationalists that their protests could be constitutional rather than violent. The land campaign was suspended and this threatened to divide the nationalist movement, as the more extreme members wished to continue their protests. Yet 1882 was still a difficult year for Gladstone in Ireland. The tragic murder on 6 May 1882 of Lord Frederick Cavendish, Gladstone's nephew and the new Chief Secretary for Ireland, brought great personal sorrow for Gladstone; but it also brought political difficulty as more coercion was now felt necessary. This brought the nationalists back together again in protest against the new measures.

What Gladstone was doing was still trying to pacify Ireland, but Ireland's mood was becoming one where pacification was more and more difficult. Gladstone had reacted to Irish protests by attempting reform on a number of occasions – Ireland was taking up more and more of his political time. What was becoming clearer and clearer was that Parnell and the nationalists saw the legislation, however helpful, as treating the symptoms and not the cause of the Irish troubles which they saw as the whole presence of the English landlord system in the country. Only self-government would now do and Parnell would campaign until it was achieved.

## WHEN DID GLADSTONE BECOME CONVINCED OF THE NEED FOR HOME RULE?

Although Gladstone had apparently ruled out the possibility of Home Rule at a speech in Aberdeen in 1871, there is evidence that his conversion to Home Rule in 1885 was not a sudden one. The events of

1881–2 seemed to have convinced him that the Irish spirit possessed a genuine feel for self-government. Gladstone never used the word 'nationalism' – or hardly any word with 'ism', as Colin Matthew, who has studied and edited all Gladstone's diaries, has pointed out. But he did accept the validity of the concept to a far greater extent than did Disraeli. This partly helps to explain his greater sympathy with Balkan nationalism in the 1870s. Moreover, Gladstone lived through a time when Liberalism and nationalism often went hand in hand and when nationalism was yet to acquire its more sinister and fascist overtones with which it became linked in the following century. Despite the fact that Ireland quietened down in 1883 and 1884, Gladstone felt that he had still not 'pacified them' and that further measures would be required.

Gladstone wanted Ireland treated as any other part of the United Kingdom; this accounts for his insistence that the provisions of the third parliamentary Reform Bill which dealt with vote extension must be extended to Ireland on exactly the same basis as in England. And this was even though he knew this would enfranchise many potential supporters of Parnell's Irish Home Rule Party. In contrast, to avoid further obstruction by Irish members he did not attempt to redistribute seats in Ireland. But this also benefited the Irish MPs as they were now over-represented in Parliament. Gladstone had come to the conclusion that the nationalists were now the only legitimate source of authority in Ireland: their demands had to be seriously considered.

## WHAT WERE THE REASONS FOR GLADSTONE'S BEHAVIOUR OVER THE HOME RULE QUESTION IN 1885–6?

Gladstone appears to have become finally convinced of the need for Home Rule after the fall of his government in June 1885, defeated on an amendment to the budget. Seventy Liberals had failed to support the government. There seemed a real – if brief and mistaken – possibility that a Conservative administration under Salisbury might consider the possibility of Home Rule. The new Irish **Viceroy** Lord Carnarvon had secret conversations with Parnell. Since Gladstone was not committing himself to Home Rule at this stage, Parnell instructed supporters of Home Rule to vote Conservative (if there was no Irish Home Rule candidate) at the election that Salisbury had called in November 1885. This may have lost Gladstone and the Liberals some 20 or more seats; it turned out to be crucial. The Liberal majority of 86 over the Conservatives was exactly matched by the number of Irish nationalist MPs. Parnell now held the balance of power. Gladstone had taken a Norwegian holiday in August 1885 and apparently made a definite commitment to Home Rule at this stage. However, he seems to have felt that it would be best left to the Conservatives if possible. The

**KEY TERM**

**Viceroy** The most senior British government official in Ireland, representing the monarch.

Liberals would not oppose and thus the issue could be kept out of party politics.

Did Gladstone act for political motives here? The Liberal Party was not in good shape. The stresses and strains of its various coalitions of interests led to disagreements and splits as had happened at the end of Gladstone's previous government in 1873–4 and indeed also in 1867 over parliamentary reform, in 1858 over the Conspiracy to Murder Bill and in 1855 over the Crimean War. Perhaps one great cause such as Home Rule could reunite them again. Yet Gladstone would surely have anticipated that a controversial bill for Home Rule could have serious consequences for the unity of the party, making their divisions worse. Moreover, there was the problem of the approval of the House of Lords. It might be felt more likely that it would reluctantly accept Home Rule if a *Conservative* leader such as Salisbury – himself – were to insist on its necessity. Gladstone did not want Home Rule to become a political football but he now saw it as, at least, a lesser evil.

### The Hawarden Kite and Liberal opposition

In the middle of December 1885 it became public knowledge that Gladstone had been converted to the need for Home Rule. His youngest son Herbert, a strong believer in Home Rule himself, made indiscreet remarks to the press and the 'secret' conversion was out. This incident became known as the Hawarden Kite. Had Gladstone from his country home in Flintshire flown a kite to discover whether he could get the Liberals back into power and regain Irish nationalist support? If so, it worked, but only in the short term. Salisbury resigned when defeated by a Liberal-inspired vote at the end of January 1886 and Gladstone formed his third ministry. Liberal cracks, however, appeared immediately. Chamberlain had no sooner been appointed to Gladstone's new cabinet in early February than he resigned in March when the terms of the proposed Home Rule Bill became known. Gladstone's Home Rule Bill split the Liberal Party and 93 Liberal 'Unionists' voted against the measure, ensuring its defeat by 343 votes to 313. Another election had to be called, in effect a plebiscite on Home Rule. It brought the clearest evidence yet of one of Gladstone's difficulties: public opinion was not sympathetic to Irish reform. The Conservatives won 316 seats, the Liberals 190, the Liberal Unionists 79 and the Irish nationalists 85.

### What effect did Home Rule have on the Liberal Party?

It was clear that a large proportion of the Whig section of the party led by Lord Hartington was opposed to the principle of Home Rule. Moreover, more Radical Liberals such as Joseph Chamberlain were too. Chamberlain was an advocate of radical reform in many ways and a strong supporter of local government in Birmingham where he had been an effective Lord Mayor in the late 1870s. He wished to see 'central

> **KEY TERM**
>
> **Plebiscite** A vote by the people to decide one particular issue. Normally elections were fought on a range of issues rather than one dominant one, though this could happen as in 1831 over parliamentary reform and in 1857 over Palmerston's style in foreign policy.

boards', which would have involved some devolution, rather than Home Rule. Historians have found Chamberlain's opposition to Home Rule puzzling and have seen in the Liberal split over it a clash of personalities. Gladstone's rather high-handed treatment of Chamberlain when he was in the cabinet, and his lack of consultation with both Hartington and Chamberlain about his changing opinions on the Home Rule issue are seen to have turned these two Liberals against him, as well as many other Whigs and a few Radicals as well. Were Chamberlain and Hartington, like Gladstone, hoping to gain power and perhaps leadership of the party with the upheaval that Home Rule was causing? Or is the Liberal split on Home Rule a sign of principle in politics? In the end Chamberlain lost his chance of succeeding Gladstone and ended up in the Conservative Party. It was the Conservatives who were the party that benefited from the Home Rule saga.

## CONCLUSION

- Gladstone tackled the Irish Question with more vigour and a greater degree of success than previous English ministers.
- He did not anticipate having to deal with the question again in his second ministry.
- His efforts to deal with the problems of Irish land, though considerable, did not really succeed in getting to the roots of the problem.
- As a Liberal Gladstone was ill at ease with having to impose coercion measures on Ireland.
- However, the need to do this only made him feel more obliged to try to pass another more constructive measure.
- Gladstone found it as hard to pacify the Liberal Party over Ireland as he did the Irish themselves.
- The precise degree of success of Gladstone's measures and his tactics over his conversion to Home Rule late in 1885 are still the subject of much controversy.

# How did the failure of the Irish Home Rule Bills affect Liberalism and Conservatism?

## INTRODUCTION

- In politics, the Conservatives dominated Irish policy in the last decade and a half of the nineteenth century and received the backing of Liberal Unionists.
- Arthur Balfour, the Irish Secretary, pursued a tough policy towards law and order in Ireland in the late 1880s.
- Balfour and his brother Gerald introduced some measures of reform in Ireland during the 1890s, though to limited effect.
- While Gladstone remained wedded to Irish Home Rule, some Liberals were far from enthusiastic by the end of the century.
- Salisbury showed less interest in, and commitment to, Irish matters, and strongly opposed Home Rule.
- Public opinion in England and eastern Ulster remained firmly opposed to Home Rule.

### Views of historians

There is little dispute that Ireland was still a significant factor in British politics after 1886 but it is generally conceded that its impact was much less dramatic. Rubinstein (1998), sees Ireland's relative lack of prominence immediately after 1886 as surprising, and it seems that a combination of the severe but effective methods of control used by Arthur Balfour and the weaknesses and divisions of the Irish nationalists, even *before* the fall of Parnell, were the major explanation. Peter Marsh, *The Discipline of Popular Government* (1978), admires Salisbury's political skill in (usually) satisfying the desires both of the Liberal Unionists and his more resistant Conservative colleagues. But Marsh admits that he failed at times to back Arthur and Gerald Balfour, his two Chief Secretaries between 1887 and 1900. He asserts that 'Salisbury's heart was not altogether with him' (Arthur Balfour). Salisbury's distaste for Irish affairs has been re-emphasised by one of his recent biographers, Andrew Roberts, in *Salisbury: Victorian Titan* (1999). Salisbury was convinced that the Irish needed firm government to make them toe the line and Roberts brings out Salisbury's reservations about the more constructive aspects of the Balfour brothers' policy. Roberts concludes that Salisbury's 'depth of … cynicism' was a distinguishing characteristic of his attitude towards Ireland.

Irish historians have, not surprisingly, been critical of Balfour's stern policies. F.S.L. Lyons, generally a most impartial historian, calls Balfour's

Crimes Act and the policy of trying to get the Roman Catholic Church to condemn the Plan of Campaign as 'insidious' (*Ireland Since the Famine*, 1973). However, Joseph Lee in *The Modernisation of Irish Society* (1973) plays down the Irish casualties under Balfour's 'bloody' rule as 'derisory' compared to those resulting from Oliver Cromwell's rampage in the seventeenth century. But Lee also sees his and his brother Gerald's reforms as lacking in major impact. Generally, the Unionism of Gerald Balfour and George Wyndham is seen as more 'constructive' though there is some dispute about the motivation. Roy Foster, *Modern Ireland 1600–1972* (1988), argues that the reforms 'did not represent a sustained **Machiavellian conspiracy** to cut out nationalist demands'. John France in Blake and Cecil (eds) *Salisbury: the Man and his Policies* (1987) plays down the difference between the parties on Irish policy more than some other historians by arguing that their policies on Ireland were only 'conceived in a context of deep political calculation' and that Gladstone was alone in seeing the landlord class in Ireland as being part of a constructive solution to the Irish Question. He also doubts the use of the word 'constructive' to describe the Conservative Irish policy, seeing it more as short-term reactions to particular problems.

## WHAT WAS THE NATURE OF THE PARTY DIVISION OVER HOME RULE?

The defeat of the Irish Home Rule Bill in 1886 ushered in a new era in British politics. The Bill had split the Liberal Party, and the Liberal Unionists remained detached from it. The division was more reminiscent of the Conservative split in 1846 over Corn Law repeal than the Liberal one over reform in 1866 where the rift was soon healed. In 1868 Gladstone applied the healing balm in the form of a new issue to unite the Liberals, Irish Church disestablishment. In 1886, however, Ireland was to prove a continued source of division. Moreover, whereas the reform question in 1866–7 *was* settled – by the Conservatives – there was no chance of this happening with Ireland. Home Rule would not be granted at Conservative hands. Nor would Gladstone forget Ireland, and his determination to settle the question, against all the odds, prevented the division from healing. Still worse from the Liberal point of view, their Unionists did not generally return to the fold. For a time, like the Peelites in 1846, they retained a certain detachment from party, but, in a process which began even before 1890, many gradually drifted over to the Conservatives.

### How did the opposition of Ulster Unionists to Home Rule help the Conservatives?

One advantage for the Conservatives was that they could now consistently rely on the support of the Ulster Unionists in an alliance that

**KEY TERM**

**Machiavellian conspiracy** A complex and devious plan to achieve your own ends by any means possible regardless of moral code. Named after the late-fifteenth-century Italian writer Niccolo Machiavelli.

**KEY CONCEPT**

**The political significance of Ulster** In around 1800 many Ulster Protestants had been prepared to ally with Roman Catholics in a nationalist movement. But by the 1880s the Protestant majority in the eastern (industrial) part of Ulster had developed more uniformly anti-Catholic views. As late as Easter 1885, however, Ulster Protestants had not believed that Gladstone really would introduce Home Rule.

continued in an amended form up to the 1960s. The **political significance of Ulster** appeared relatively suddenly in 1885–6, since Home Rule was not really regarded as practical politics until Gladstone took up the cause. The people of eastern Ulster had never succumbed to the charms of their fellow Protestant Parnell and their opposition, once roused, was vigorous, with Colonel Edward Saunderson at the head of it. In 1885 he had invited Lord Randolph Churchill to Belfast. Churchill – ever the political opportunist – saw potential support for the Conservatives from Ulster, where religious suspicion of Roman Catholic rule, political concerns regarding safety and security, and economic reservations regarding the backwardness of much of the rest of Ireland had produced a profound opposition to the latest Home Rule proposals. Not for nothing did Churchill comment on the question of Protestant Ulster's opposition to Home Rule: 'Ulster will fight and Ulster will be right.' The fighting occurred with serious rioting in 1886 in Belfast. The early signs of extreme opposition were apparent in discussions about taking a solemn oath and the possibility of military resistance. Not selling the Ulster Protestants short provided one of the main justifications for Conservative opposition to the whole concept of Home Rule.

## What was Salisbury's attitude towards Ireland?

Churchill was not alone: Salisbury argued the same in less militant language. 'We cannot desert the loyal people of Ulster' he argued, and he was concerned about the effects on the rest of the Empire such as India – for Salisbury regarded Ireland as part of the Empire in the same way. Salisbury was careful to keep Ulster Unionists on his side as the 1890s went on, with a privy councillorship for Colonel Saunderson and a post in government for the rising star and future leader Edward Carson, who was appointed Solicitor General in 1900. Salisbury could also rely on some Scottish votes, from Glasgow Protestants for instance, who sympathised with their fellow **Presbyterians** in Ulster. A quarter of successful candidates in Scottish seats in the 1892 election were Liberal Unionists.

Salisbury, like many other leading political figures of the century, never showed much sympathy for the Irish or much sign that he understood the full nature of their demands. He certainly felt them to be incapable of self-government and caused a stir in 1886, when he referred to their demand for Home Rule as being about as sensible as giving it to **Hottentots.**

He had the advantage of using the parliamentary devices (such as the guillotine to prevent obstructionism) developed in Gladstone's second ministry in the early 1880s to bring debates to a rapid halt. When selecting Balfour for the position of Irish Secretary in 1887, Salisbury made clear the change of direction. The day before the appointment he made a speech in which he argued that as regards Ireland 'too much softness has crept into our proposals' and that Ireland 'could not be governed by platitudes and rosewater'.

### Salisbury's continued opposition to Home Rule

Salisbury's opposition to Home Rule never faded. At the time of Gladstone's second bill in 1893 his country home Hatfield House was used as the venue for a large demonstration against the legislation with over 1500 Ulster people present. Salisbury then made two anti-Home Rule speeches in Ireland, in Belfast and Londonderry. He argued that it would be untrue to the Empire to allow the Bill through and to the 'duty which has descended to you from a splendid ancestry'. The majority of 30 in the Commons was less than the number of nationalist MPs (38) associated with agrarian outrages, he asserted. He continued to regard Home Rule as a delusion. He was privately critical of some of the reforms his own administration introduced.

## ARTHUR BALFOUR BECOMES IRISH SECRETARY

**Conciliation**
Trying to obtain an agreement between two warring sides by rational talk and calm discussion.

The Conservatives, far from disunited about Ireland, not only had the reassurance of Liberal Unionist support, but they also possessed the advantage of a public opinion which did not in the main favour major concessions to Ireland, as the election in 1886 had indicated. Salisbury, with not uncommon pessimism, seemed to view the Irish Question as virtually insoluble. When further economic depression caused more agrarian disturbances in the winter of 1886–7, the Irish Secretary Hicks Beach was inclined to **conciliation** as well as imposing coercion. But on his retirement in 1887 Arthur Balfour, Salisbury's nephew, was appointed in his place. Relatively young, and anxious to win his political spurs, Balfour would be faithful to his uncle's wishes. This meant following a policy of dealing harshly with the disturbances and only when law and order had been fully established would concessions be made. At the very least the 'solution' to the Irish Question would be some time coming.

This delay was politically quite convenient for Salisbury. Whilst Irish issues remained prominent, they reminded the electorate of the upheaval in the parties in 1886 and this made it more likely that the Liberal Unionists would not return to their original party. Balfour's aim was to toughen his political reputation so as to be seen as heir apparent to Salisbury in the coming years. His task was difficult in the extreme but it was made slightly less daunting by the fact that Parnell was now committed to gaining Home Rule by political means and thus had the support of the Liberals. Parnell therefore disapproved of the extreme measures in the **Plan of Campaign** begun in October 1886 and conceived by Irish nationalist Tim Harrington and run by William O'Brien and John Dillon. As Parnell would not support the Campaign, its effects were limited both geographically and politically.

Another government tactic was ultimately less successful. This was to seek a Roman Catholic condemnation of the Plan of Campaign and related activities. The outlawing of the Plan of Campaign by Pope Leo XIII in 1888 was accepted reluctantly by the hierarchy of the Irish Church, though ordinary parish priests, closer to the heartbeat of the ordinary tenants, were often in opposition to it.

Balfour had the advantage of a much weakened and divided nationalist movement. At one stage there was a threefold division between John Redmond, carrying the flag for the old Parnellites (and who was eventually to lead the reunited movement after 1900) and the rest, divided between Justin McCarthy and Tim Healey. Leading supporters such as John Dillon and William O'Brien suffered spells in jail in the early 1890s.

## What was the extent and nature of Balfour's legislation?

The nickname 'Bloody Balfour' referred to the overall severity of the policy rather than to the number of fatalities. There were some, however, such as at **Mitchelstown**. Balfour's Crimes Act was to be a permanent law rather than an Act of Emergency which would have to be renewed every year. It increased the power of both the Viceroy and local magistrates to deal with the landlord–tenant relationship. Tenants' boycotts, refusal to accept eviction and intimidation of landlords were all to be illegal. However, Balfour also followed a more constructive policy with the Irish Land Act of 1887 which extended Gladstone's 1881 Act to **leaseholders** – over 100,000 of them. This reflected Liberal Unionist influence. Their opposition to Irish Home Rule did not mean opposition to fair and constructive treatment for the Irish. Political realities had forced Salisbury to concede. The reality was that this was not a period of Conservative government but of a Unionist one. The differences were significant, as the principle of the Land Act of 1887 shows, and, despite the apparent unity over the issue, applied to Irish policy, if not the principle of Home Rule itself.

Land purchase was also encouraged. In 1888 £10 million more was made available for it and in 1891 £33 million. The government made buying land from the landlords easier by giving tenants a 100 per cent loan; before this it had been a loan of up to a third and then two-thirds in 1880. Balfour introduced a light railway scheme in 1890 and a

Congested Districts Board the following year. Both were designed to aid the poverty-stricken areas of western Ireland. After 1890 agrarian outrages declined sharply: a decline which was directly related to the number of land purchases.

### What was the degree of Unionist co-operation?

Lord Hartington gave what might be described as an independent support to the government. 'He will support the present Government on all critical occasions', Salisbury assured the Queen, soon after he had formed his second ministry. This meant a broad support for Salisbury's policy of coercion. Liberal Unionists were no longer only opposed to Home Rule. About half a dozen Liberal Unionists opposed coercion sufficiently strongly in 1887 and 1888 to return to the Liberals, but this made the rest more united in backing government policy. This strengthened Salisbury's hand, but may also have tempered the severity of his measures at times in order to preserve unity on the issue. Reluctantly he agreed to changes to the Land Bill in 1887. More formal links came with the Arlington Street (London) compact of 1890 when Salisbury, Hartington and other party chiefs agreed to combine the constituency committees of the two parties and to call themselves Unionists. They would not oppose each other at election time. Indeed the word Conservative, while never disappearing, was to take something of a back seat while Irish issues remained prominent. Salisbury, as a staunch Conservative, was probably a more effective leader of this alliance than a more moderate Conservative. His mere presence reassured the more traditional landowning members that there would be no sell-out on issues like Ireland and yet he could make realistic compromises when they were necessary.

## WHAT WAS THE NATURE OF THE POLITICAL DIVISION AMONG THE LIBERALS?

Not all of the English Liberal Unionists were from the moderate, Whig-dominated, landowning group led by Lord Hartington. As well as Radicals Chamberlain and Trevelyan (the latter soon to return to the Liberals), there were also prominent city financiers such as George Goschen and a flurry of supporters from the universities and academic world which had backed Gladstone so strongly over the Bulgarian atrocities in the previous decade. This included the constitutional expert A.V. Dicey and the historian J.R. Seeley. But unlike the Peelites in 1846 the Unionists did not take *all* the men of talent with them. Among those prominent in the Liberal Party now were Radical figures such as **Harcourt** and Morley. Of the leading Whig aristocrats, only Earl Spencer stayed loyal to the Gladstonian idea of Home Rule. Thus the social differences between the parties became more marked. The trend towards the Conservatives in middle-class suburbia was thus confirmed.

### KEY TERM

**Congested Districts Board**
Set up to invest money in poorer areas of western Ireland where the size of the population could not be sustained by the relative poverty of the agriculture in the area. Technical help with agriculture would be given, as well as help with migration and the encouragement of the amalgamation of very small holdings.

### KEY PERSON

**Sir William Harcourt 1827–1904**
Liberal politician who first became an MP in 1868. Home Secretary 1880–5 and Chancellor of the Exchequer 1886 and 1892–5; party leader 1896–8. A very capable but sometimes awkward colleague.

Another social development was also accelerating at this time. The decline in landowning Liberal MPs was particularly noticeable as lawyers such as Herbert Asquith, who came from a middle-class, Yorkshire background, and businessmen such as Sir Thomas Brassey and Walter Runciman rose rapidly in the party's ranks. This trend was general and not unknown in the Conservative Party, but there it was not seen to such a marked extent. Clearly there was a battle for the middle-class votes, and here the defection of Chamberlain to the Unionists was significant. Asquith brought all his analytical skills to the Liberal attack on Conservative policy in Ireland, pointing out the gulf between the wishes of the elected representatives in Ireland and how they were being treated by the English government.

## What was Gladstone's attitude to Home Rule after 1886?

There was little doubt that Gladstone, with the aid of his Irish Secretary John Morley, intended to attempt another Home Rule Bill if possible. The party was bogged down in the details of what this might include. Whigs like Spencer wanted to see a renewed emphasis on land purchase and there was also discussion about whether the objection that Joseph Chamberlain had raised to Home Rule in 1886 – that Irish MPs were no longer to be **represented at Westminster** – could be modified. In 1887 Gladstone considered that the Irish MPs might be retained provisionally and the 1893 proposals did allow them to remain. But this did not induce Joseph Chamberlain to support the Bill.

## WHAT EFFECT DID THE DOWNFALL OF PARNELL HAVE ON THE PARTIES?

Events concerning Parnell between 1887 and 1890 ensured that the political focus would remain on Ireland. As the news developed of the **Pigott letters**, the fortunes of Liberals and Unionists swayed back and forth. It was alleged that Parnell had claimed that the Under-Secretary T.H. Burke (one of the Phoenix Park murder victims in 1881) had received his 'just deserts'. This was initially to the advantage of the government and was exploited by Salisbury. He pointed out that the association between Gladstone and Parnell could imply that Gladstone was consorting with one who had connived at murder. The revelation of the Pigott letters as forgeries was something of a setback for them, but any increase in sympathy for the wronged Parnell soon evaporated when the news of the O'Shea divorce came through in November 1890. The political alliance with Gladstone had become close when Parnell visited Gladstone at Hawarden at the end of 1889; now it was over for good.

Gladstone, under pressure from his nonconformist supporters, suggested in his roundabout fashion to one of Parnell's leading supporters, Justin

### KEY CONCEPT

**Irish representation at Westminster**
Gladstone had argued that, if given their own Parliament, the Irish would not require to be represented at Westminster. However, Chamberlain felt that they should still be allowed some say because their country would be affected by the imperial foreign and defence decisions that would be taken in the Westminster Parliament.

### KEY TERM

**Pigott letters**
Pigott was the forger of the letters published by *The Times* in 1887–9 to try to blame Parnell for the Phoenix Park murders in May 1882, i.e. associate him with Fenianism and bring about his fall politically.

McCarthy, that if Parnell remained Irish leader the Liberal Party would not be elected next time round and Home Rule would be fatally delayed. The nonconformist conscience also reared its head: Wesleyan Methodist Hugh Price Hughes made it clear that support for the Liberals would not be forthcoming if they remained in alliance with the adulterer Parnell. Gladstone wrote to Morley, asking him to tell Parnell that he, Gladstone, could no longer lead the Liberals if Parnell continued as leader of the National League. There was some confusion over whether Parnell had read the letter's contents, but when it was clear he was to be re-elected Irish leader, Gladstone took the major decision to publish his letter. This destroyed Parnell. Irish nationalists now faced a choice between continuing to back Parnell who had achieved so much, or clinging to the Liberal alliance that offered the only realistic hope of Home Rule. Professor Lyons' researches suggest that the total support for Parnell was 32 members of the parliamentary party, leaving 54 against, a clear majority to remove him.

The circumstances surrounding the fall of Parnell doubtless affected the by-election at Bassetlaw (a north Nottinghamshire mining district) in December 1890. Despite two major speeches from Gladstone in the constituency the Conservative majority increased. This was a setback for the Liberals.

## WHY DID THE SECOND HOME RULE BILL FAIL?

The fall of Parnell produced a split in the Irish Home Rule Party but it was not at first an even division. With the election of 1892 the Liberals were able to displace Salisbury. They had the support of the Irish nationalists while they still remained committed to bringing in a bill. Eighty nationalists were returned, a total figure little different from their number in the Parnell days, but only nine were Parnellites; the other 71 were initially supporters of Justin McCarthy and this made links with the Liberals somewhat easier.

Gladstone's insistence on bringing forward a bill in 1893 kept the focus on Ireland for a little longer. Once he had been defeated, however, the issue began to fade in the public mind. Although Morley wanted to run a campaign which would attack the House of Lords his colleagues overruled him. Gladstone's request that Parliament be dissolved again to focus on Home Rule was rejected by his cabinet. The question simply lacked popular concern. An appeal to the will of the people and a criticism of the hereditary nature of the House of Lords could perhaps strike a chord with a substantial section of the voting community, but not on this particular question. Previous omens were not good. In 1888 Gladstone had urged Liberal electors to vote for Wilfred Scawen Blunt even though he was in jail for defying the Crimes Act. But the electors of Deptford in south-east London preferred the Unionist candidate. There seemed to be little support for the cause of Irish nationalism. An increasingly literate and newspaper-reading public devoured sensational stories in national English newspapers of intimidation by Irish 'Moonlighters'. Their conclusion was that the Irish were not fit for self-government.

More than this was the imperial mentality of the day. The Irish were seen as part of a United Kingdom, who could not, on a 'whim', demand self-government. The country of the multi-national Empire did not accept that the nationalistic feelings of the Irish were valid. In any case the proposed degree of independence was seen as economically foolhardy.

## What was the effect on the Liberals of the second Home Rule defeat?

Rosebery soon outlined the trend. This was to delay moving further until a majority of English public opinion could be brought round to Home Rule. This was an interesting notion, since it does not appear to have applied to previous Liberal legislation, some of which had not been particularly popular. Moreover, when the Liberals obtained a majority in England in 1906, there was no sign of Home Rule forthcoming, perhaps because there *was* such a large majority and the Irish nationalists could be ignored.

## What was 'kill Home Rule by kindness'?

'The government would of course be very glad if they could, by kindness, kill Home Rule' as new Irish Secretary Gerald Balfour (Arthur's brother) asserted in October 1895. The 1896 Irish Land Bill would be seen as the first practical attempt at this policy. Thus it provided £36 million for land purchase as well as removing some of the higher rents that had been imposed in previous legislation as security against failure to maintain payments. It removed some of the bureaucratic complications associated with the Bill of 1891.

Landlord influence also declined politically. Local government reform was introduced in 1898, ten years after its English equivalent. But this was not surprising. Salisbury had promised as much, even before the election of 1885. It could be seen as treating Ireland as nearly as possible the same as England – now the naughty child was behaving better – quite the reverse of acknowledging the differences between the countries stressed by nationalists. The Act created county councils and rural and urban district councils, increasing the power of elected officials at the expense of landlords and granting women a vote at local levels. What Asquith called waiting for 'the sanction and sympathy of British opinion' seemed very close to Salisbury's view that England – as the predominant country in the Kingdom – must be seen to be willing to grant its assent. In 1899 a new Irish Department of Agricultural and Technical Instruction was set up by Gerald Balfour. This emphasised the constructive side of the policies of the two Balfours.

## WHAT WAS THE POLITICAL SITUATION IN IRELAND BY 1900?

By 1900 Ireland was relatively quiet and took second place in the election of that year to the Boer War. It seemed incongruous to talk about giving away power from the centre of the Empire when it was fighting so hard to retain full control so much further from home. Land purchase, now increasingly desired by the Anglo-Irish landowning class, had proved more successful in the 1890s and culminated in Wyndham's Act in 1903. Ireland was starting to develop into a land of peasant proprietors, the most effective long-term solution to the whole land question. But Home Rule, while subdued immediately after 1900, was a sleeping giant. Land purchase was starting to turn Ireland into a country with a high proportion of peasant proprietors, whose general outlook was less radical than in Parnell's time. But none of these development would stifle the growing nationalist feeling, increasingly affected by a cultural renaissance among the Irish and a revival of the Gaelic language and culture.

The 'kill Home Rule by kindness' policy – a sharp contrast to just ten years earlier – had been based on the assumption that reform should follow control. Demands for Home Rule were also being killed by the continuing divisions of the Irish nationalists and the uncertainty of Gladstone's Liberal successors. If in power would they actually introduce a Home Rule bill? Were they to be feared? Ironically this was to end the period of the Irish bogey, when all right-thinking Unionists would hold fast, the Conservatives and their Liberal Unionists allies. In 1906 when many ex-Liberals returned to the fold they did so in the knowledge that Home Rule was not a burning issue and that voting Liberal again would not bring back the spectre of an Irish Parliament in Dublin.

But the idea that the Irish demands for self-government would go away with better treatment from Westminster and economic improvement proved mistaken. Too many years of ill-treatment and neglect and exploitation had ensured the development of nationalist feelings that would not be assuaged by some land purchase bills and a relaxation in coercion. When Queen Victoria visited Ireland in 1900 it was partly an attempt to recruit more patriotic Irishmen to fight the Boers. Perhaps her relative lack of success was based on the irony of asking the Irish to help suppress a 'small nation struggling to be free'.

## CONCLUSION

- The English attitude to the treatment of Ireland had undergone considerable change in the last quarter of the nineteenth century.
- The Liberals had become a divided party over Ireland and were to spend much of the period in opposition.
- The Conservatives never really recognised the Irish claims to nationhood but found Ireland easier to control in the 1890s than it had been in the 1880s.
- Liberal weaknesses, Gladstone's near obsession with Irish Home Rule, the fall of Parnell leading to the subsequent divisions in the Irish nationalist groups, and the loyal support of much of Ulster, helped to ensure Unionist dominance.
- Tenant purchase of land was beginning to solve some of the economic and social problems in Ireland.
- A strong nationalist feeling nonetheless remained and a battered and bruised Irish nationalists would revive to make further major impact on British politics within a few years.

# Why were the Conservatives such a successful party in the period 1886–1900?

## INTRODUCTION

- A broad-based coalition helped to bring Conservatives their success. The alliance with the Liberal Unionists was clearly crucial. Informal at first, it became fully operational in 1895 but was of significance throughout the period.
- As Prime Minister, the Marquess of Salisbury won three elections in fourteen years, a Conservative record unmatched between Lord Liverpool in the 1820s and Margaret Thatcher in the 1980s. He handled both opponents and awkward political customers on his own side with considerable political skill.
- The party attracted voters from all social ranks, the landed interest, the increasingly wealthy middle class and from the working class in areas where popular Protestantism and/or imperialistic fervour ensured the regular return of Conservatives.
- The Conservative Party was efficiently organised as a mass party in an increasingly democratic age. It seemed more coherent and united than the Liberal Party and presided over an age of relative political stability despite having to deal with major disturbances in Ireland and some serious working-class protests in London.
- Conservative achievements in local government, careful stewarding of the nation's finances and Salisbury's experienced hand at the tiller in foreign policy helped to boost their popularity.

### Views of historians

Until recently historians have not been over-generous to Lord Salisbury, seeing him as a cynical, negative and even reactionary figure who, somewhat oddly, presided over Britain when the country was becoming at least semi-democratic in its political structure. John Belchem in *Class, Party and the Political System in Britain 1867–1914* (1990) felt that 'Salisbury sought to polarise politics' and that his defence of established interests was 'uncompromising'. Feuchtwanger in *Democracy and Empire: Great Britain 1865–1914* (1985) concluded that Salisbury only passed two reforms of note in his 1886–92 ministry and that these 'could be equally well justified from the point of view of Conservative resistance'.

However, Paul Smith, in *Lord Salisbury on Politics,* argues in his long introduction to Salisbury's political writings for the magazine *The Quarterly Review* from 1860 to 1863 that 'he has not occupied the place in the Conservative hall of fame or received the attention from historians that might seem to be his due'. What praise there was for Salisbury related to his undoubted diplomatic abilities as illustrated in J.A.S. Grenville's *Lord Salisbury's Foreign Policy* (1964). It is true that Lord Blake in his *Conservative Party from Peel to Major* (1996) – first published as *The Conservative Party from Peel to Churchill* – felt that it was misleading to assume that Salisbury 'got away' with 'a long period of cautious negativism in domestic affairs', but he argued that the reforms were passed because of the demands for change from his Unionist allies and because of the fears of a Liberal revival. Salisbury's domestic reputation really began to rise with the publication of Peter Marsh's book *The Discipline of Popular Government; Lord Salisbury's Domestic Statecraft* (1978). His outmanoeuvring of Lord Randolph Churchill, some shrewd appointments in government such as George Goschen and W.H. Smith, and his ability to accommodate Unionists as different as Hartington and Chamberlain illustrated his ability in this area. He was, argues Marsh, 'a master without superior in the arts of cabinet management'. But Marsh still saw Salisbury as 'more of a diehard than any Conservative leader since his godfather the Duke of Wellington'.

It was only in 1999 that two major and complete biographies of Salisbury appeared: *Salisbury: Victorian Titan* by Andrew Roberts and David Steele's *Lord Salisbury: A Political Biography*. Roberts sees Salisbury's views maturing from his 'somewhat reactionary High Toryism of his youth' to a more pragmatic and realistic version of what was broadly a similar philosophy: 'he never reneged on his earlier beliefs'. He fought 'an impressive lifelong rearguard action' against the forces of modernism. Salisbury, he argues, should not be criticised for not doing things 'he thought either undesirable or impossible'. In fact his achievements were considerable. He did 'an astonishingly successful job' in 'attempting to channel and civilise the forces of democracy' after 1867.

Steele, however, goes further and, asserting the 'lack of substance' of the **Tory democracy** of Disraeli and Lord Randolph Churchill, sees Salisbury as re-establishing the Conservatives as the party of government for the first time since 1832. He argues that Salisbury adapted the party's ideas and policies to the new era after 1885, arguing that 'little was left of their old Conservatism'. Over Ireland, Steele sees Salisbury as more far-sighted than Gladstone in that he regarded land purchase and the development of peasant proprietors as the solution to the Irish Question. Salisbury was not against Home Rule in principle, Steele argues, but felt the time was not right and the Conservative Party not ready for such a step. Steele also sees Salisbury as more progressive in domestic policy than he has been made out to be in previous assessments, quoting a number of contemporaries who testified to the radicalism of Salisbury's social legislation.

## HOW DID THE THIRD REFORM ACT HELP TO TRANSFORM CONSERVATISM?

The handling of the third Reform Bill crisis in 1884 was the time when Salisbury really showed his political craftsmanship and influenced future political development. He had already appreciated the growing support for the Conservatives in the new middle-class suburbs and now he entered upon a piece of hard negotiation in order to obtain what advantages he could from the new Redistribution Act. Here, Salisbury's pragmatism was seen at its most prominent. He had opposed reform in 1867 but since the change had gone ahead it had to be accepted and the best had to be made of the new situation.

Salisbury regarded the eventual passing into law of the household franchise in rural areas as inevitable and was trying to make the most of it for his own party. Initially, however, he encouraged the House of Lords to hold up the Bill to emphasise its right to play a major part in political decision-making. A separate Redistribution Bill was insisted on by the House of Lords led by Salisbury. This would separate town and country clearly and introduce more single-member seats, weakening the Whig element in the Liberal Party who could no longer share a two-member seat with a more radical Liberal. Substantial redistribution from country to town would not be to the Conservatives' disadvantage. Taking into account the Secret Ballot and Corrupt Practices Act and the extension of the vote to the more independent rural householder, they could no longer rely on controlling the rural vote. They would do better to rely on the growing middle-class urban Conservative support, which would come into its own once the Redistribution Act became law.

## WHAT WERE THE POLITICAL QUALITIES OF LORD SALISBURY?

**The fall of Lord Randolph Churchill and the rise of W.H. Smith.** From the time of the Redistribution Act in 1884, and the defeat of the pro-Home Rule Liberals at the election of 1886, Salisbury was increasingly seen as a shrewd political operator. He held together a wide alliance very effectively and often handled men and measures with considerable aplomb. Lord Randolph Churchill had been allowed to have his head in the early 1880s when it could be argued that he was angling for Salisbury rather than Stafford Northcote to be the leader of the party. But Salisbury's acceptance of Churchill's hasty offer of resignation as Chancellor of the Exchequer at the end of 1886 was a well-timed masterstroke. For Churchill never recovered. Salisbury had shrewdly accepted a casual resignation from Churchill on a significant issue – that of allowing the army extra funds. A dispute on this issue was hardly likely to bring Churchill sympathy from the mass of the Conservative Party. It should be argued that Salisbury had already identified the inconsistencies and unreliabilities in Churchill's behaviour which were a sign of his oncoming syphilitic illness.

Salisbury's selection of **W.H. Smith** in 1887 to be First Lord of the Treasury (a post usually reserved for the Prime Minister) and run business in the House of Commons showed his shrewd judgement of men from a social group different from his own. Smith proved a most reliable and loyal colleague until his untimely death in 1891, after which he was sorely missed by Salisbury. The downfall of the duke's son and the rise of the newsagent's boy had brought the social changes in the party into stark relief. Salisbury's appointment of peers from a business background also showed a thoughtful assessment of the changing political situation. Only a handful had been appointed before 1886, Gladstone having traditional views on this matter, but over 200 were in the Upper House by 1914; and it was Salisbury who led the way after 1886. His numerous appointments included a brewer such as Henry Allsopp from Burton-on-Trent who was created Baron Hindlip in 1889, and a textile manufacturer like Bradford's Samuel Cunliffe-Lister, creator of the vast Manningham mills, who became Lord Masham in 1891.

## HOW GOOD WERE SALISBURY'S RELATIONS WITH THE LIBERAL UNIONISTS?

**The appointment of Goschen.** Liberal Unionists brought valuable advantages for Salisbury's governments on many occasions. In Salisbury's second ministry 1886–92, the government was in theory a purely Conservative administration relying nonetheless on Unionist support. The appointment of Unionist Goschen as Chancellor of the Exchequer at the start of 1887 was an isolated one at this stage. Goschen had been unhappy in the Liberal Party for some time and had been the only prominent member of the party to oppose the third Reform Bill. His financial expertise was universally acknowledged, however, and he could help Salisbury's government to acquire a reputation for fiscal competence. Moreover, Liberal Unionist leader Hartington gave his approval for Goschen's appointment and this brought the two groups closer together.

Goschen's own views, based on strict laissez-faire economics, made sure that there would be no immediate move towards any kind of protection, fair trade or even retaliation, for which Salisbury was known to argue at times. Moreover, Salisbury found Hartington 'cordial and loyal', and, perhaps more surprisingly, got on remarkably well with the Radical Liberal Unionist Joseph Chamberlain, admiring his 'absence of cant'. Yet Salisbury had earlier shown contempt for the Liberal Unionists who were, he felt, often 'spineless'. His controversial **Manacles and Manitoba speech** at the time of the Home Rule crisis was designed to put them in a weak position politically. Ever the realist, however, Salisbury increasingly came to accept their presence.

**Other Liberal Unionists.** Unionists were the beneficiaries of the wide-ranging patronage that Salisbury possessed. For instance Lord Lansdowne was appointed Viceroy of India, Lord Dufferin was made Ambassador in Rome and Sir Henry James would have been made a High Court judge (he later became a Unionist minister) if Salisbury had not discovered at the last moment that his leaving the House of Commons would have produced an awkward by-election. Unionists brought direct financial advantages to the Conservative Party and in 1892 party funds were up at least £100,000 over 1880. These Unionists were often from the business world rather than the landed classes and the shift from one to the other inside the Conservative Party was speeded up. In 1900 only 20 per cent of Conservative MPs were still exclusively from a landed background; 52 per cent were from commerce and industry.

**Joseph Chamberlain.** The Conservative–Liberal Unionist relationship was complicated by the fact that the Unionists themselves were not united. The towering Radical figure of Joseph Chamberlain looked down uneasily on the fray. Immediately after 1886 the leading issue was whether he and his Birmingham supporters would reunite with the Liberals. At the same time, however, Chamberlain and Hartington hoped to influence Salisbury's government in the direction of social reform at home and a more constructive approach towards Irish questions. Their return to the Liberals seemed more and more unlikely after Goschen's acceptance of office. It is significant to find that by 1891 Chamberlain was praising the social reforms of the Salisbury government: the extension of free elementary education was brought in that year and housing, public health and factory acts the previous year. Even more significantly he had congratulated the Conservative government on its decision to retain Egypt. Imperialism was beginning to edge out social reform in occupying the most prominent part of Chamberlain's political agenda.

When Salisbury returned to office for his third ministry in 1895 the alliance with the Liberal Unionists had become a formal one. Hartington, who had become the Duke of Devonshire in 1891, became Lord President of the Council – a post of some prestige but no specific departmental responsibilities. Chamberlain was offered any post he wished and took the post of Colonial Secretary, indicating the way his interests were moving. In the next few years Chamberlain found himself increasingly free to operate as he wished and policy became more adventurous than Salisbury had ever allowed before.

## WHAT WAS SALISBURY'S PERCEPTION OF THE ROLE OF GOVERNMENT?

Salisbury was a notable person to be the dominant political figure in the period after the third Reform Act when democratic politics were becoming essential in order to play the political game successfully. He came from the heart of the English aristocracy but presided over the country at a time when the landowning influence in the country was declining. However, he was adaptable. Even before he became Prime Minister he had in the early 1880s begun to speak more frequently 'out of doors'. Three days of speaking engagements in Edinburgh, for instance, showed how he could tailor his speeches to a potentially supportive, middle-class, northern audience, hardly one he was used to mixing with in his own social life. Since popular participation in government was a reality, he took the line of Robert Lowe after the second Reform Act that 'we must educate our masters'.

With Goschen and subsequently the cautious Hicks Beach as Chancellors, public expenditure was hardly likely to run wild and Salisbury was generally to follow the Liberal path of laissez-faire, except in the area of housing. Yet as Prime Minister he presided over a period when these principles were being challenged, not least as a result of the exposure of the sheer volume of the scale of poverty that existed up and down the country, as demonstrated in the surveys of Charles Booth in London and Seebohm Rowntree in York. After Salisbury's departure the demand for an extension to the range of social reform was to become overwhelming.

**National Union of Conservative Associations** A 'caucus' similar to the National Liberal Federation and adopted by Lord Randolph Churchill as the seat of his rapidly increasing power in the party. In 1884 he challenged his official leaders by resigning from the chair of the National Union, only to be triumphantly re-elected within a fortnight.

Salisbury frequently disliked the more extreme manifestations of his party followers. As a high churchman he never cared for popular Protestant (and sometimes anti-Catholic) demonstrations. He also found the more jingoistic of his supporters somewhat embarrassing and tried to restrain them. He took a cautious middle of the road position on 'fair trade' (see Section 4) questions opposing the wholesale introduction of protection but accepting the justification of 'retaliatory' tariffs for those who imposed high duties on British exports. The Conservative **National Union** carried protectionist motions in 1887 and 1891 and Salisbury walked a tightrope on the issue. Following the politically most effective line was a very delicate issue, and this is clearly shown in the days before the 1892 election when Salisbury allowed himself to be seen as a fraction less committed to free trade than the electorate seemed to want him to be. Joseph Chamberlain (later to split the party on this very issue) had the temerity to complain that Salisbury's comments on retaliation may have lost a dozen crucial seats to the Liberals at the election.

## WAS SALISBURY A SIGNIFICANT SOCIAL REFORMER?

In 1885 at the start of his first ministry Salisbury said he saw social reform as more significant than imperialism. Traditionally, his period of office has not been regarded as a great period of social innovation. Yet he did regard this area of political life as important. Some of this interest was a question of adapting realistically to circumstances. Since elementary education had effectively become compulsory in 1876, Salisbury argued that, logically, it ought to be free. Thus he could easily justify the grant of free universal elementary education in 1891. If the Liberals were to pass a similar measure it would most likely remove or restrict Church influence and control over schools which Salisbury, as a good churchman, was anxious to maintain. Help was also at hand for the other end of the educational spectrum. In 1889 Treasury grants to university foundations other than Oxford were granted and subsequently extended. The Westminster government was prepared to help elsewhere. To reduce local expenditure, grants in aid to local authorities were considerably increased rising from £4 to £8 million in the seven years after 1887. During the interlude of Liberal government (August 1892–June 1895), Salisbury did not oppose the controversial Death Duties Bill brought by William Harcourt in 1895, not only because he was wary of the Lords opposing a Commons' financial measure, but also because he acknowledged the government needed to raise additional revenue for the armed forces.

The Houses of the Working Classes Act in 1890 strengthened the compulsory purchase aspects of the 1875 Artisan's Dwelling Act. Salisbury's argument was that because of the building of new streets, railway buildings and the Thames Embankment, the space for working-class living had been reduced and the balance needed redressing. He wanted to promote good relations between capital and labour and the 1896 Conciliation Act provided for the appointment of arbitrators in industrial disputes if both sides agreed. His education bill of 1896 fell foul of Chamberlain's opposition because of its proposal to provide state help for Church schools. This was a great disappointment to Salisbury.

But at times Salisbury could be intransigent and take a strict laissez-faire attitude. He opposed the clause in an Allotments Bill with provision for compulsory purchase in stark contrast to his attitude on housing. He was reluctant to include London in the Local Government Reform of 1888 and only did so on the strong insistence of his Chancellor Goschen. He could not be persuaded by Joseph Chamberlain to take immediate action on the recommendations of the 1898 report for old age pension provision. Then the Boer War made it too late to take action. Salisbury preferred uncontroversial legislation: he argued that if it was contentious then public opinion was not ready for it. He disliked the manifesto idea that had taken hold since 1868. Yet he appeared to accept **Churchill's Dartford programme.** With the fall of Churchill this was not replaced, yet much of it was still carried through.

## HOW EFFECTIVE WAS CONSERVATIVE PARTY ORGANISATION?

Conservative Party organisation improved rapidly after the 1880 election.

**Churchill's Dartford programme** A speech made by Churchill in October 1886 at Dartford in Kent, putting forward – Chamberlain-like – a radical programme of reforms which he felt the government should take up. The reforms included democratic local government, free elementary education and land and agricultural reform.

As a result the party was able to take advantage of the opportunities that recent political changes had brought to the Conservatives. It was thought that the 1880 election was lost because of the Liberals' superior management of the electorate through the 'caucus' machine. The Conservatives did not intend simply to imitate this: Conservative organisation always remained driven from the top compared to the more grass-roots Liberal approach, but organisation was now seen as the key to success. In addressing bodies such as the South Essex Registration Association in 1882 Salisbury argued 'it is here, in associations of this kind, that the policy of the Empire is made'. 'Captain' Richard Middleton proved an astute choice as Party Agent in 1885: he soon took over the organisation of the National Union as well, remaining in charge until 1903. As the new organiser, he advised Salisbury on all matters electoral including the choosing of a suitable date for a general election. His analysis of turnout, seasonal variations and local differences has a late twentieth-century ring about it. He kept Salisbury in touch with grass-roots opinion in the party, who should be sweetened and who disciplined, and advised the Prime Minister on honours.

Middleton worked in effective tandem with Aretas Akers-Douglas who became Chief Whip at about the same time. Both were from west Kent and knew the suburban world of the new potential Conservative voter. Akers-Douglas advised about the selection of suitable Conservative candidates and the use of the national party budget. The Corrupt Practices Act in 1883 had limited expenses only in each *local* seat; so national fund-raising at election time was beginning to take on the increasingly significant role it has had ever since. Akers-Douglas and his successor Sir William Walrond were most efficient at persuading the Conservative MPs to turn out for a high percentage of parliamentary votes. This was not an easy task. A vote on a budget clause in 1890 was almost lost because so many Conservative MPs were at the Ascot races. 'Douglas and Middleton have never put me wrong' said Salisbury, not a man given to false praise. They provided him with an efficient stream of information and analysis without ever wanting to take over from the politicians in areas of policy. Salisbury played his own part. As early as 1884 he was complaining that his own epitaph would read: 'Died of writing inane letters to empty-headed Conservative Associations'. He continued to tour the country on the speaking tours that were becoming increasingly common for prominent politicians, speaking in a lively style, though prone to indiscretions at times.

### What was the nature of middle-class Conservative support?

**Economic interests.** What kind of people were attracted to this urban Conservatism? They covered a considerable social range. Salisbury himself saw the more plutocratic in the wealthy London suburb of Maida Vale as he made his journey from Westminster back to his country (still just country) seat at Hatfield in Hertfordshire. Henry Pelling's analysis of the

56 wealthiest constituencies – calculated by the number of servants employed – shows them to have been heavily Conservative. The number of Conservative MPs in London went up from 35 to 51 between 1885 and 1895. However, this was not just because of the wealthy middle class. The more modest lower middle-class bank employees, clerks and modest shopkeepers were increasingly coming to join the Conservative ranks as their own social position and economic stability increased. Clerks, 95,000 strong in the country as a whole in 1850, were to grow to a total of 843,000 by 1914.

**The role of women.** Though there was no female franchise, middle-class Conservative women were active for the party, especially in the Primrose League. Usually with no paid employment, prepared to 'muck in' now that electoral activity was becoming a more civilised affair, and much in demand for the substantial increase in popular political activity, they performed an invaluable role for the Conservatives in administration and money-raising. Conservative Party membership stood at one and a half million by 1900, truly a mass party. The growth of the Primrose League was also striking. Standing at 237,000 in 1886, it had risen to 1 million plus by 1891 and possibly approached 2 million by 1910, though Martin Pugh (*The Making of Modern British Politics*, 1993) thinks contemporaries may have exaggerated the figures.

**Working-class Conservatism.** Though the Conservatives were officially a free trade party, the degree of support for fair trade (see Section 4) meant that workers in trades such as Coventry ribbon weaving, Sheffield cutlery and Lancashire textiles were likely to look to the Conservatives. Twelve out of thirteen cotton spinning towns in Lancashire regularly returned Conservatives. Workers also joined the numerous Conservative clubs where (frequently) alcohol flowed more freely than in Liberal ones. In some areas the public house was the vital component in attracting potential members to meetings. Since Gladstone's Licensing Act, the drink trade had generally been very happy to let out its premises for Conservative rather than Liberal meetings. Yet the Conservative central organisation showed a sensitivity to local conditions. Middleton took a great interest in the detailed arrangements for such clubs, advising local Conservatives to furnish them plainly if comfortably so that working men would not feel out of place in them. In parts of Liverpool teetotal clubs would be set up where this was felt to be more appropriate.

**Popular Protestantism and Conservatism.** The development of Conservative clubs with their mix of social and political agendas had a distinctively religious tinge in Lancashire, where the Conservatives attracted large numbers of working men in towns such as Bury and Bolton. Unlike Yorkshire, where nonconformity was strong, working-class Anglicanism, often of the Evangelical variety, remained predominant in Lancashire. Popular Protestantism, was, however, exactly that – Protestant and not just low-church Anglican. The growing number of nonconformists in the Conservative ranks was becoming apparent as Wesleyan Methodists in particular – quite comfortable with the principle of establishment – joined the Unionists after the Home Rule split in 1886. Moreover, Salisbury was wary of too much ecclesiastical legislation after the controversies of the Public Worship Act of 1874 in Disraeli's ministry.

**Popular imperialism.** The association of Conservatives with imperialism also attracted support. Thus there were keen Conservative supporters in dockyard towns such as Chatham, Plymouth, Portsmouth, Southampton and the great shipbuilding centre of Newcastle, and among the manufacturers and labourers in the armaments factories in towns such as Woolwich (with a large arsenal and a good football team). The imperialist mood influenced the teaching of history and geography, and the style and content of popular adventure stories in what was becoming the great age of reading (taught in all primary schools thanks to the Education Act of 1870 but not yet subject to the rival influences of radio and TV, let alone computers). The Golden Jubilee celebrations in 1887 marked a high point of pride in the Empire and were, almost despite Salisbury, extremely popular.

Salisbury himself had a somewhat cynical attitude to the democratic process and what he perceived as the potentially dangerous influence of an unrestricted – and in his opinion semi-ignorant – public opinion on diplomacy. He did not particularly go out of his way to court popularity in his diplomatic activities, probably his favourite aspect of his public life. His foreign policy was hardly Palmerstonian in style; he was generally cautious and non-committal, and reluctant to get involved in large-scale undertakings, especially in the 1886–92 ministry. Indeed, he gave up the island of Heligoland in return for territory in East Africa, which was just the sort of possession that Palmerston might have used gunboats to defend. Salisbury's second ministry *coincided* – and this is the correct word – with the most dramatic stage of imperial expansion, not only in Africa but also in the Pacific, with the joint ownership of the New Hebrides with France in 1888 and sole control of Tonga the following year.

## HOW EFFECTIVE WAS SALISBURY'S FOREIGN POLICY?

Just as Gladstone always wished to be Chancellor of the Exchequer as well as Prime Minister so Salisbury always desired to hold the post of Foreign Secretary. He did so in his brief first ministry in 1885–6 and then not long into his second ministry at the start of 1887 when he **removed Stafford Northcote – now Earl of Iddesleigh.** Salisbury avoided formal alliances in a period when they were common, but this did not mean that Britain was friendless. Salisbury's pact with Italy and Austria in

## KEY EVENT

### The removal of the Earl of Iddesleigh

Salisbury was anxious to take the Foreign Office himself and to accommodate Liberal Unionists. Seeing that Iddesleigh was unwell and past his best and had written to Salisbury rather mildly indicating his willingness to stand down, Salisbury decided to drop him from the government. Unfortunately Salisbury carelessly leaked the sacking to the newspapers before Iddesleigh got to know of it. He was very offended and refused offers of any other post. A few days later he suddenly collapsed and died in the Prime Minister's presence. This was an embarrassing time for Salisbury, who was criticised for his insensitive handling of the situation.

1887 to defend the status quo in the Mediterranean was a secret one and not formally known about (though suspected in some quarters for a number of years). Such was the respect in which Salisbury was held that the Liberal opposition, though suspicious that there had been a secret agreement, accepted his assurances that no fundamental change had taken place in British commitments to other powers. Salisbury always refused attempts in the late 1880s by Germany's Chancellor Bismarck to draw him into the Triple Alliance of Germany, Austria and Italy. He believed that Britain's lack of definite alliances and commitments was to the country's advantage.

In the first part of his third ministry, after 1895, Salisbury did not lose his touch. His handling of the Fashoda crisis in 1898 (see Chapter 7, page 123) was seen as masterly as the French effectively were forced to back down. Salisbury continued to get on well with both Hartington and Chamberlain, his handling of the latter being in sharp contrast to Gladstone's inability to deal with his former Liberal colleague. However, Chamberlain's tentacles as Colonial Secretary widened as the decade drew to a close when Salisbury, in poorer health than hitherto, gave him a freer hand. The South African troubles leading to the Boer War in 1899 were to blot Salisbury's record of success, respected by Conservative, Unionist and many Liberals alike. From the time of the outbreak of this war the Conservative star began to fall. Even though Salisbury's timing of an election in 1900 proved successful, Conservative ascendancy was not to last much longer. The Liberals appeared to be in the wilderness as much as ever but in fact their period of opposition was soon to come to an end.

## CONCLUSION

- The Conservatives owed a good deal of their success in this period to the political statecraft of Lord Salisbury, a somewhat mysteriously underrated political figure for many years in view of his achievements and prominent position.
- Although Salisbury's domestic policies were cautious, he was not quite the diehard reactionary that he has sometimes been called.
- The Conservative Party adapted successfully to the changing political climate in widening its appeal and streamlining its organisation.
- Though Salisbury was never himself a 'jingo' he benefited from the popularity of the imperialistic mood of expansion at the end of the century.

# SECTION 8

## Liberalism: reassessment and revival
## Conservatives: success and split
## 1886–1906

### INTRODUCTION

- The Liberal Party, split and weakened by the Home Rule crisis in 1886, went through a difficult and divisive period for the rest of the century.
- Until 1894 the presence of Gladstone, intent on passing a Home Rule bill, was a complicating factor in Liberal development.
- The political and economic effects of the Boer War transformed the prospects for the Liberal and Conservative parties.
- Balfour's ministry between July 1902 and December 1905 appeared to be a disastrous one for the Conservatives.
- The Liberals recovered much of their old strength and nonconformist support as a series of traditional issues was highlighted in the period before the general election of 1906.

### Views of historians: the Liberals

Some of the weaknesses of the Liberal Party in this period have been traditionally ascribed to Gladstone's increasing determination to cling to the leadership of the party, despite his age. There is little dispute that he was obsessed with attempting a final settlement of the Home Rule question with Ireland, but did he go along with the more radical developments in the party in the early 1890s? Philip Magnus in *Gladstone* (1954) remarked that 'collectivism, construction (a mixture of socialism and social reform) and socialism were all anathema to Gladstone until the end of his life' and this has been a common view ever since. In a succinct overview, *Gladstone and the Liberal Party* (1990), Michael Winstanley referred to Gladstone's dislike of Chamberlain and Dilke's radicalism and also says he 'railed against what he regarded as the "selfish instincts" behind new appeals to the working-class voter'.

However, a detailed examination of the Liberal Party between 1885 and 1894 in Michael Barker's *Gladstone and Radicalism* (1975) saw Gladstone by no means as hostile to all new radical forces. Barker argued that Gladstone ultimately agreed with the general thrust of the taxation proposals of Chamberlain's Unauthorised Programme. Barker also asserted that, in continuing to push for Irish Home Rule after 1886, Gladstone 'chose also to espouse with enthusiasm the new radical claims stimulated by the example of Ireland'. Gladstone described the victory of the unions in the 1889 London dock strike as 'a real social advance' and in 1891 spoke sympathetically, if indirectly, about old age pensions. A more recent essay by Simon Peaple and John Vincent, 'Gladstone and the Working Man', in *Gladstone* (ed. 1998 by Peter Jagger) backs Barker, and portrays Gladstone as 'ahead of the times' in encouraging the idea of greater direct representation for the working man.

## Views of historians: the Conservatives

As far as the Conservatives are concerned it is tempting to see them falling apart as soon as the shrewd and experienced Salisbury left the helm in 1902. Few used to dispute the personal failings of Balfour as a leader both in anticipating the consequences of events and in his personal dealings with some of the leading figures of the day. But did he inherit a position that was to prove impossible to deal with?

E.H.H. Green's study, *The Crisis of Conservatism: The Politics, Economics and Ideology of the British Conservative Party, 1880–1914* (1995), is a complex book whose end date lies outside the confines of this volume. However, Green does argue that tariff reform was seen as a potential answer to the tensions within the party. These tensions had arisen from different economic interests at home, and from the questions raised by the Boer War. In difficult circumstances, Green argues, Balfour did not do as badly as some have perceived and was right to hang on to the idea of tariff reform. The importance of the tariff reform debate in the party during the earlier fair trade arguments which took place after 1880 is stressed by Green, although it was an issue given only a one-line footnote 25 years previously in Lord Blake's classic study, *The Conservative Party from Peel to Churchill* (1970).

Does this further enhance the reputation of Salisbury in holding the party together or make him responsible for failing to confront issues earlier? David Steele, in *Lord Salisbury: A Political Biography* (1999), asserts that 'there was no "crisis of Conservatism" while Salisbury led the Tories', but John Ramsden in *An Appetite for Power: A History of the Conservative Party since 1830* (1998) is influenced by Green when he sees 1900–2 as crucial: 'by the time that Salisbury was succeeded by Balfour ... the Party had ... moved significantly away from the comfortable world in which the parliamentary majority of 1900 had been achieved'.

## WHY WERE THE LIBERALS OUT OF OFFICE FOR MOST OF THE PERIOD 1886–1905?

In the late 1880s Liberals were frequently optimistic about soon returning to office. Although they had lost the general election of 1886, within eighteen months they began to win by-elections at a variety of places from Ayr to Southampton and Barrow to Spalding and were confident of

victory whenever the next election was called. But this optimism was not to last.

**Gladstone and the Liberals.** Salisbury's statesmanship, essentially conservative but not unprogressive at times, did not allow the Liberals a crusade round which to come together against him. Gladstone's plea 'Remember Mitchelstown' (see Section 6, page 215) was a call for some sort of moral outrage campaign against Salisbury's Irish policy. It never got anywhere near the Bulgarian-type excitements of the 1870s. Neither the scale of the deaths nor their location could produce that kind of reaction. Unlike earlier times, when Irish Church disestablishment had provided the rallying ground, the Liberals could not find that elusive, uniting issue. Gladstone was only remaining in politics to try to deal with Ireland through granting Home Rule and the Liberals had lost a number of their ablest supporters as a result of the Home Rule split. But not only had men like Chamberlain and Hartington departed from the party, **Sir Charles Dilke**, a match for Chamberlain in ability, also suddenly faded from the political scene in Parnell-like manner in 1886, when cited in a divorce case.

'The speedy concession to Ireland of what she most justly desires.' To replace it with another matter 'cannot even be contested'. Gladstone's view tended to be that, until Irish Home Rule was dealt with, there could be little concentration on other reforms and policies. He had convinced himself that if Home Rule was not connected to a land bill, as it was in 1886, it would get through. Without the dominant Chamberlain there was constant public debate in the Liberal Party over the next policy move that it should make. The 'Celtic fringes' became more dominant in the party circles, with Welshmen such as Stuart Rendel and the young David Lloyd George, and Charles Cameron in Scotland.

## What was the Liberals' relationship with the labour interest?

One hope Liberals possessed was that the growing political interest of the skilled working class was being expressed by the term **Lib-Lab**. The prevailing view in the 1880s was that, through Lib-Labism, the labour interest would continue to find political expression through the Liberal Party as it had first done in 1874 when Alexander McDonald and Thomas Burt had been elected as **working-class Liberal MPs** for mining communities. The split of the Liberals in 1886 over Home Rule and the detachment of many aristocratic Whigs gave hope to the more radical elements in the Liberal Party that they could incorporate strong, social reforming opinions within the party, and offer a radical alternative to the Conservatives and Unionists. But the Liberal Party was in some upheaval at this time. In the late 1880s there was still the hope that the Unionists might reconnect with the party and it was clear that, with Gladstone still at the helm, Irish Home Rule was not going to go away as an issue.

Moreover, the **rise of socialism** in the 1880s threatened to provide an alternative haven of support for the working-class voter.

**The rejection of working men.** Some Liberals, notably Gladstone, *were* keen to see working men as candidates for the party but few were selected. A well-connected Liberal with a private income was always a more attractive proposition than a working man, where the lack of a parliamentary salary would handicap him. The rejection of men like Keir Hardie – for the mid-Lanarkshire seat in 1888 – was to prove damaging in the long term. Within a few years future Labour Party leaders Ramsay MacDonald and Arthur Henderson had received similar treatment. Hardie's immediate response was to form the Scottish Labour Party. In the election of 1892 only 25 working men had been selected and of these a mere ten were successful. Only Hardie showed any degree of independence from the Liberals. Those that had been elected, like William Randal Cremer and George Howell, attached themselves to mainstream Liberalism on the majority of questions.

**Independent labour?** Some socialists had clearly decided they could not live in a Liberal Party where major employers of labour such as Sir Alfred Illingworth, MP for Bradford, and Sir James Kitson, the Leeds president of the National Liberal Federation, were so prominent. John Morley, a fervent believer in laissez-faire, found labour campaigners against him at Newcastle in the 1892 election. But the gradual development of the idea that unemployment and poverty could be related to the general state of the economy rather than individual failings was gaining ground. A radical movement outside the Liberal Party was beginning to grow. In the long term this was to benefit the Conservatives. Radicals who had broadly attached themselves to the Liberals from about 1850 to about 1890 were now becoming detached. Later, as their numbers grew, the middle-class electorate judged that these radicals could be most effectively opposed by the Conservatives. The degree of Lib-Lab co-operation varied. In London the **Progressive Party** on the London County Council showed them working together to the greatest extent. It is hardly surprising that some socialists decided to start their own **Independant Labour Party**.

## WHAT WAS THE NATURE OF LIBERAL DIVISIONS?

In the 1890s the divisions in the Liberal camp were considerable. Some strongly laissez-faire Liberals such as Morley remained suspicious of any reforms which involved an increasing role for the state; he also opposed the increasingly important imperialistic wing of the party, in which Lord Rosebery was prominent. The Imperial Federation League founded by Rosebery in 1889 indicated the direction in which some Liberals were going.

New Liberals, however, complicated the situation: men like Asquith, for example, who was something of an imperialist, but who also saw the need for the state to play a part in fostering better social conditions through educational, housing, factory and insurance reforms. Yet some labour representatives had already made up their mind that Lib-Labism would not do. The Liberal vote again became fractured. In 1890 the archetypal Lib-Lab exponent Henry Broadhurst (Under-Secretary at the Home Office in 1886) decided to retire as Secretary of the Parliamentary Committee of the TUC, making way for the more radical trade union figures like Tom Mann (engineering) and Ben Tillett (dockers) who were looking for separate labour representation.

One Liberal, Sydney Buxton, did raise the cry for more state intervention in sweated trades: but Conservative Home Secretary Henry Matthews, in his Factory and Workshops Bill of 1891, was very cautious. Liberals were more prepared to help children – the Commons agreed to raise the age for part-time child workers from 10 to 11 – but on questions of adult labour regulation, such as the eight-hour day for miners, they remained obdurate and voted against. They followed Gladstone's line that these issues were best left to voluntary agreements between employers and workers.

Finally the loyalty of nonconformist support for the Liberals was becoming less conspicious, though it lingered into the 1920s. Not only were the numbers of nonconformists growing more slowly than before, but many of them disliked the obvious Liberal association with what they saw as lawless Catholic Ireland. Methodist Hugh Price Hughes and Baptist John Clifford led the assault.

### What was the Newcastle programme?
One effort to bring about some co-ordination in policy was the Newcastle programme agreed at the party conference in Newcastle in 1891. But a good deal of this involved traditional Liberal causes such as Welsh and Scottish disestablishment, temperance reform through **local option**, an extension of democracy through further local government reform, Parliaments every three years instead of every seven and an end to plural voting at national elections, though not female suffrage. Little was said about social reform other than very cautious statements about restricting hours of work in some trades and a possible extension of employers' liability for accidents.

### Why was so little of the programme enacted in the Liberal government 1892–5?
When the Liberals were again briefly in power between 1892 and 1895, Home Rule dominated. After the defeat of Home Rule in the Lords (see Chapter 8, page 134). Gladstone was always likely to resign as he did in

1894. True to form it was over the excessive spending of public money: he thought the National Estimates too high. With Rosebery a very ineffective successor and the government a minority one, another election was inevitable in 1895 and it produced a comfortable return to power for Salisbury and the Conservatives, now more formally allied to the Unionists. None of the TUC's Labour Electoral Committee got elected. This led to a Liberal underestimation of labour potential in the next few years. The winning of the election by Salisbury and his Unionist coalition in 1895 has traditionally been attributed to the negative factor of Liberal unpopularity but it could also be claimed that the new middle classes were now enthusiastically supporting their party and saw Salisbury as a bedrock against the growth of socialism. The Liberal organisation certainly left much to be desired and 131 seats were left uncontested, nearly 100 fewer seats being contested than in 1892.

### Why did the Liberals suffer further defeats?

The Liberal Party was led by the sensitive but irresolute Earl of Rosebery until 1896 and then the ill-tempered Sir William Harcourt until he rsigned in 1898. The Liberals were uncomfortable as to the party's future direction and the nature of its membership. The nadir for the Liberals was reached during the early stages of the Boer War in 1899. The new leader Sir Henry Campbell-Bannerman had a difficult task in keeping the party together, with David Lloyd George adopting a pro-Boer stance in contrast to the more imperialistic views of Rosebery and Asquith. The election of 1900 was clearly called at a time of maximum inconvenience for the Liberals and resulted in another comfortable majority for Salisbury. The new century, closely followed by a new monarch in the rotund shape of Edward VII, did not immediately find a new Prime Minister or a new party in power. But this situation was not to last long. In the aftermath of the 1900 result, future electoral prospects for the Liberals looked bleak. They had just lost their second election running, and they seemed a divided, confused and uncertain party. However, the political tide soon turned and by 1906 the Liberals were back in government with a strong majority. How had this turnabout occurred?

## WHAT WAS THE EFFECT OF THE BOER WAR ON LIBERALS AND CONSERVATIVES?

At about the time of the death of Queen Victoria at the end of January 1901, in the middle of the Boer War, the tide began to turn for the Liberals and against the Conservatives. The struggle to defeat the Boers had to take the form of **attrition**. A slow advance across Boer-held territory entailed farm-burning and **internment** of the civilian population in 'camps' into which they were 'concentrated', and gave Britain the unenviable reputation of coining a phrase that retained a chilling

**KEY TERMS**

**Attrition and internment**
Attrition: wearing away or grinding down. In a military context, a slow and painstaking cornering of the opponent.
Internment: confining within prescribed limits. In this context, detention and imprisonment without trial.

reputation through the twentieth century. In June 1901, the Liberal leader Sir Henry Campbell-Bannerman denounced the internment tactic as pursuing 'methods of barbarism'. At the time it was made, this speech was controversial, but it marked the point where the pro-imperialist public mood began to fail. Campbell-Bannerman's speech would never produce the effect of Gladstone's outpourings on the Bulgarian atrocities in the 1870s: but on this occasion it was Britain itself that was accused of being barbaric.

## What was national efficiency?

One of the main social consequences of the war was the discovery that the young men who had been medically examined when they volunteered to join the army in 1899 and 1900 were largely unfit for service. General Maurice, exaggerating somewhat but not ridiculously so, reckoned that approaching 60 per cent of the new recruits had been rejected on medical grounds. If 'methods of barbarism' and 'slave labour' questioned Britain's *moral* superiority and fitness to rule other races, then these findings questioned its *physical* fitness to do so. It gave a new impetus to social reform on grounds of 'national efficiency'. 'New' Liberals, armed with the statistics from the surveys of Rowntree and Booth, now had more ammunition for launching a peacetime war on poverty. Although social reform has not been regarded as a major issue in the election campaign of 1905–6, research has shown that nearly 70 per cent of Liberal candidates did mention it in their pre-election pronouncements. This usually included Poor Law reform and old age pensions.

**Bushel** A measure of wheat, in liquid terms equivalent to a little over 100 litres.

**KEY CONCEPT**

**Imperial preference** The idea of imposing tariffs on foreign goods but favouring goods from the Empire by making their tariffs lower or non-existent.

Nor were Conservatives unaffected by public concern over the issue. The Balfour government set up two committees in 1904 and 1905. The first, unsurprisingly, was on physical deterioration; the second, on the working of the Poor Laws, suggested that the feeling that social provision needed to be extended beyond Poor Law relief was an idea widely shared.

## WHAT WAS THE ORIGIN OF THE TARIFF REFORM DEBATE?

It was the financial pressures brought about by the war that produced the most dramatic political upheaval and eventually brought Balfour and the Conservatives crashing to a comprehensively lost election at the start of 1906. Before his political retirement at the same time as Salisbury (in July 1902), the Chancellor of the Exchequer Hicks Beach was struggling to achieve a balanced budget and pay for the war. He reintroduced a (temporary) fixed duty on corn imports of 10d (about 4p) per **bushel** in his final budget. It was made clear that this was done purely for revenue-raising reasons, but it brought up the fair trade/free trade issue that had been quietly simmering away in Conservative ranks since the 1880s. Back in 1897 the idea of **imperial preference** had been discussed at the London

Colonial Conference held during the Queen's Diamond Jubilee celebrations. After the imposition of the tax in 1902, Sir Wilfred Laurier, Prime Minister of Canada, suggested that if the new duty was not imposed on Canada his country would, in turn, remove its duties on British goods. Joseph Chamberlain warmed to this idea and now saw imperial preference as the solution to British economic ills.

**Britain's relative economic decline.** That there were economic 'ills' was not really disputed. Britain's dominant world economic position was declining in relative terms as Germany and the United States, in particular, came to challenge it. In the 1890s the change was particularly noticeable. Britain had a 35 per cent share of the world trade in manufactured goods in 1890; this had been reduced to 28.4 per cent ten years later. Production of British steel had risen from 3.6 million tonnes in 1890 to 4.9 million in 1900 but the German increase in the same period was from 2.2 million to nearly 6.3 million. Would tariffs reverse the trend?

## What were the arguments over tariff reform?

**Arguments for.** Chamberlain was convinced that tariff reform, in the shape of imperial preference, was the solution. Three quarters of a million British workers, he claimed, were dependent for their employment on colonial trade. Moreover, Chamberlain argued, some 50 million white people, many of British origin, lived overseas in the Empire. (Chamberlain showed little interest in the non-white Empire in general and the Indian Empire in particular.) It was logical to make one large economic area of this world on which the 'sun never set'. British growth had almost stopped and was becalmed by foreign tariffs, while other countries' goods literally sailed into British ports. The Radical still inside the now Unionist Chamberlain argued that tariff reform would not only lead to further economic development, but would also distribute wealth better among all classes of the British community. Cherished aims such as the introduction of old age pensions would be brought nearer. Germany, France, Austria and Russia had all had tariffs since the early 1880s and the United States raised theirs dramatically after the election of President McKinley in 1896. Chamberlain asserted that it was folly for Britain not to retaliate in some measure.

**Arguments against.** But free traders did not agree. Prominent among their arguments was a concern that food prices would rise. This was a most sensitive subject. Consumer-oriented twenty-first century men and women might find a rise in the price of bread a minor irritant, but for the large number of the population on the breadline, who had to spend a high proportion of their income on food, price rises in this area spelt potential economic disaster. Free trade Liberals argued the reverse of Chamberlain: that the poor would be the ones to suffer from tariffs and

**Arthur Balfour: was he a disaster as Prime Minister?**

there would be more unemployment, not less. The growth of countries like Germany and the United States, they argued, was not connected with tariffs but with their size, vast resources and rapidly increasing population. Free trade had made Britain great and had assumed for these people an almost divine status. Significantly, however, the arguments on both sides were couched less in terms of party principle than in what policy would best benefit the people. The age of democracy was dawning.

In fact the backing for tariff reform tended to come from those who felt they had most to gain from it. Support was strong in Chamberlain-dominated Birmingham and the West Midlands where the various iron and engineering tradesmen felt tariffs would end cheap foreign competition. In 1900 about a quarter of the value of British imports came from manufactured items, a sharp increase over the previous generation. By contrast, much of the cotton textile trade and the shipbuilding industry saw their markets disappearing if other countries were to retaliate. In Lancashire the traditional Conservative support began to fade, as it was apparent that the Liberals would never desert free trade for tariff reform.

### Tariff reform: what was the political fallout?

It was indeed the Liberals who were to benefit most from the debate and the Conservatives who were to lose their dominant political position gained under Salisbury. The potentially divisive nature of the issue for Conservatives, the uncertainty of Prime Minister Balfour's political touch over it, and the overweening ambition of Chamberlain to control the direction of party policy, all combined to produce a profound and complex division.

After the retirement of Hicks Beach from the Exchequer, Balfour, as the new Prime Minister, selected C.T. Ritchie as his new Chancellor. Ritchie, who had flirted with the fair trade movement at the end of the 1880s, was now a convinced free trader, but found Chamberlain determined to raise the issue of tariff reform. In the winter of 1902–3 Chamberlain paid a long visit to South Africa and returned having become even more convinced of the necessity of imperial preference. Balfour, however, though partially convinced by Chamberlain's arguments, was reluctant to put pressure on his new Chancellor and so Ritchie, in his first budget in 1903, was allowed to go ahead with his chosen policy of removing Hicks Beach's temporary corn duty. Balfour's unwise decision to promise a review of the tariff policy *after* Ritchie's budget persuaded Chamberlain not to resign and continue his fight for tariffs from the inside. This soon had dramatic consequences. In May 1903 Chamberlain made a speech at Birmingham where he argued that 'a review of our fiscal system was necessary and desirable'. The battle was joined and it was the Conservatives who were battling.

Balfour's indecisive leadership was now fatal. He promised an unpopular compromise policy on retaliatory tariffs but no imperial preference, at which point in September 1903 Chamberlain resigned in order to organise a national campaign for tariff reform. Chamberlain was unaware that Balfour was, at the same time, accepting the resignation of the leading free trader in the cabinet, the Duke of Devonshire (formerly Lord Hartington). Devonshire had been offended by a speech from Balfour which suggested tariffs *would* be introduced when the time was ripe.

The party was now hopelessly divided. The young Winston Churchill **crossed the floor of the House** to join the Liberals. Balfour had lost some of his ablest ministers. Chamberlain claimed that 174 Conservatives supported him and of the other 200 only 27 were in outright opposition, but the Unionist Free Fooders, as they became known, put up a vigorous fight. By 1905 the Liberals were in a strong position. At the first two by-elections, fought at the end of 1903, with tariff reform as an issue, the Conservatives had done well; but in those fought in 1904 the Liberals were universally triumphant. The whole affair had enabled them to re-unite on one of their cherished beliefs, free trade.

## WHY WERE THE LIBERALS SO UNITED?

By the end of 1905 the Liberals possessed considerable political advantages. Balfour chose this moment to resign, in December. However, he did not call an election. Perhaps he hoped the Liberal leader, Campbell-Bannerman, would have difficulty forming a united government; but in complete opposition to the Conservatives, Liberal tensions and dissensions had melted away. Political circumstances had indeed been favourable to them.

## Chinese 'slavery'

Another factor linked to the Boer War produced the possibility of a moral crusade for the Liberals and a further chance to recover their old confidence. As a result of the post-war labour shortage in South Africa, High Commissioner Sir Alfred Milner decided to import Chinese labour in the Rand gold mines. Initially resisted by Chamberlain as Colonial Secretary, it was introduced early in 1904 after he had resigned. It involved the Chinese being hired as **indentured** labourers and living and working in appalling and overcrowded conditions. The Liberal humanitarian conscience had been aroused once more, oddly combined with more racist feelings that the Chinese had prevented British workers from emigrating to South Africa for another employment opportunity. It gave the Liberals and Campbell-Bannerman a chance for more emotive language with the phrase 'Chinese slavery' and it certainly damaged Balfour's government at what was already a difficult time.

## Education: another unfortunate subject for the Conservatives

One valuable link that had strengthened the Liberals again in the first years of the new century was the nonconformist one. Here, Balfour inherited trouble rather than created it. Shortly before Salisbury retired in July, a new Education Bill had been presented to Parliament. On similar lines to the proposal that had been dropped in 1896, its aim was to bring help to the voluntary Church schools which were in danger of closing because of lack of funds. 'Many of the voluntary schools are ruined', Salisbury bewailed, 'they can only be saved by contributions in some form by the state'. That 'form' had been the central government in the past, so the principle of state aid was not new.

However, the Bill's proposal for the ratepayers to fund the schools was different and more far-reaching. It brought nonconformist opposition from those who had no intention of allowing 'Rome on the rates', as Baptist leader John Clifford put it. The High Church Oxford Movement had spread well into the Anglican Church, making nonconformists suspicious of 'ritualising' clergymen who, they believed, would spread their beliefs in schools. Resentment and suspicion were particularly strong in Wales, where a religious revival in 1904–5 added a passionate intensity to the debates. Anglican schools were seen as particularly intrusive in many areas of the principality and in the county council elections in Wales in 1904 Liberals completely swept the board. The old correlation between nonconformity and Liberalism had been restored in fullest measure. At its height resistance to the Act involved refusal to pay the part of the rate calculated to be the amount subsidising an Anglican school. Imprisonment sometimes resulted after a refusal to pay the subsequent fine.

### Why did the Licensing Act of 1904 produce a political dispute?

With the nonconformist conscience thoroughly aroused there was also excitement over the Licensing Bill of 1904. It had been increasingly common to find local authorities refusing to renew licences in towns where there were large numbers of public houses already. This refusal to re-license was generally supported, and not just by teetotal and abstemious Liberals. But, because of some legal uncertainties, the compensation traditionally given to the unlucky landlords had not been paid in recent cases, effectively taking away their livelihood. Trouble ensued over the Bill's proposed compensation to the unfortunate landlords. In quieter times the Bill would have been seen as acceptable. But these were not quieter times. No matter that the money was coming from a levy from the luckier ones who did have their licences renewed, and who would now presumably receive more trade. The very idea of money going to suppliers of the demon drink produced more protests at the actions of the by now weakening government.

## WHAT WERE BALFOURS'S SHORTCOMINGS AS PRIME MINISTER?

Balfour, the Prime Minister since Salisbury's retirement, seemed to have gone from one disaster to another. His assumption of power had been surrounded by suggestions of **nepotism** as he was Salisbury's nephew. When he invited Salisbury's son into the government in 1903, he had four relatives of one kind or another sitting around the cabinet table. The phrase coined around 1900 to describe this development, the 'Hotel Cecil' (Cecil being the Salisbury family name), still seemed to apply. Although a man of considerable intellectual ability, Balfour's rather languid style of governing attracted criticism. He did not always anticipate reactions to some of his measures, as when Chamberlain vainly warned him about nonconformist reaction to the Education Act, but he was shown at his worst in the tariff reform dispute where he managed to lose the most able supporter of the idea – Chamberlain – and one of free trade's staunchest defenders, the Duke of Devonshire (Hartington). On reflection Balfour should perhaps have changed Salisbury's cabinet rather more and stamped his own authority more forcefully on the new government.

The result was that the real achievements of his relatively short ministry have been largely missed. The Education and the Licensing Acts operated well. A new relationship was forged with France thanks partly to the Parisian visits of the new King Edward VII – with whom Balfour got on better than his uncle had done; Salisbury, in his final year as Prime Minister, had never quite come to terms with the fact that Queen Victoria was no longer alive. The Irish Land Purchase Act of **Wyndham**

**KEY TERM**

**Nepotism**
Appointing one's relations to posts of importance.

in 1903 was another outstanding success. Moreover, it is unfair to blame Balfour for Wyndham's resignation in 1905 when some Conservatives criticised the possibility of future reforms seen by some as dangerously close to Home Rule. Balfour had tried to keep him but Wyndham had insisted on resigning.

There were other significant reforms. In the armed services greater efficiency was produced by the creation of a new Army General Staff in 1904 and the abolition of the old post of Commander-in-Chief as well as the start of major naval reforms. There was also the re-organisation of the recently created Committee of Imperial Defence in 1903–4. More controversial was the Aliens Act of 1905 which sought to modify the traditional British welcome to all comers, without turning away genuine asylum seekers, a debate continuing 100 hundred years later. Balfour was also aware of unemployment problems and one of his last pieces of legislation was his brother Gerald's Unemployed Workmen's Act of 1905. Unemployment committees linked up with borough councils and Poor Law guardians to help find work for those without and to investigate emigration possibilities. However, in areas of social reform it was now the Liberals who had more to offer.

## WHAT WAS THE NATURE OF THE LIBERAL RECOVERY?

The Liberal Party that took office when Balfour resigned in December 1905 was a very different body from the squabbling party of the 1890s. It was transforming its frequently negative creed (especially over the removal of privilege) to a more constructive ideology; one based upon seeing the necessity for protection for the less fortunate in society as the true creation of a free society, achievable through some redistribution of taxation. The stronger leadership of Campbell-Bannerman since 1898 had certainly helped this development, though in the 1892–5 ministry there had been a few early signs of legislation that moved in this direction. These included the Inspection of Railways Act and Employers' Liability Act (heavily modified in the Lords) as well as the better-known death duties legislation which had been imposed at 1 per cent on estates of £50 and graduated to reach 8 per cent on those of £1 million or above. The Rainbow Circle, founded in 1893 by such young Liberals as Herbert Samuel and Charles Trevelyan, restored both intellectual activity and social concern to the forefront of the party's thinking.

Although Liberal imperialism was still present, the tensions and divisions between imperialists and anti-imperialists had faded by the end of the Boer War. Moreover, so had the financial problems that had led to Liberals failing to contest 163 seats firmly controlled by Conservatives or Liberal Unionists. They were attracting a younger generation of Liberals and, in their triumphant victory in the general election of January 1906, 205 out of the 405 Liberal MPs elected had never sat in Parliament before.

### Lib-Labism again? The pact of 1903

Another important political development of the first half-dozen years of the century was also benefiting the Liberals, at least in the short run. The development of the Labour Party – known from 1900 to 1906 as the Labour Representation Committee – was seen at this stage as helping the Liberals rather than the Conservatives in electoral terms. At first sight this may seem surprising. The breakdown of Lib-Lab co-operation in the 1890s and the eventual emergence of a separate labour representation group by the end of the decade could have spelt difficulty for the Liberals in attracting the support of working men away from them. In the long run this was indeed the case but at first a mutually beneficial link between the two parties was forged. Perhaps because of this very threat Herbert Gladstone – son of the ex-Prime Minister and Liberal Chief Whip – undertook secret talks with LRC Secretary Ramsay MacDonald in 1903 to develop an electoral pact. The LRC would be given a free run in seats where a split in the anti-Conservative vote would give victory to the Tory. In return Labour would also stand aside in places where the Liberals had a chance of edging out the Conservatives if their vote was unaffected by the appearance of a third party.

There was a pressing reason for Labour to agree to this pact. For the Liberals also promised that, if elected, their first task would be to introduce a Trade Disputes Act, a piece of legislation the labour movement desperately required. In 1901 the House of Lords had made the final decision in a long-running legal case concerning the Taff Vale Railway Company and the Amalgamated Society of Railway Servants trade union. In August 1900 the company had sued the union for loss of earnings after a strike and it was this verdict in favour of the company that the House of Lords, overruling the Appeal Court, had confirmed. It would seem to make strikes almost impossible for fear of legal action and throw into doubt the legal position of trade unions since the passing of trade union acts by Liberals and Conservatives in the 1870s. Only a fresh piece of legislation confirming the right of trade unions to withhold labour in a trade dispute would settle the question. Balfour's government had showed no signs of taking action on the matter and so representatives of labour held out hopes for a Liberal Party victory and suitable legislation on its election in January 1906. They were not to be disappointed: it was one of the first major pieces of legislation passed by the new Liberal government later in the year.

## CONCLUSION

With 400 Liberal MPs elected in 1906 and a majority of 243 over the Conservatives, the Liberals were enjoying one of their greatest-ever successes. A number of factors had favoured the Liberals in the period immediately preceding the election: the Conservative split over tariff reform, the revival of nonconformist support for the Liberals and the Liberals' pact with the new Labour Party.

These should be seen as the most significant factors in the result. The Conservatives, in contrast, had suffered their worst-ever defeat with only the election in the aftermath of the first Reform Act in 1832 being anywhere near as bad. As then, a left-of-centre government was about to embark on a series of major reforms and the attitude of a Conservative-dominated House of Lords was to become an issue for discussion. The Conservative leader Balfour was only too well aware of another historical parallel: the split in the Conservatives over protection had happened before in 1846. Would it take them as long to recover as it did then? Or would they even survive as a party? At this stage few would have predicted the collapse of Liberalism in the 1920s and the domination of many twentieth-century governments by Conservatives.

When attempting a document question as the first question in an examination, you need to warm up your brain as quickly as possible. You must allow some time for reading and digestion of the extracts, and so you should not plunge into writing about them too quickly. On the other hand, you don't want to take up an *excessive* amount of time on the reading and comprehension. So, how do you read through the extracts as swiftly but also as thoroughly as possible? Different approaches suit different people but you might like to consider a set format which, if followed, should minimise the effects of early nerves. One possibility is outlined below.

- Read the source descriptions of all the extracts: this will only take a few seconds but you will immediately gain a good idea of the broad subject matter and your brain can begin recalling your ideas about this area of the course. In this case 'Conservative policy on post-1886 Ireland' is clearly the focus.

- Now read through the two questions you are asked to answer. Again this will not take long. They clearly involve a comparative assessment of two politically opposed speeches, and an overall assessment of Conservative Irish policy.

- *Only now* read the extracts themselves; but as you do so you should be reading them with the questions in mind instead of reading them worrying 'what on earth are they going to ask me in relation to this extract?'

# SOURCE-BASED QUESTIONS IN THE STYLE OF AQA

Read the following sources and then answer the questions which follow.

### Source A
Two clear, positive intelligible plans are before the world. There is the plan of the [Liberal] government; and there is the plan of Lord Salisbury. Our plan is that Ireland should, under well-considered conditions, transact her own affairs. His plan is to ask Parliament for new repressive laws, and to enforce them resolutely for twenty years; at the end of which time he assures us that Ireland will be fit to accept any gifts in the way of local government or the repeal of the coercion laws, that you may wish to give her ...

Gladstone's address to the electors of Midlothian June 1886. Quoted in John Wroughton, *Documents on British Political History 1815–1914* (1971).

### Source B
(In the seventeenth century Oliver Cromwell brutally suppressed an Irish rebellion against English control.)

Cromwell failed because he relied solely upon repressive measures. That mistake I shall not imitate. I shall be as relentless as Cromwell in enforcing obedience to the law, but at the same time I shall be as radical as any reformer in redressing any grievances, and especially in removing every cause of complaint in regard to the land. It is on the twofold aspect of my policy that I rely for my success. Hitherto, English governments have stood first upon one leg and then upon the other. They have either been all for repression or all for reform. I am for both; repression as stern as Cromwell; reform as thorough as Mr Parnell or anyone else can desire.

Arthur Balfour outlines his policy as Chief Secretary for Ireland 1887. From B. Alderson, *Arthur James Balfour: The Man and his Work* (1903), quoted in Michael Willis, *Reading Historical Documents: Nineteenth Century Britain 1815–1914* (1990).

### Source C
When Salisbury appointed his nephew, Gerald Balfour, Arthur's younger brother, to the Chief Secretaryship for Ireland in early July 1895, he did not realise the extent to which ... [Gerald Balfour] was committed to a new form of constructive, engaged Unionism. ... In a speech at Leeds he [Gerald Balfour] candidly admitted 'the Government would of course be very glad if they were able by kindness to kill Home Rule'.

A modern biographer looks at Lord Salisbury's Irish policy. From Andrew Roberts, *Salisbury: Victorian Titan* (1999).

## Questions

> 1 Study sources A and B. How far does Arthur Balfour's speech confirm Gladstone's comments about Conservative policy in Ireland in 1886?
>
> (10 marks)

> 2 Study all three sources and use your own knowledge. Discuss the view that Conservative policy towards Ireland between 1886 and 1905 was to 'by kindness kill Home Rule' rather than follow a 'repressive policy'.
>
> (20 marks)

**Question 1.** Firstly you need to examine what Gladstone's comments are and *then* go on to consider the content of Balfour's speech. Try to think of a summary word for the mood of Gladstone's extract: possibilities are 'critical', 'hostile', 'accusatory'. Use of the odd word such as this in your answer would be useful. Now think in terms of two or three ways in which Gladstone is critical, hostile or accusatory. Some possibilities are:

- the proposed 'repressive laws';
- their resolute enforcement;
- the long delay before any more beneficial and constructive legislation is introduced.

Now examine Balfour's comments. What evidence is there of 'repressive laws', their resolute enforcement and a delay before the introduction of constructive reforms? The following points may occur to you if you undertake this assessment in a methodical way.

Remember that if you are asked to comment on the *degree* of similarity between two extracts the likelihood is that there will be some similarities and some contrasts. So, in what ways does the Balfour speech confirm Gladstone's critical comments?

- Balfour uses the word 'relentless' to describe part of his policy which is not inconsistent with Gladstone's use of the word 'resolute'. He also admits indirectly to the use of repression; he refers to Cromwell's policy by this name and then suggests his own policy will in some ways be similar. It seems clear that Balfour is going to follow the line of policy to which Gladstone refers, though not clear whether he will do this for as long as Gladstone fears: i.e. 20 years. You can make these points.

However, Balfour makes it clear that, in contradiction of Gladstone's accusation, he will not introduce a long period of repression pure and simple but will introduce 'reform' at the same time as the harsher policies. In this important respect, Balfour's speech does not confirm Gladstone's comments. Now you should be in a position to write out an answer to this question. You can quote from the extracts, but if you do:

- make them very brief: a short phrase or even just one significant word (see a few examples quoted above);
- try to work it naturally into the sentence rather than bringing your answer to a halt to fit it in.

To reach the higher levels your answer needs to be properly comparative. You should avoid making a series of points about one extract followed by a series of points about the other. Make a point that will relate to both extracts in order to obtain the maximum degree of comparison with the other extract. Do this at the beginning of a paragraph, following up your general assertion with specific references to the extracts. For instance, your paragraph might begin:

*One way in which Balfour's speech appears to confirm Gladstone's assertion, is that Balfour accepts that certain aspects of his policy will be repressive.*

Go on to illustrate this point before dealing with another one. If there is another point which confirms the correctness of Gladstone's assertion, use linking vocabulary such as 'moreover', 'in addition' or 'as well as this'. However, if you are going to make a contrasting point and argue that there are differences between Gladstone's comments and the actual policy of Balfour, then you need to use language that indicates the contrast, with words or phrases such as 'however', 'nevertheless' or 'despite this'. These immediately indicate a change of mood in an economical fashion.

In this way you should be able to display the skills required to reach the highest level of response – level 4 – where you are required to select the appropriate material from the sources, analyse the extent of similarity or difference in them and reach a careful judgement based on this material.

**Question 2.** Most assertions used for examination purposes will have some truth in them but generally go too far (or not far enough) in their comments. This gives you an opportunity to plan an answer, with some points confirming the judgement and others not. For instance, in this case you could use the following evidence to suggest a degree of truth in the assertion.

Mention for example some of Arthur Balfour's more constructive policies as Irish Secretary between 1887 and 1891 such as land purchase, the Congested Districts Board and the investment in new railways. However, for the top levels you need to avoid mere reproduction of these. What you need to do is assess how far these policies can be seen to be 'kind' and to what extent they killed the desire for Home Rule. You also need to examine how far the policies of the Balfour brothers (with Gerald Balfour as Chief Secretary from 1895 to 1902) were designed primarily to establish law and order in Ireland. But whatever your precise assessment on this point, you could use this material and contrast it with Gladstone's prediction in Source A to show that the Conservative policies in these years were not all repressive. The end date of the question allows you to include George Wyndham's important Land Purchase Act of 1903.

But you would also need to examine the harsher aspects of Conservative polices. You could refer to Arthur Balfour's own admission of this in Source B and give some examples. After all, Balfour was not known as 'Bloody Balfour' for nothing, and reference could be made to the harsh new Crimes Act of 1887 and the deaths in the same year of nationalists at Mitchelstown, an incident much criticised by Gladstone, who saw this event as the epitome of the policy of pure repression he mentions in Source A.

Whilst you would be wise to mention some points in favour of the assertion and some points against, you do not have to sit on the fence in your conclusion. You can weight the evidence more in one direction than another. At the very least it is not a bad idea to question the absolute truth of an assertion. When you are asked about the truth of an assertion *over a period of time* one approach is to argue that the assertion may be truer of one part of the period. Here, for instance you could argue, referring to Source C, that as the 1890s went on the 'kinder' aspects of government policy were arguably more apparent than they had been in the late 1880s. The fact that Lord Salisbury was never as enthusiastic about Irish reform as the Balfour brothers can also be made, referring to Source C.

To reach the higher mark levels 4 and 5 – 16 out of 20 and above – you need to select material from both the sources *and* your own knowledge, provide an analytical response to the question and, therefore, be able to reach an effectively sustained judgement appropriate to the demands of the question. The best way to do this is to make a point of your own first and then use a reference to one of the extracts to illustrate it. For example, you could begin one point:

*Arthur Balfour's policy as Chief Secretary 1887–91 was a repressive one in some respects; as indicated in Source B, he admitted this himself, referring to repression 'as stern as Cromwell'.*

For the highest level of marks evidence of independent judgement is required. For instance, you could argue that Irish nationalist feeling had become so strong by the turn of the century that no policy, however constructive or however kind, was ever going to satisfy it if it fell short of Home Rule.

# SOURCE-BASED QUESTIONS IN THE STYLE OF OCR: THE PRINCIPLES BEHIND GLADSTONE'S AND DISRAELI'S FOREIGN POLICY

## Source A

Before 1868 Gladstone and Disraeli had often found themselves in entire agreement on foreign affairs. This was easier when they were both in opposition to Palmerston. ... Both also stressed the need for Britain to co-operate with the other European powers, especially France, if war in Europe was to be avoided. Their sane attitude to France was to be one theme on which the two rivals never clashed. ... In his Guildhall speech of 1879 Disraeli outlined the principles on which he had acted. He stressed ... Britain's duty as the wealthiest of Empires to honour her obligations to Europe. Despite his flirtation with Imperialism, Disraeli recognised Britain's decisive role in Europe. Indeed when Disraeli spoke of Empire he did not mean merely colonial annexations, but the whole power of Britain which was based on both her territorial possessions and her moral influence in the world. Gladstone in his Midlothian campaign summed up his attitude to Britain's part in international relations in much the same way. He sought to strengthen and use the Empire to preserve the 'blessings of peace'... acknowledging the rights of all nations.

A British historian sees similarities in the foreign-policy principles of the two men. From B.H. Abbott, *Gladstone and Disraeli* (1972).

## Source B

In foreign affairs, Disraeli followed very much in the footsteps of Palmerston. His overriding concern was the protection of British interests. He never shared any of Gladstone's grand ideas about countries working together in a Concert of Europe. This was clear from his approach to the Eastern Question. Here Disraeli's basic aim was to prevent the Russians exploiting the terminal decline of the Ottoman Empire to their own advantage. His anxiety was that, as Turkey's hold over its Balkan and middle eastern territories weakened, Russia would move in, thus menacing ... Britain's strategic and commercial position ... Disraeli was following the established British line. [He] criticised Gladstone for his failure to respond to this renewed Russian threat. Gladstone, however, was not mobbed by strategic concerns but by moral ones ... his condemnation of Turkey for its savagery and his contempt for Disraeli's government ... polarised opinion in Britain. The nation divided between Gladstone, the protector of oppressed peoples and Disraeli, the guardian of the nation's interests.

A more recent writer contrasts the views of the two men quite sharply. From Michael Lynch *An Introduction to Nineteenth Century British History* (1999).

## Source C

When Disraeli took office in 1874, it is doubtful whether he had any clear ideas on foreign policy other than doing something – it did not matter what – to re-assert Britain's power in Europe. He had been highly critical of Gladstone's allegedly inactive attitude during the last six years. Failure to mediate in the Franco-Prussian War, to prevent the Russian denunciation of the Black Sea Clauses or to modify the result of the Alabama arbitration, all were cited as instances of Britain's isolation and general decline; and as Leader of the Opposition Disraeli naturally made the most of them. He was therefore in the mood to seize the first chance which came his way of demonstrating that the tone of British policy had changed.

Disraeli's principal biographer searches in vain for Disraeli's principles in foreign policy. From Robert Blake, *Disraeli* (1966).

## Source D

I will tell you what I think to be the right principles of foreign policy. ... The first thing is to foster the strength of the Empire by just legislation and economy at home ... and to reserve the strength of the Empire, to reserve the expenditure of that strength, for great and worthy occasions abroad ... my second principle .... ought to be to preserve to the nations of the world ... the blessings of peace. ... The third principle is ... to strive to cultivate ... what is called the Concert of Europe ... my fourth principle is that you should avoid needless and entangling engagements ... my fifth is to acknowledge the equal rights of all nations. ... And ... [the] sixth is ... [that] the foreign policy of England should always be inspired by the love of freedom.

Gladstone sets out his foreign-policy principles in a Midlothian speech in 1879. Quoted in Michael Scott-Baumann (ed.), *Years of Expansion: Britain 1815–1914* (1995).

## Questions

> 1 Study sources A and B. Examine and explain the differences in the two historians' views expressed.

> 2 Study all the sources. How helpful are the sources in examining the view that Gladstone followed clearer principles in foreign policy than did Disraeli?

**Question 1.** In answering this question, the contrasting views need to be clearly identified. Here it would be useful to bring out the differences by use of specific phrases from the extracts to illustrate your assertions. For example, the closeness of Gladstone's and Disraeli's views argued for in Source A, and the substantial difference of opinion apparent from Source B, could be brought out by setting the phrase 'entire agreement' in Source A against 'nation divided' in Source B. In addition, differences could also be brought out by reference to the permanent agreement over attitudes to France in Source A compared with the diametrically opposed viewpoints over the approach to Russia and Turkey in Source B.

The extracts are of generous length so try to use as wide a range of points from them as possible. Thus, you should contrast the difference in the use of the word 'moral': Source A relates Disraeli's view of Empire to this word, and implies Gladstone has a similar view. However, in Source B this same word 'moral' is reserved for Gladstone's approach to the Russian-Turkish question, and Disraeli, by implication, is only concerned with 'strategic concerns'.

A carefully constructed evaluation of the differences – with close reasoning – will receive credit. This approach should help you to avoid paraphrase, which will receive little credit. However, for the highest band of achievement, candidates also need to make some qualifying remarks that *explain* some reasons for the differences. Here, the differences in the timeframe will help in constructing a convincing argument. Source A makes a point of referring to the pre-1868 period, when it is admitted there was less to disagree about in foreign policy. By contrast, Source B specifically refers to the post-Palmerston period, that is, after 1865. Here, a candidate's *contextual* knowledge can be put to good effect. Differences between extracts may be less clear-cut than at first sight, and so might be explained by looking at which aspects of the policies in question are being highlighted. Different criteria, with a wider or narrower vision of the subject in question, may have been adopted. Moreover, the fact that the subject matter is not entirely the same, could also be used to help explain the differences in the two accounts. For instance, Source B focuses on the issue – the Eastern Question – and the time – the late 1870s – when the bitterness of the division between Gladstone and Disraeli was at its greatest.

Try to work very short quotations (often just one word) from the extracts into your answer. For instance:

*The apparent contrast between the two pieces, however, is modified by the fact that the 'entire agreement' of Source A is confined to the period before either of the two men became Prime Minister. It therefore excludes the time when, as Disraeli was later to put it, all principles of foreign policy had to be re-cast because of the changed nature of Europe after the Franco-Prussian war and the subsequent unification of Germany. Moreover, Source B focuses on the issue where Gladstone's sense of outrage at the 'savagery' of the Turks and his concern for 'oppressed peoples' was likely to maximise his different approach from Disraeli to the Eastern Question.*

**Question 2.** Here it is important to make reference to *all* the extracts if the highest level of marks is to be obtained. The context of the sources needs careful examination. The date, the precise source and the subject matter may all provide clues that might be helpful in answering the question. The careful analysis of each extract is clearly important, but this skill needs to be combined with your own wider understanding and knowledge.

So, Source A would be seen as helpful because it suggests similarities rather than differences between the policies over a wide time span, and its definition of Empire, although from a late twentieth-century source, gives a clear idea of the phrase that relates to the context of the time 100 years earlier. By contrast, Source B is more concerned with the specific case of the Eastern Question of the 1870s. However, it does give us a sense of the continuity of foreign policy in what was a rather different Europe in the 1870s, by making a reference to the Palmerstonian past and linking Disraeli's more adventurous foreign policy to this tradition.

Source C has the advantage of focusing on a specific period of time for examining Disraeli's principles in foreign policy and presenting the valuable political context of seeing Disraeli's idea as essentially aiming to be more active in foreign policy than Gladstone. Gladstone's own outline of his principles in Source D has the merit of the clarity of a list and of giving us a first-hand view of his principles. However, contextual knowledge could be used to bring out partiality here. Gladstone is campaigning against what he called Beaconsfieldism and in particular what Gladstone saw as the wilder excesses of Disraeli's foreign policy. This may have influenced Gladstone's choice of principles, to maximise the contrast with his political opponent.

Make your own point, use the extracts to illustrate it and be aware of the context of the piece. For instance:

*Gladstone's clear statement of his principles in foreign policy in Source D does give us a valuable insight into the working of his mind. The caution whereby expenditure is restricted to 'worthy occasions', the vision of a co-operative, free and equal Europe and his belief in the 'blessings of peace' – also confirmed in Source A – all suggest a far-sighted and principled policy. However, as the context of the speech is the Midlothian campaign, one of Gladstone's aims may be to emphasise principles which he can accuse Disraeli of failing to keep to in his latest adventures in Afghanistan and Southern Africa.*

# FURTHER READING

## AS SECTION

These books are often also suitable for reading and research for the A2 section.

Eric Evans *The Complete A–Z Nineteenth and Twentieth Century British History Handbook* (Hodder, 1995)

Eric Evans *The Birth of Modern Britain 1780–1914* (Longman, 1997)

Michael Lynch* *Gladstone and Disraeli* (Hodder & Stoughton, 1991)

Michael Lynch *An Introduction to Nineteenth Century British History* (Hodder & Stoughton, 1999)

Malcolm Pearce *Sources in History: The Nineteenth Century* (Bell & Hyman, 1986)

R. Pearce and R. Sterne *Government and Reform 1815–1918* (Hodder & Stoughton, 1994)

W. D. Rubinstein *Britain's Century: A Political and Social History 1815–1905* (Arnold, 1998)

M. Scott-Baumann (ed.) *Years of Expansion: Britain 1815–1914* (Hodder & Stoughton, 1995)

John Walton *The Second Reform Act* (Routledge, 1987)

John Walton *Disraeli* (Routledge, 1990)

Duncan Watts *Tories, Unionists and Conservatives 1815–1914* (Hodder & Stoughton, 1994)

Duncan Watts *Whigs, Liberals and Radicals 1815–1914* (Hodder & Stoughton, 1994)

Michael Willis* *Gladstone and Disraeli: Policies and Principles* (Cambridge, 1989)

Michael Willis* *Reading Historical Documents: Nineteenth Century Britain 1815–1914* (Blackwell, 1990)

* = A modern collection of documents

## A2 SECTION

Paul Adelman *Gladstone, Disraeli and Later Victorian Politics* (Longman, 3rd edn, 1997)

Michael Barker *Gladstone and Radicalism* (Harvester, 1975)

John Belchem *Class, Party and the Political System in Britain 1867–1914* (Blackwell, 1990)

Robert Blake *Disraeli* (Eyre & Spottiswoode, 1966)

Robert Blake *The Conservative Party from Peel to Major* (Fontana, 1996)

Muriel Chamberlain *Lord Palmerston* (GBC Books, 1987)

E. J. Feuchtwanger *Democracy and Empire: Great Britain 1865–1914* (Edward Arnold, 1985)

E. J. Feuchtwanger *Gladstone* (Penguin, 2nd edn, 1989)

R. F. Foster *Modern Ireland 1600–1972* (Penguin, 1988)

E. H. H. Green *The Crisis of Conservatism: The Politics, Economics and Ideology of the British Conservative Party, 1880–1914* (Routledge, 1995)

Eric Hobsbawm *Industry and Empire* (Penguin revised edn, 1999)

Peter Jagger (ed.) *Gladstone* (Hambledon, 1998)

Roy Jenkins *Gladstone* (Macmillan, 1995)

T. A. Jenkins *The Liberal Ascendancy 1830–1886* (Macmillan, 1994)

P. T. Marsh *The Discipline of Popular Government: Lord Salisbury's Domestic Statecraft* (Harvester, 1978)

P. J. Marshall (ed.) *The Cambridge Illustrated History of the British Empire* (CUP, 1996)

Colin Matthew *Gladstone 1809–1874* (Oxford, 1986) and *Gladstone 1874–1898* (Oxford, 1995)

J. P. Parry *Democracy and Religion* (Cambridge, 1986)

J. P. Parry *The Rise and Fall of Liberal Government in Victorian Britain* (Yale UP, 1994)

Martin Pugh *The Making of Modern British Politics* (Blackwell, 2nd edn, 1993)

John Ramsden *An Appetite for Power: A History of the Conservative Party since 1830* (Harper Collins, 1998)

Andrew Roberts *Salisbury: Victorian Titan* (Weidenfeld & Nicholson, 1999)

S. Saul *The Myth of the Great Depression* (Macmillan, 1969)

Paul Smith *Disraeli: A Brief Life* (Cambridge Canto, 1996)

David Steele *Lord Salisbury: A Political Biography* (Routledge, 1999)

Robert Taylor *Lord Salisbury* (Penguin, 1975)

John Vincent *The Formation of the British Liberal Party* (Penguin, 1966)

John Vincent *Disraeli* (Oxford, 1990)

Duncan Watts *Joseph Chamberlain and the Challenge of Radicalism* (Hodder & Stoughton, 1992)

Michael Winstanley *Gladstone and the Liberal Party* (Routledge, 1990)

## Websites

Examples of key websites are suggested below. Although these were up to date at the time of writing, it is essential for teachers to preview these sites before using them with pupils. This will ensure that the URL is still accurate and the content is suitable for your needs. We suggest that you bookmark useful sites and consider enabling pupils to access them through the school intranet. We are bringing this to your attention as we are aware of legitimate sites being appropriated illegally by people wanting to distribute unsuitable or offensive material. We strongly advise you to purchase screening software so that pupils are protected from unsuitable sites and their material.

_www.spartacus.schoolnet.co.uk_
This contains an Encyclopaedia of British History 1700–1900 with sections on Monarchy, MPs, Political Parties, Election Results, Prime Ministers, Religion and Society, Parliamentary Reform and Parliamentary Legislation – 30 Acts passed between 1846 and 1906 are described.

_www.bbc.co.uk/history_
This is an opening to a wealth of constantly updated information.

_www.victorianweb.org_
You can move with ease through a range of information on Victorian Politics, Society, Gender, Philosophy, Religion, Science, Technology and much more.

_www.Historytoday.com_
This has useful encyclopaedic resources, book reviews, online articles and revision guidance.

# INDEX